Leaping the Abyss

Putting Group Genius to Work

Gayle Pergamit and Chris Peterson

"For what can the teeming molecules that hustled themselves into self-reproducing metabolisms, the cells coordinating their behaviors to form multicelled organisms, the ecosystems, and even economic and political systems have in common? The wonderful possibility, to be held as a working hypothesis, bold but fragile, is that on many fronts, life evolves toward a regime that is poised between order and chaos. The evocative phrase that points to this working hypothesis is this: life exists at the edge of chaos. . . Networks in the regime near the edge of chaos--this compromise between order and surprise--appear best able to coordinate complex activities and best able to evolve as well."

—Stuart Kauffman, *At Home in the Universe*

©1997 Gayle Pergamit and Chris Peterson. All rights reserved.
DesignShop™ is a trademark of MG Taylor Corporation. The *Scan, Focus, Act* model was developed by Frank Burns and Linda Nelson, ©1983 MetaSystems Design Group, Arlington VA.

Contents

1.........Chapter 1
Slaying Monsters, Saving Kingdoms

compressing time to action and generating orders of magnitude returns... bringing collaboration out of conflict and a scarcity mentality... the structure must evolve because structure wins... you must start with the current "DNA" and go from there

11.........Chapter 2
Beginning the Quest

everything speaks... setting the tone in the music of our lives and our work... folding many different perspectives and individuals together in the work... employing a process to focus as much data and energy as possible... creating a neutral space for discovery and interaction

27.........Chapter 3
Freeing Time & Attention

shattering the limitations we accept regarding time... employing techniques to provide the focus and discipline necessary for breakthrough creativity... balance intensity, immersion, concentration, attention, rhythm over time... executing multiple cycles of the creative process leads to geometrically increasing returns

43.........Chapter 4
Exploring New Terrain...

learning to scan individually and in teams... stretching mental muscles... employing a comprehensive toolkit instead of looking for the silver bullet... you can't drive change and still be careful... what it means to participate in a design process

61.........Chapter 5
...And Expanding Your Universe

the difference between scanning and planning... employing the first half of the creative process for learning so that good decisions can be made in the second half... the importance of managing knowledge... increasing the flow of the data stream... using scanning to outframe the situation

81........Chapter 6
Using the Power of Space and Place

using changes in the physical environment as aids in making mental leaps and emotional shifts. . . managing the environment so that people become naturally and spontaneously creative, productive and cooperative

101.......Chapter 7
Facing the Abyss

creating the game. . . engendering collaboration. . . the discipline of the change agent. . . the role of the facilitator. . . embracing the risk of starting with a blank piece of paper. . . asking the right questions. . . living with uncertainty, ambiguity, and paradox. . . embracing discomfort as a precursor to fundamental change. . . solving problems instead of assuaging conditions. . . getting out of the box by being a kid again

125........Chapter 8
Leveraging Complexity

employing complex metaphors to illuminate complicated problems. . . using indirect and nonlinear approaches to understanding complex systems. . . understanding that the problem is so complex that it requires the consideration of hundreds of options instead of just a few

139........Chapter 9
Inventing the Problem

following the process of iteration: design, test and redesign. . . avoiding a limited solution set . . . broadening the definition of the problem. . . building models

159........Chapter 10
Magic Behind the Scenes

the science and art of facilitating the creative process. . . flocking and swarming. . . exemplifying the behavior you want to see established. . . supporting the creative process by being invisible. . . being in the game as a collaborator, never an observer. . .

177........Chapter 11
Tactical Planning at Warp Speed

making deep changes—avoid exhausting yourself in the little changes... the art of assembling the high performing team... envisioning the preferred future state and then bringing a little of the future back to here every day

199........Chapter 12
Designing the Ride

embracing wholeness in the process: there is no single point or event that triggers the solution to precipitate... creating a balance between scripting and improvisation... building a design for an event instead of an agenda... using the scan focus act model as a template for designing a session

223........Chapter 13
Giving Up the Illusion of Control:
Fear, Frustration, and Other Forms of Loathing

how to sponsor a DesignShop... overcoming the fear of embracing true collaboration without exerting control... letting the vision, plan and the implementation emerge

237........Chapter 14
Bringing the Future Back Home

how to bring the results of a DesignShop back home... structure wins... determining which structures to change in order to redirect and loosen the hold of the status quo

259........Axioms

the assumptions underlying collaboration, creativity, planning, and the emergence of enterprise

261........Further Reading
Acknowledgments
Index

Leaping the Abyss: Putting Group Genius to Work

Authors' Preface

Since this is a rather unusual book, you deserve an explanation of how it came to be.

A few years ago we got an email from someone saying they were using our first book in some kind of management seminar called a DesignShop. Now, that first book was about nanotechnology, not business, but this email implied that they were finding the book useful in getting people to think creatively about the future and change their companies' strategies to adapt.

Well, this was flattering, but we couldn't figure out how it would work. What could this mean—that DesignShop participants were using our book—and what is a DesignShop? We put in a phone call to satisfy our curiosity, and so discovered MG Taylor: Matt Taylor with his background in architecture and design processes, Gail Taylor with her experience in accelerated learning and creativity with individuals, and how this combination evolved into DesignShops.

The techniques, environment, and thought underlying their work were fascinating. Now we were more curious than before—could reducing barriers to performance make as much of a difference as they claimed? Did environment really count so heavily in structuring group dynamics and promoting—or inhibiting—creativity? How could a short workshop make such a dramatic difference to organizations? Our list of questions only got longer. But we heard enough examples of solid success to want to understand the process better.

The more they told us, the more curious and interested we became. They were pulling together insights from fields as diverse as architecture and brain chemistry and applying them to business. They were also incorporating insights from the best business theories around. They seemed to have brought it all together in a completely unique three-day format that sounded challenging, fun, and actually generated solid work product.

Leaping the Abyss: Putting Group Genius to Work

Could this be real? Could complex problems be solved that fast? It was hard to believe. We decided we had to see this in action for ourselves. Enquiring scientific, journalistic, and business-oriented minds wanted to know whether this had really delivered hard-core, bottom-line results as claimed. So we went and checked it out.

Our initial reaction to this first event was to start a thought experiment, applying this process to past situations. It was definitely a case of "If I'd known then what I know now, here's what I would have handled differently." Our second reaction was "Here's how I'm going to start using this knowledge today." Then the next thought was "We want our friends and business colleagues to know about this." Practically all the interesting people we know are trying to accomplish something difficult—from CEOs to non-profit executives, they are all working on challenging problems, and we felt they could make great headway by applying the DesignShop process.

Those who are in Fortune 100 companies may well encounter DesignShop-style processes as MG Taylor and their colleagues at Ernst & Young carry it into the corporate world. But most managers aren't in Fortune 100 companies, and a way was needed to get the word out. The DesignShop concept takes a while to explain, so someone really needed to write a book.

We suggested that MG Taylor write the book. They suggested that we do it. Eventually, we saw this made sense, for two reasons:

- First, our background in nanotechnology: we already knew that an immense technical, business, and social tsunami is coming along shortly, so we're always looking for great new techniques to help people and organizations cope with change. And here in Silicon Valley, companies are already being forced to deal with a blinding rate of technological change. This speed-up will likely increase, and definitely spread.

- Second, we've been around in business for long enough to know that it's tough out there, and we all need whatever help we can get. In high-tech startups, no matter how smart, talented, and hard-working you are, you need to use every possible advantage to succeed. In more traditional companies, such as large military contractors, it's tough to continually reinvent what you're doing instead of fighting fires and sinking beneath endemic problems.

Authors' Preface

So we agreed to spend a month writing this book. Instead, it took two years.

But it's been worth it, because—for a change—this is something really new, really profound. Even if all you take away from this book is a handful of techniques and insights—even if you never use the full-scale DesignShop process—knowing these techniques can make a big difference for you and your company.

When we ran the book draft past our favorite B School professor, who's seen every piece of change literature since Noah got off the ark, she said "wow, this is actually new!" Part of what's new here is bringing insight from other fields—such as architecture and education—into business. The other part is synthesis—taking the well-known insights of business theorists like Drucker, Deming, and so on, and getting them to play together in a new way.

This book was based on interviews with DesignShop participants and the information they provided. They have shared their secrets and opinions on the nature of the process and how it turned out for them. This account reflects their opinions and their knowledge of what it is that makes their businesses work, rather than official statements by their respective organizations. For example, the words and opinions expressed by Colonel Bill Rutley are his own and do not necessarily represent the position of the US Air Force or its agencies.

So there are ideas here that you can extract and use immediately. We've provided some pointers to the sources of inspiration for the DesignShop concept, but this is not an academic-style tracing of the intellectual roots of the process or its components. You'll find some supporting theory to show the logic of the process, but this is not a textbook. Instead, the purpose of this book is to bring to your attention this new tool and some examples of its success.

You'll find that we focus on MG Taylor, the company that originated this process. That's because the original work was done largely by Matt and Gail Taylor, and by the facilitators who have worked on their team for a long time. To tell you this story, we wanted to go to the source—the originators—and give you as immediate a feel from them as possible.

You hear a lot about Matt and Gail in this book, but they've trained up lots of other facilitators, who are now training more. Soon, you be able to get great facilitation from a variety of sources. Which is a good thing, given how many organizations need this process, and urgently. Nobody needs to tell us all how increasingly desperate everyone feels: swamped, overloaded, operating right on the edge—or over the edge. And it's only going to get worse. We wrote this book to help.

So, have fun with the ideas, and use them profitably.

Gayle Pergamit and Chris Peterson
gayle@pergamit.com, peterson@foresight.org
Palo Alto, California
April 1997

Slaying Monsters, Saving Kingdoms

How often do you operate at your personal best during the business day? Are there times when you really hit your stride? You can resolve challenges with ease and power. A "problem" no longer strikes you as problematic. Instead, it's swept away in the solution that you are creating.

Sometimes you've been part of a group or a team that had that same kind of magic—call it "group genius." You might have to search your memory back to college, high school, or even beyond to remember when everything came together and your team delivered a first-rate performance on the sports field, in a school play, in an outdoor adventure.

Why isn't it like that more of the time in the business world—both for you as an individual and for your organization? Instead, too often you find that groups won't change as needed. People are intractable. Problems are insurmountable. You find yourself fighting against creativity blocks, against oppressive work environments that wear you down, or against coworkers' or management's resistance to change. Sometimes, after massive effort, you reach the conclusion that the structure of the organization just won't budge and you walk away thinking "you can't fight City Hall."

This book is an invitation to try a different way of working that enhances your individual and group productivity and creativity. This way of working brings environment, processes, and tools into concert to produce some amazing results. This is more than just a powerful new tool to add to your managerial toolkit. It's a process used to tackle big challenges, and it works for all kinds of organizations. You can also use it to change how you work and live day to day.

Seven Domains Model
http://www.mgtaylor.com/mgtaylor/glasbead/sevndoms.htm

Would you consider testing a process that routinely gets your group or company to reach agreement on key issues—and produces a detailed, written operating plan—in days rather than the current three months...six months...or more?

You can try it out in condensed form, a three-day experience from which there is a high probability you will emerge with spectacular results. It's not a seminar that teaches you how to accomplish things. It's a process that actually accomplishes an astonishing result in three days.

Our goal here is to take you on a tour of one of these events and survey the achievements of many others. And, if you like it, you can incorporate this way of doing things into your daily working environment.

It's different enough to merit a special name: the DesignShop™ process.

Glossary A-M
http://www. mgtaylor.com/mgtaylor/glossary.htm

This technique for change and creativity began as a method to enable individuals to enhance their creativity and solve difficult problems. It then expanded to address the dilemmas and opportunities faced by groups. Since the mid-1980s, it has evolved in the marketplace, being tested by companies working to improve bottom lines. Use of this process has spread almost exclusively by word of mouth, as one manager or CEO tells a friend, "You've got to try this process. It's unusual, but it works for us."

Groups of all sorts, ranging from large to small, military to counter-culture, manufacturing to entertainment industry, have used it to design successful solutions to challenging, complex, seemingly intractable problems in every area of business. Many have used the DesignShop process for solving single problems. Others have implemented the DesignShop environment and processes back at the office to create an ongoing change in their ways of working.

The improvements come about not by changing the people, but by changing their environment. Intelligence-suppressing factors and creativity-suppressing factors have been removed. People are given an enhanced set of knowledge tools and processes that let them be more effective—they are using power saws and drills instead of rocks. People operate closer to their maximum capacities.

Overcoming Barriers

Many barriers—time, embedded beliefs, and the physical environment—have been around so long that you no longer recognize their costs to your productivity and creativity. You are trapped by a set of assumptions, barriers, and concepts that systematically produce results you don't want. Many of these barriers are deeply enmeshed with current norms of work. "Getting rid of distractions and barriers is probably the foundation level for all the rest of the work," is how one senior manager describes it.

It's not that our current patterns aren't productive—they just aren't productive enough—and we know it. We still have problems in our organizations for which current techniques aren't providing solutions. The market demand for TQM, leadership courses, time management courses, and so on serves as direct feedback saying—"still not good enough, we need more." Current workplace habits keep us trapped in areas of local maxima, unable to move to higher levels of productivity. In the process of evaluation, we need the honesty to recognize that one of the barriers to change is fear of loss of control—or, more accurately, the illusion of control.

Here are some examples of real-world results from the DesignShop process:

- Carl's Jr. hamburger chain used the process to create their redesign plan for the next decade. Instead of spending two years and $1 million designing, they achieved spectacular results through a three-day Design Shop at a fraction of the cost. Their plan generated even more benefits, including innovations that cut implementation time by 50%—to six months instead of a year.

- A contract dispute had labor and management hostility raging on—long after the new contract had been signed. They needed to bury the

A DesignShop, hosted with trepidation by the FAA, produced previously-unimaginable cooperation and sharing of information between airlines, and an unprecedented win-win solution that decreased delays by 50% in less than 120 days.

Design Build Use
http://www. mgtaylor.com/
mgtaylor/glasbead/dbumodel.htm

hatchet, not keep sinking it into the other side's car tires. A DesignShop session resolved the emotions, built trust, and forged warring parties into a productive team. It was so successful that the management and labor involved took this problem-solving process on tour throughout the U.S. and as far as South Africa.

- Colorado counter-culture types with a dream, but with little business experience and tight funding, used it to design a rapid implementation plan to open a natural foods store. In three months, the first store was up and running, and became the basis of their multi-million dollar grocery chain—which is so successful that they now have to fight off hostile takeover attempts.

- Using the process intensively over 22 months, a technical test center completely revamped their vision, their business, and their profitability. Arnold Engineering Development Center turned a 30% reduction in government funding into a 30% increase in commercial business, locked in $750 million in new business, entered strategic alliances that brought tens of millions of dollars worth of donated capital structure improvements by partners, and transformed a financially-crippled entity into a creative, dynamic, profitable center of technical excellence.

- An opera company used the DesignShop process as a last ditch effort to prevent bankruptcy. Instead of the usual agonizing over how to raise funds, the process revealed a corporate taboo that had prevented the team from realizing that they were already sitting on a pot of gold. They discovered untapped financial resources, reconceived proper use of their assets, and became consistently viable again.

- Pan Am, United Airlines, American Airlines, TWA, and other U.S. air carriers were losing and frustrating customers due to delays, and losing lots of money in the process. U.S. air traffic control procedures were causing the delays, but the roots of the problem between the airlines and the FAA—and between the rival airlines themselves—were so fundamental that everyone knew no win-win situation was possible. A DesignShop event, hosted with trepidation by the FAA, produced previously-unimaginable cooperation and sharing of information between airlines, and an unprecedented win-win solution that decreased delays by 50% in less than 120 days.

- High school principals—competitors for the same scarce funding—met as adversaries. During a one-day event, they restructured their relationships and moved into a pattern of profitable cooperation with no legal barriers. Years later, they continue to share resources and have made their resource pie even bigger.

- Avis Rent-A-Car went into this process hoping to smooth the relocation of a large percentage of their reservations work force to a soon-to-be-built second reservation center. They left the DesignShop event having reconsidered the traditional solution of building a second reservation center and replaced it with a completely new approach that saved millions in land and construction cost, lowered operating costs, reduced employee turnover, boosted productivity, and smoothly handled Avis's growing reservation load.

- National Car Rental used the process to develop a powerful and prescient Total Asset Management System for automobiles. In the six years since, as more of the major car rental companies and auto manufacturers implement components of the plan, it is clear that the National Car Rental event accurately identified the future of these industries.

- In Colorado, the Boulder County Development Office found that a one-time use of the process provided their organization with enough vision and energy to drive them strongly for over seven years.

- Inspired by the DesignShop process, employees of an insurance and financial services conglomerate were able to overcome their fear and redesign the organization without their department. By doing so, they transformed their attitudes from those of potentially-obsolete functionaries to flexible "gold-collar" workers—valuable in any organization.

- The Air Force's F-15 team had a complex problem—one for which no one wanted to step up and claim ownership. Ongoing evolution of their software and hardware platforms was causing enough problems to seriously inhibit communication between members of this global organization. Using the process, they revamped their old ways of organizing which had gotten them into the mess. They invented new ways to organize their people into a virtual team that solved the problems.

How can dramatic improvements happen so quickly?

Imagine that a team of Disneyland or Industrial Light & Magic engineers had gone to the site of your upcoming vacation and custom-made a ride just for you. They orchestrated an active journey to let you have peak experiences—a river rafting trip paddling through wild Class V rapids. As the ride progressed, the engineers modified the journey to suit your immediate needs—maybe they added a stretch of quiet beauty and calm water for a needed rest after your team successfully carried the rafts through a difficult, boulder-strewn portage. Imagine that they constructed a journey that became a venture of discovery and achievement. In literature and cinema, journeys of this sort become the tales of heroes from Odysseus to the Three Musketeers to Indiana Jones, and the achievements are slaying the monster, saving the kingdom, and finding the treasure.

Scan Focus Act Model
http://www. mgtaylor.com/
mgtaylor/glasbead/SFA.htm

The DesignShop experience can be likened to taking your mind, and your coworkers' minds, on a custom-tailored, problem-solving adventure voyage using the whole world of ideas as your theme park. The journey is crafted to the needs of your organization and its business challenges. The design rules for creating a good voyage are used by the engineers, but never brought to the riders' attention. The technical mechanisms are hidden underneath and not allowed to intrude on the travelers' experience. The quality of the results comes from engaging fully in the unique experience of the journey.

The DesignShop process is full of turbulence. Ambiguity and complexity are added before the process moves to a manageable elegance. It requires a different criteria set than the ones normally used to judge whether or not a meeting is "going well." It is deliberately a high-variety environment that is vastly more demanding than the standard business setting.

Slaying Monsters, Saving Kingdoms

As you take the DesignShop ride, you are placing yourself in a state of ambiguity and risk as you move toward the future state that you desire. You are fully engaged in a physical process surrounded with the appropriate metaphors—you have stepped onto the boat and cast off from the shore. This is much more than a mere exchange of information.

Placing yourself in this state of ambiguity is stressful. Creative people are accustomed to doing it, but still experience the stress. Most of modern civilization has focused on how to run away from risk. The average person or organization is habitually working to *reduce* variety, ambiguity, and risk—not embrace it. The usual solution is to ignore it, not experience it.

DesignShops manage the risk, and allow you to focus on creating solutions. The reason DesignShops achieve success is that participants are being carried forward by the entire structure of the whole experience, like passengers in a boat traveling down a river. Instead of focusing on their individual, day-to-day concerns—including internal politics, egos, and jostling for career advancement—team members are caught up by an intense group effort in problem-solving.

Often when a group needs to find a new solution, they try a brainstorming session. Sometimes this works; often it doesn't. The DesignShop techniques can be thought of as a way to take such a session and multiply its effectiveness by an order of magnitude. It uses a combination of practical exercises and a few simple tricks, along with an environment optimized for problem-solving, to greatly increase the odds of success.

We will give you the sensation of the experience, and we will also show you the behind-the-scenes mechanism of a DesignShop event so you can begin to recreate the environment and processes for your organization.

In retrospect, we were convinced that we would have reaped significant benefits from using DesignShop techniques in complex business situations in our own past—with software companies from Autodesk to Lotus, with military contractors, and troubled nonprofits. It's a case of "I wish I knew then what I know now." Now that we've experienced the DesignShop, these new insights, tools, and processes will be part of our future tool kit.

Designing Sessions
http://www. mgtaylor.com/
mgtaylor/jotm/spring97/
session_design.htm

The Wharton DesignShop

We attended our first DesignShop activity in Philadelphia. We arrived early to see the staff set up the physical environment and design the sequence of exercises. Sponsored by the Center for Advanced Studies in Management at the Wharton Graduate School of Business, this was one of many uses of the process. Multiple organizations attended instead of just one organization and its stakeholders.

The attending organizations came to work on two issues:
- The question posed by the sponsor, the Wharton Graduate School of Business: What is the structure of the 21st century organization?, and
- An organization-specific challenge that each group needed to address.

This event turned out to be well-suited for our task of analyzing the process' effectiveness. The multiple organizations in attendance gave us the opportunity to speak with a large and diverse set of people who routinely use the process to work on problems specific to their businesses and technologies. We talked with experienced participants and extracted from them their past results from the process. We watched the first-time attendees' reactions, noted how similar they were to our own "first-timer" reactions, and how they changed as the event progressed. We also saw the behind-the-scenes staff action that made this journey possible.

Over three days, we saw over forty business executives, engineers, management consultants, military officers, and university professors get frustrated, angry, annoyed—well, the first-timers did—then excited, enthusiastic, engaged, cooperative, productive, and above all…creative.

We saw business groups generate solutions—often dazzling solutions—to problems that had plagued them for up to four years. If they had brought a proposal with them from home—fine, respectable proposals that had been labored over for months or years—they replaced them with solutions that were vastly better.

Business acumen, inventiveness, ability to recognize opportunities, and tactics for capturing opportunities kept improving throughout the event. We saw these patterns consistently, in group after group, whether they were military personnel, management consultants, fast-food restaurant franchisees, or purveyors of education.

On our return home, we made some immediate changes in our personal work environments and processes. Even without holding a DesignShop and getting the full benefits, we could still quickly adapt many insights to give productivity gains day to day.

Without having attended the event—and discovered for ourselves both the costs imposed by some of our traditional procedures and the benefits that are possible within 72 hours—we would have remained curious, but not moved to action. By sharing enough of this experience and analysis with you, we hope you'll be moved to include these new techniques and insights in your tool kit for working on tough problems. Better yet, we hope you'll choose to restructure your environment so that it is supportive of you and your work in these fast and complex times.

Challenge

Beginning with this chapter, and continuing with every chapter in the book, readers are invited to participate in a "Take-a-Page" exercise. We'll provide the blank pages and some guiding questions. You provide the creative energy and responses.

One further note before beginning: most of these challenges will be more difficult to solve if you're doing them alone. They're not impossible to do alone, but some collaboration will increase the creativity. If you can find a friend to work with, all the better.

Let's begin.

1. You've just finished Chapter 1. Without referring back to it, simply record your impressions. Don't necessarily analyze or debate what you've read, merely record impressions. You may do so through a drawing, a few words, a mind map, whatever method you choose. What puzzled you? What resonated with your previous experiences?

2. Now that you've recorded your impressions, if there are items of curiosity or question, refer back to the text for clarification and record any new observations on this page.

3. How do you currently approach working with others, and designing and building with others? What stages do you and your fellow collaborators tend to cycle through on your way to creating a problem and subsequently solving it? What strategies do you employ in working with other people, not necessarily to get something out of them, but to collectively leverage each other's abilities? What are your assumptions about creativity? What are your assumptions and beliefs about collaboration; about people working together to create incredible value? You may need to think about these questions over a series of days, watching your life through a different lens.

4. What is possible to accomplish in three days? What factors keep it from being more?

Beginning the Quest

It's 8:00 AM Wednesday morning, and the beginning of the journey through the DesignShop process. Over several days of intensive setup, the support team has worked magic on a standard, large hotel meeting room—you can still pick out aspects of the old space: the ceiling, the carpet, and parts of the walls are visible.

But the standard "start of conference" ambiance is missing: no lines of chairs and skirted tables (equipped with paper, pens, glasses, and water pitchers) facing an empty podium (equipped with overhead projector) from which wisdom will be dispensed.

The space is now transformed into something entirely different. It's been segmented into a warren of smaller spaces, connected by avenues lined with displays of information. Everywhere you look are intriguing articles, graphics, quotations, even comics—a closer look reveals that they all have some relevance to the broader issues we're here to work on.

Although the chairs, as well as the tables that hold the buffet breakfast, are standard hotel issue, all the other furniture is unusual. It's clearly special. Each piece is mobile—usually wheeled—and esthetically pleasing, often of beautiful woods with flowing lines. Some pieces are unrecognizable. A special stand holding a computer with a World Wide Web link is so attractive that it belongs in a museum of modern art or design. Instead, it's here for our use—just one more piece of an inviting and energizing environment.

On display are various 3D objects: art, puzzles, simple games…many of them are, well, toys. This is somewhat shocking—we're here to tackle important company problems, and we're being presented with toys. How can this be necessary or helpful? At this early stage we are asking ourselves, "What executive or military officer would be seen playing with one of these toys?"

As becomes clear over the next three days, the toys, the posted materials, and art objects are more than just decoration, although they perform that purpose too. Everything has a purpose, either to inform, to stretch the mind, or to introduce new perspectives on the issue at hand.

All possible standard signals have been changed in order to send the message that this is not business as usual: not a conference, not a seminar, not a workshop, not like anything else we've experienced.

Not only the visual environment is unusual, but the auditory environment is as well. Music is being played—not canned Muzak, but real music. Though most participants don't realize it, and may never consciously notice the music at all, the selection of which pieces we're hearing has been carefully made to enhance each stage of the event. In these few minutes, before the group gathers for the first time, the staff has chosen "Primal Magic" by Strunz & Farah, "Rio Amazonas" by Chuck Jonkey, and "Dance the Devil Away" by Outback, with the goal of setting a tone of upbeat, energetic concentration as we prepare to launch into our work.

All possible standard signals have been changed in order to send the message that this is not business as usual: not a conference, not a seminar, not a workshop, not like anything else we've experienced.

The most obvious signals are the playful ones: toys, music, books. Another signal is the clothing of the arriving participants. All the participants have been informed in advance that casual clothing is preferred. No need for suits and ties—or high heels and hose—the goal is to maximize comfort as the level of physical activity fluctuates, and to help reduce traditional status and role signals.

Even small signals have been changed. The standard conference registration protocol is deliberately missing. Name badges are available, but alphabetized by first name. And this badge—along with breakfast—are all the participants pick up as they enter. No notebook, no package of materials, and most important, no schedule of events.

Participants get their badges, and staff members collect—and move to secure storage for the day—the briefcases, cellular phones, beepers, and all the other paraphernalia that carry the message of "business as usual." (Women participants are even encouraged to store away their purses; surprisingly, this often works.) Beepers, phones, briefcases: even if they aren't used, they all give the impression that their holder may be mentally called away at any time to higher priority work—he or she may even choose to leave. These objects send a subliminal message of noncommitment to full participation in the event at hand.

Carrying around these items would also slow participants down. As we'll see, the process to come involves a lot of physical movement from space to space, and within each space. It's important to relieve the participants of burdens: both the physical burden of lugging stuff around and the mental burden of worrying about its security. Far better to lock it all up and free everyone for focusing on the task at hand.

And it works. Having been rid of the need to carry things around, the participants have their hands free to pick up breakfast and wander out into the space, as they are meant to do at this stage.

As people begin milling around, one thing is very clear: we're not in Kansas anymore.

Creating an Atmosphere

This dispersion of the participants into the setting, as well as the background hum of activity by the staff, are deliberate components of the event. When the participants walk in the door, they are coming from different organizations, or different parts of the same organization. They have different things on their minds—career agendas, personal concerns—some may not have even wanted to attend at all.

So the first order of business is focusing everyone's attention, getting all these different individuals aligned to working together on a common set of challenges. How do you get people to drop those differences that act as barriers, letting them focus on productive work?

Experience has shown that the staff—termed "knowledge workers" in the Taylor organization—helps set the tone immediately, even before the first session starts, by focusing on tasks and avoiding the temptation to chat with the participants.

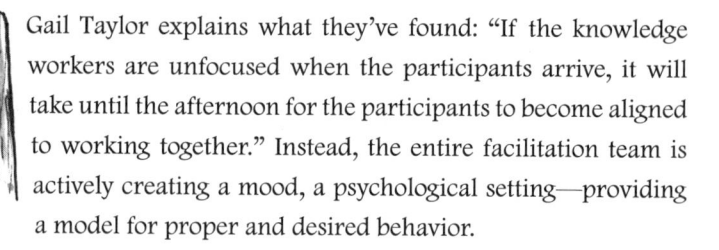

Gail Taylor explains what they've found: "If the knowledge workers are unfocused when the participants arrive, it will take until the afternoon for the participants to become aligned to working together." Instead, the entire facilitation team is actively creating a mood, a psychological setting—providing a model for proper and desired behavior.

So, the team is on site early, and while they're friendly to arriving participants, they avoid social conversation and don't discuss the process to come. Each team member is intent on work. This structuring of the atmosphere by the team transmits a complex message to the arriving participants, and they pick up this work-focused mood quickly.

Participants, with portable breakfast in hand, disperse into the space, picking up books and other objects, reading things posted on the walls, poking around on the computer display of the World Wide Web. The information being made available in all forms is high quality, irresistibly intriguing. Even we, as writers and long-time book collectors, were seduced by the 350-volume collection of books there. We like to think that we're familiar with most of the best books in our various areas of interest, having been vacuuming up titles for many years. But it had been a long time since we had run into such a high concentration of interesting books that were new discoveries for us. This exploratory process continues as a background action during the meals and transition points throughout the session, making every moment in the space an active mental exercise, an opportunity to learn new concepts and relevant information.

Who Comes to a DesignShop? Bringing Stakeholders Together

As the participants explore the room, browse through books and scan the information posted on the walls, it's unclear what positions they hold in their organizations. The badges give no titles. The casual attire gives no clues. What kind of participants does an organization need to send to one of these events to make it work?

Beginning the Quest

For a standard DesignShop event, where one organization is tackling a large challenge, the answer to this question is—at least one representative of each affected group. This can include suppliers, contractors, customers, employees from all levels and departments, as well as the VPs and division managers who usually come to strategic planning events.

Elsa Porter, a Wharton participant who has sponsored DesignShop events in the past, feels strongly: "The most important thing about a DesignShop is how you put together the people. You must have project managers, stakeholders, all of the different perspectives in there."

A "stakeholder" is anyone who will be affected by the outcome of your business decision. This means including people who are normally excluded because they are thought to be adversarial or unwilling to participate, or are considered to have no need to know, or are vendors and not company insiders. They start as separate individuals with their own agendas and their own concerns. They become team members of the company, all pulling towards a win-win solution. The results, instead of being injurious because of the disclosure of proprietary information, or turbulent with perpetual personal conflict, end up producing cost savings, increased profits, increased creativity. The new work relationships forged during the DesignShop are capable of transforming the nature of the post-DesignShop business relationship into something new, different, and even better than the previous relationship.

Over the next few days, we interviewed many Wharton participants about their previous experiences with the process. Clearly, including a broad variety of participants was important to success. Bill Espinosa, at that time in charge of strategy for CKE, told us of an experience using DesignShops in the fast-paced and competitive world of the fast-food business. The key to success, he felt, was getting all the relevant stakeholders represented. It created an expanded participant pool of stakeholders that produced new perspectives and unexpected savings in time and cost.

Business of Enterprise Model
http://www.mgtaylor.com/mgtaylor/glasbead/busofent.htm

Carl's Jr.
Going Beyond Hamburgers to
Bring Its Stakeholders Together

In the Western states, the name "Carl's Jr." is readily recognized as a long-standing and significant part of the fast-food landscape. CKE is Carl's Jr.'s parent company. Generations have grown up buying hamburgers and charbroiled chicken from the 650 "stores" decorated with a snazzy star logo. Bill Espinosa gives the overview:

> We are a sandwich concept. Our main products are hamburgers and charbroiled chicken. We have this really nice dining room. We already do partial table service. We emulate the aspects of a nice place to go. The stores are in good locations, but were hardly used other than at lunch time.

Bill Espinosa joined the large regional fast food chain in June 1994 as Vice President of Strategic Planning to help straighten out a situation needing immediate and major changes. Sales had declined for four years in a row.

One of Carl's Jr.'s problems was that it was primarily seen as a lunch establishment. This means that the units were used heavily at only one part of the day. Bill explains:

> We basically do a lunch business. McDonald's does breakfast, lunch, snack, dinner, and late-night snack. We had to take a look at how we could introduce something that would bring in existing customers more frequently, or bring in more new people.

The new image of Carl's Jr. has two parts—we want to optimize what Carl's Jr. is now, and we want to offer a major new "day part." We do lunch, and now we want to optimize by going into another day part. We looked at how to develop another day part.

Breakfast was an option, but we felt dinner was the way to go. Dinner is a profitable, high ticket item. People come in for lunch or breakfast and want to spend only 99 cents. Dinner was the way to go and fit better with our image: the really nice dining rooms, partial table service, a nice place to go, good locations. We decided to pursue that.

Beginning the Quest

Because Bill had done DesignShop activities at his previous company, he was able to use a subset of those techniques to help kick off the dinner project:

> I simulated some mini-DesignShops—call them "DesignSessions." We had a training project that needed a jump start, and I used the techniques as a facilitator for one of our vice presidents to help her pull together an environment in which she could quickly accomplish a lot. I conducted one on the dinner project. We were working with Long John Silver to bring in their food, equipment, etc. into a Carl's Jr., and create a "dual brand" restaurant.

Although these weren't complete DesignShop sessions, didn't include all the stakeholders, and were done in a highly modified form, the results were beneficial. At this point the organization was successfully moving toward serving dinner. In parallel, they had made a number of improvements based on consumer feedback, but Bill knew there was a major element missing:

> We had already fixed labor, readjusted prices, and done everything the customers said we had to do in order to get back into phase with competitors. Yet, when I walked into a clean, freshly painted store, it looked old.
>
> Those of us who've been in the food business knew what the problem was— the stores had not been renovated or enhanced in 10 to 12 years. The service systems, the physical plant, the logo, all sorts of elements in the 650 units had not been remodeled or image-enhanced.
>
> What happens is that over the course of ten years, we blend into the environment, and our customer will drive by us. We no longer stand out. Players in the food industry find they need to reposition their image. It tells people "come in—we are new and fresh." The cycle is increasingly shorter. The rule of thumb now is an image enhancement every five to ten years.

Design Build Use Model
http://www.mgtaylor.com/mgtaylor/glasbead/dbumodel.htm

It was one of those tasks which one human could not figure out, solve, and implement alone. It was going to require the input and skill sets from many different disciplines from inside and outside of the organization.

This was a make-or-break project for CKE, and Bill, brand new to the company, had the responsibility to make it work. He chose to bet the company's future— and his own reputation—on the DesignShop process.

Although Bill had given people a sample of what was to come with his modified "DesignSessions," no one else had ever experienced a full-fledged DesignShop event. Bill explained the full process to the president "as much as you can describe it in advance."

> When it came to "Store 2000"—the new image enhancement and remodel program—we had to assume everything in the restaurant was up for grabs.
>
> We would have to take in a ton of new information on where we are and where we should go in the future—augment our capabilities and skill sets. All this had to converge and come together to give us the specifications for the Store 2000. In order to make that very large jump, I needed a process that would help focus as much data and energy as possible.
>
> The best process that I had experienced was the DesignShop process. This was far too important and complex a project to just dump on a group of architects and managers. The capital cost to remodel was $100,000 per store across 650 stores—that's $65 million. We needed the DesignShop process to make it all work. It had to work! So I persuaded management that a DesignShop was the way to do it.

Bill stressed that his experience had led him to the conclusion that a key point is getting all the stakeholders together:

> The aspect of the process that really produces the value is the openness to ideas from all areas, free of the usual biases. That is what you need in order to feel like you've bathed yourself in enough data, with the right people, in an environment that supports the work.
>
> The other part is that the process sends the message that there is no one in charge. The participants aren't trying to please any particular manager. Otherwise, there is a tendency for people to come in and think, "What do you want to hear?"

The goal of the "Store 2000" event was to get all the stakeholders participating to project themselves and the company into the future—to envision what a Carl's Jr. should be in the year 2000. So a wide range of stakeholders was invited to attend the event in late November at the Hilton in Anaheim right across from Disneyland.

A key part of the success would depend on having someone from each group of stakeholders present and participating—effectively representing their interests throughout the process.

The goal of the "Store 2000" event was to get all the stakeholders participating to project themselves and the company into the future—to envision what a Carl's Jr. should be in the year 2000.

Beginning the Quest

There were about 45 people. We invited people from every major business processing group involved with the company. We invited the person who had done some of the major documents we would be reviewing at the event. We invited a typical customer. We also invited a number of consultants—marketing, packaging, building.

We explained to the vendors and consultants that their participation would be pro bono. "It is a DesignShop where we will be trying to exchange ideas, not where you would be trying to sell us something." We wanted them to get involved, and there were no guarantees that they would be the uniform company, etc., that would ultimately be selected. The benefit to them would be that they would understand the direction in which we were going. Of course, they all wanted to know whether the others were coming for free. So all the outside participants had to come for free.

Some vendors turned me down and chose not to attend. They did not get penalized. No one was required to come. There were about 45 people who agreed to come.

The DesignShop process would result in the design specifications for that store—the Carl's Jr. store of the future. In accordance with the importance of the event to the company's future, a great deal of preparation took place:

Required advance reading was over 1,000 pages: our menu strategy, which the marketing department had just published; a database of marketing research, which we have on a continuing basis; a position paper by an outside consultant on trends in the food industry; data on competitors; five years of financials; and a couple of books to stimulate creative thinking.

It was proprietary information. A lot of people read all the 1,000 pages of required read-ahead material—particularly people from the outside.

About a month before the event, everything was coming together, when there was a change in presidents. The one who hired me, and approved the DesignShop, left in October and went to Hardy's. We had other changes happening at the same time. The marketing vice president had left. The holidays were approaching fast. We were either going to do the DesignShop session as planned or wait quite a while.

The new president and COO is Tom Thompson. Tom is also a franchisee and owns sixteen stores; his perspective is unique and well-grounded. I went to Tom and asked him what he wanted to do. Because we had announced the event to the franchisees, he was already aware of the plan. He had always

---

We really cannot sensibly disagree when we are standing in two entirely different vantage points. A vantage point is like a scientist's microscope or telescope: an instrument that sets the range of our observations, and separates and highlights events in which we're particularly interested.

—Thomas Gilbert,
Human Competence

Vantage Points Model
http://www.mgtaylor.com/
mgtaylor/glasbead/vantgpts.htm

endorsed the image enhancement, and had recognized what we had to accomplish in the DesignShop. He took it on faith that we needed this process.

Was Bill nervous about the DesignShop? He was betting his personal reputation on this. If it succeeded, he was golden, but if it failed...

Yes. That is exactly right. This was incredibly strategic, because you do not get more than one shot.

In late November 1994 the Store 2000 event got rolling, with Matt and Gail Taylor facilitating and forty-five participating stakeholders from every category gathered for the three-day session. Not only would they envision what a Carl's Jr. should be in the year 2000, the goal would be to leave the DesignShop on the last day with actual design specifications for that store.

This was the critical challenge. CKE's goal was to start building the Store 2000 immediately.

The next step in the process was to say what elements of that Store 2000 can we afford to bring back into the remodel program? How many things stay and how many move? The objective was to design four prototype stores: interiors, uniforms, everything. We told the participants that they should address the whole gestalt. The people, product, environment—not just paint and plastic.

The end product had to be a design for a new-image store that creates the needed sales response from the customers: they rediscover what we are. It had to be complete enough to provide an exterior that would tell people we were there and an interior that made it a nice place to come back to, that was not tired. It had to be fresh and fun.

There was a ground rule with which we went into the DesignShop session—technology that could not be implemented in sixty days would not be in the remodel. For example, touch screen ordering in the drive-through is not yet available. We needed to roll out the new image by third quarter.

There were high levels of energy. Many people had seen the mini-DesignShops I had facilitated. They liked the technique. When they saw it in the full form they thought it was really powerful stuff.

This was a way to get people comfortable with the idea that they were empowered to help with the design. They do not have to wait for blueprints from someone else.

Note this point about whom you include on your list of stakeholders: it is vital to have the decision makers included in the event. That way if you have a question or need a decision, you just walk across the room and get it.

I told our internal CKE participants, "Get as much out of these people in the three days we have them locked in this room as you can. Extract every bit of data. Afterwards you will have this project book and you can refer back to it—the DesignShop documentation—and know when we talked about packaging, for example, what specific issues were discussed."

As an experienced DesignShop participant, Bill was able to see that it was going well.

The team had a feeling of empowerment. They got the best input from all of the key players.

Besides the energy, there were also high levels of conflict. At one point the franchisee representative said the franchisees could not afford to make these changes to all their stores. So there was the need to find a balance. We worked it through.

Several times people came to me and said, "I can't deal with what is going on in my breakout group. People are saying this and this…" I would have to say "We will deal with this later. Let's keep drawing this on paper. I would rather make a hundred mistakes on paper than build three stores and find out none of them work, or that they will not be implemented because they are too expensive."

These people were experiencing high levels of energy and conflict—doesn't sound like fun, does it? But remember, these people were surrounded by one of the most playful-looking environments they had ever experienced as adults—which sounds like goofing off and wasting time, doesn't it? The two extremes sound completely contradictory.

It certainly doesn't sound like what we traditionally consider a "productive or normal business environment," or behavior that is usually considered "productive or normal." This is precisely not a typical business environment.

It is, instead, a design environment.

Matt Taylor observes:

A world-class design environment often looks very chaotic. There is often a high degree of confrontation and disagreement with people testing different alternatives, switching sides and dialoging back and forth. It's also a happy environment, with people having breakthroughs. It is an emotional experience.

Appropriate behavior rules within a traditional organization do not allow for this type of emotion, confrontation, contradiction, and the attendant level of discomfort. But without these dynamics, you cannot have a design process. Instead, you have a bunch of people sitting politely maintaining conversation within a very narrow band width of propriety.

For most people, being within a creative process is signalled by a feeling of discomfort at some point. and discomfort is something we are usually trained to avoid.

Like Matt, Bill was also able to recognize the energy and conflict as a normal characteristic of working in a high-performance design environment. Pulling from knowledge of what this interaction meant, Bill was able to put aside his natural nervousness about the process and focus on making the high level of performance happen. The result—group genius.

They got into it and delivered in three days. They produced designs, uniforms, color schemes—the whole bit. They even went further and developed the training system.

We put the focus on the food. Our restaurants had not really highlighted the food enough. We opened up the stores physically. A major objective was to put the food on center stage. At the end of the DesignShop event, we had design specifications for this.

We also had a plan to cut costs by doing a test remodel, checking what pays off there, doing the second at a lower cost, checking again, and so on through four stores. In this way we will test each concept, and the things that seem to have the most customer impact will survive as the basis for our remodel. [As positive results came in, the need for a fourth "validation" store was dropped, and only three test stores were built.]

These three prototype stores will take it down to what we feel are the absolute essentials for a remodel program. What we will provide is the option for a restaurant owner or franchisee to choose a full-blown enhancement with confidence, because they will know they are going to get their money back.

Sidebar notes:

Seven Stages of the Creative Process Model
http://www.mgtaylor.com/mgtaylor/glasbead/7stagcrp.htm

Appropriate behavior rules within a traditional organization do not allow for this type of emotion, confrontation, contradiction, and the attendant level of discomfort. But without these dynamics, you cannot have a design process.

Design Build Use Model
http://www.mgtaylor.com/mgtaylor/glasbead/dbumodel.htm

Beginning the Quest 23

The support of the franchisees was critical. Bill was careful to watch the reaction of the franchisee representative at the DesignShop session:

> She looked at the design and said, "This is very good because I have my personal livelihood at stake." The franchisees are very tough customers, because they may have to mortgage their homes or take money out of their child's college fund to do the remodel. They needed to see us be successful.
>
> So the pressure to keep costs down and get sales up was intense. One way to do this was to speed up the project.
>
> We set an incredibly aggressive timeframe. It was deliberately unrealistic because we were using time budgets as the means to set priorities. "Since I cannot do everything, what do I need to do first?" The aggressive deadlines helped everyone focus. In a project, the longer it runs the more money it costs.

Bill Espinosa did some consensus-building at CKE after the DesignShop, to make sure that the new vision was spread beyond the forty-five participants.

> Especially because we were doing things a lot faster than the norm, I had to go to each constituency group and share with them the process and show them the objective.
>
> At this point we said, okay, now we have the design specifications. The next step is to get the core competencies and skills. We then invited different designers to come in and take a look at the plan and provide proposals.
>
> Interestingly enough, Bill Babcock, the designer who agreed to come to our DesignShop event, agreed to do the project. The other proposals that came in gave us twice the timeframe and two to three times the cost to do the project. Babcock's company had done the previous Carl's Jr. image enhancement ten years earlier—which worked—and they felt they could do it again. We too wanted the partnership to go on.

As a result of the thinking done at the DesignShop, CKE wanted to do the contract differently this time.

> What was really interesting about this is the way we approached them. I was not going to approach them the usual way. In fact, I said that if they spent $15,000 on extra design effort and found a way to engineer $10,000 out of the cost of store, I would want

them to do that extra work. And I said, "I am willing to pay you more for that." That is a different mindset.

By August 1995, CKE was part-way through implementing the results of the Store 2000 DesignShop. Could they judge its success at this stage?

The first prototype store opened only seven months after the DesignShop, and in its first full week of operation sales have already come up 10% over last year, without advertising or changing menus or the crew.

Although we did not meet our aggressive time schedule, when you take a look at the way other businesses do it, and the schedules proposed by top designers, we are far ahead of the curve.

Once the president got up there and sat in the store, he was comfortable. That store had many of the elements of the totally new store. We have pre- and post-market research showing the improvements are being well received by our customers.

We are now going into our second prototype, in Sacramento. As planned at the DesignShop event, we will go through the process of listening to the customer and to the operators and see what works and what does not work. We are going to get all of that feedback and cost-engineer it down. Basically we hope to cut the cost in half by only focusing on the changes that make a difference. Then the final prototype—the third one—will again cut the cost in half.

This cost-cutting was part of the intent of the DesignShop activity. Our target budget was going to be a certain dollar amount. When we introduced that number to our own internal people, they said it was impossible to cut the costs that much.

Last week we met in the new store. We wanted to get the most sensory feedback—the customers talking, the awnings buckling—pluses and minuses. The same people who had said that we could not operate within that budget were now saying, "We can do it."

Bill's alternative for coming up with the remodel plan would have been to do the "safe" and "clearly possible" thing by hiring a well-known, highly-respected consulting firm to do the job.

If we had hired someone, it would have been one of the top firms. They said it would take a minimum of a year to do the design and open the first store.

We got quotes of about $1 million. Using one of them would have worked, because we would have spent enough money to make it work.

Instead, using the DesignShop process, we spent about half of that and opened our remodeled store in a little over half the time they quoted. It was a very good experience.

Now that the store design has been successfully completed, Bill Espinosa and the CKE team are here at Wharton to keep pushing forward issues of overall business development. They hope the next three days of uninterrupted immersion in the DesignShop process will bring them similar levels of benefit for improving the structure of the CKE organization to cope with the coming decades.

Time to Begin the Group Process

This hope of achieving benefits for their own organizations has brought the other companies and individuals to the Wharton DesignShop event. In a sense, this unusually varied range of businesses, backgrounds and goals—ranging from the CKE hamburger people to Air Force leadership to health care providers—is an expansion of the "stakeholder" concept. What could an aerospace engineer contribute to a business school professor? What insight does a former nurse have for a management consultant? This wide span of stakeholders in 21st century organizations will certainly test the ability of the DesignShop format to extract value from a participant pool. We'll see if the variety helps or hurts.

The participants are still roaming the space, jump-starting their minds with the information all around them, and picking up an attitude of focus from the staff. Then a deep bell sound is heard, signaling that it's time to begin. Everyone drifts into the largest space, the "radiant room," defined by the half-circle of gray walls enclosing a set of chairs facing inward. Matt and Gail Taylor are at the front as key facilitators. Time to begin.

Employing the Environment
http://www.mgtaylor.com/mgtaylor/jotm/spring97/envir_creative.htm

Challenge

Welcome back.

These challenges will continue the pattern started in the previous chapter. Take a few moments to record your impressions of whatever struck you in this chapter. After you have finished, if you wish, refer back to the chapter to fill in any gaps or clarify any ideas. What questions are provoked?

1. Sketch one of the environments that you live or work in and describe how people behave in it. How does this current environment stimulate or inhibit the processes of individual or collective action? What is the soundrack you life and career is set to? What works for you and what doesn't? Include taste, touch smell, noise, visual aspects, etc.

2. Now sketch the environment as it could be and describe the new ways of work and behavior that it evokes. What changes make it a better place to work and live, changes that appeal to the heart and support the spirit as well as the mind? If you don't know how to do this, that's OK; you've identified a new realm of personal exploration just waiting for you.

3. Your sketch from Challenge 1 is the condition. Your sketch from Challenge 2 is the vision. The difference between condition and vision creates the problem. The problem is not the condition. The problem is how to bring the vision to the condition. What steps can and will you take to bring a part of your vision to you today?

Freeing Time & Attention

A key element of the DesignShop process is to eliminate blocks—identify and clear away the overhead that displaces creativity.

An environment that gives your mind and body what it needs most is likely not what you get under daily circumstances. Instead, your brain is required to pay attention to time management issues, social norms, home worries, recordkeeping, and burdens from the physical environment—at the same instant you are demanding that it be insightful, creative, decisive, communicative, or otherwise productive. All of us underestimate how strongly results are shaped by the structure or the boundaries of our surrounding environment, or how our structures and boundaries shape the results we seek.

Executives need to increase their creativity—their problem-solving, solution-generating ability—and judgment. But their way of working ties them firmly to a mode that undermines their ability to do so. Observe the effects of typically "structured" use of time and attention on executives:
- Their usual mode becomes one of rushing, very short meetings—averaging nineteen minutes—with condensed information transfer.
- They are expected to be "in command at all times," including running the meeting.
- They are expected to have the answers and make the decision, because "the buck stops here."
- They are expected to balance all competing interests, inside and outside the organization, at all times.
- While doing all of the above, they are supposed to be creative.

Because all of us have learned to bend our brains to the benefit of time, we no longer recognize time as a strong boundary condition impeding our ability to

After examining his data, the psychologist [Roger Barker] came to a startling and most un-American conclusion: Their settings were more important determinants of his subjects' behavior than their personalities.

—Winifred Gallagher
The Power of Place

think nor as a major source of mental overhead. We have all been trained to save time, to make things happen on time, to schedule time, calendar events, and build tight time structures.

We don't ask ourselves what happens when decisions on how to use time are instead prioritized for the benefit of your brain.

DesignShops construct a complete environment for the benefit of your mind, including the full scope of time issues. The DesignShop process answers the question: "How do you work with time to benefit your brain?" Consider what can be done with the many time-related variables to make you more productive:

- Manipulating hours, minutes, and number of days dedicated to each task,
- Changing the length of the days, including starting time and ending time,
- Giving participants a schedule, or keeping it hidden,
- Altering who is paying attention to time issues,
- Taking into account the role of sleep time, and the rising and falling of attention spans throughout the day,
- Experimenting with different rhythms and paces for all of these.

The brain and body respond strongly to the time called out by music—the tempo. "Sound," points out Stanford University professor of music Leonard Ratner, "touches us physically, as vibrations in the air. Physical and emotional responses to the movement of music are touched off by its pace, its regularity, its force, and its flow." Tempo enforces a mood. Timing and intensity communicate arrival or crescendo.

According to Dr. Georgi Lozanov's research into accelerated learning techniques, Baroque music's tempo and patterns help the brain stay focused on work while allowing the body to relax—an ideal state for long, intense learning periods. Depending on the nature of the task at hand, we must ask ourselves what music, tempo, and timing should be provided.

These issues have been woven into the structure and details of a DesignShop event.

Rhythm and harmony find their way into the inward places of the soul.

—PLATO

Freeing Time & Attention

We'll start by highlighting the biggest and most dramatic of the time-use techniques. We saw a three-day event, each day starting at 7:30 AM for breakfast, and ending at 8:00 PM, except for the 6:00 PM ending on the final day. Every day, for three days, the people in the room got smarter. By the end of those three days, when the teams pulled together to work on solutions to their specific problems, they were sizzling. Repeatedly, people reported having accomplished the equivalent of a year's worth of decision, design, and planning work during the course of an afternoon. It took them two days of concentrated preparation to put them in good enough mental form, with enough new tools and enough new information, to deliver a dazzling performance.

There's a jocular saying among psychologists that all the important stuff happens in the last fifteen minutes of the session. If so, it seems reasonable to ask—why not just hold fifteen-minute psychology sessions?

Similarly, at DesignShop events, the actual tactical solution to the problem gets done right at the end. So it seems reasonable to ask: why not hold fifteen-minute DesignShops? Why not expect breakthrough creativity in the same length of time as the average management meeting?

Scan Focus Act Model
http://www.mgtaylor.com/mgtaylor/glasbead/SFA.htm

This is why: There seems to be a certain amount of concentrated time—hours or days—which must be available to focus on a problem. A sizable chunk of that is spent in preparation for designing a solution, in the same way that an athlete spends more time warming-up, stretching, training and preparing than actually running the race. How much time does a brain need to be in peak form?

By the end of three days, you've dropped the extraneous mental baggage you carried in the door, you've loaded up your head with the complexity of the situation, you've got more

*The gods confound the man who first found out
How to distinguish hours!
Confound him, too
Who in this place set up a sundial,
To cut and hack my days so wretchedly
Into small portions.*

—Platus c. 200 B.C.

tools to work with, you've got more solutions to choose from, you're in top shape mentally.

The DesignShop requires the long hours and the multiple days precisely so that participants can stay focused on the present and the issues involved, rather than continually shift context to deal with the rules and demands of the standard office environment. Time issues affect intensity, immersion, concentration, attention, and rhythm.

Time issues are a sore spot for a lot of people. Matt Taylor observes:

> We have rarely had a client argue with us on a major process issue, but they will argue like hell about time.
>
> Sponsors will say in all seriousness, "Solving this problem is critical to our company—it is our top priority and you can do anything you want. But here are your boundaries: the DesignShop is going to last two days, and we'll meet each day from 8 AM to 6 PM." They argue whether it should be an eight or a ten or twelve-hour day. They get upset about whether or not a schedule is posted—all time-related issues.
>
> When the focus is placed on time, competing demands for attention immediately come to the fore. "What! Do you mean I am going to get home late?" Family demands are challenging bids for time. For individuals, the complaint might stem from not wishing to forgo the home environment. For single parents, going even an extra hour is really difficult. Or managers often say, "I want to get on an airplane and go someplace else tomorrow, so let's keep the last day's session short."
>
> Looked at objectively, if solving this problem really is top priority, aren't the other concerns secondary problems to be facilitated, and not allowed to block major achievements that the company urgently needs?
>
> The manager who wants to pare down the hours on the last day of the DesignShop, the day when everyone is finally working in peak form, is thinking of time as a constant. Although 'time' in the abstract is a sliceable, segmentable, uniform entity, time isn't all the same for us humans. We are biological creatures. The manager seems to be thinking two hours off of a three-day DesignShop is trivial and couldn't matter.
>
> Cutting down to ten hours on the last day means we lose 20% of the result of that one day. No—you lose 80% of the total result. He's not seeing the effect on the

brain, the nonlinearity of the situation, the discontinuity of the result. What you can achieve in a one-day event is not one-third of what you can achieve over three days—it is more like one-tenth.

Bryan Coffman, who has facilitated DesignShop events for over ten years for organizations ranging from the Commissioner of the IRS to components of Walt Disney World, agrees:

> Only a small percentage of people will break through to enhanced creativity during a one-day session. They have not had the benefit of sleeping on the problem two nights, not been forced to work hard on it from different vantage points. They have had time to come in, listen politely, and go home.

"Sleeping on the problem" is a deliberate use of time as a problem-solving technique. You've spent the day in "accelerated learning" or "immersion learning," loading up your head with complexity, new information, new paradigms, and vast new sets of tools to apply to your problem. That night's sleep will shift the learning into long-term memory. When you are handed a creative challenge at 8 AM, your mind comes to work with a different integrated tool kit, and perhaps with a restructured view of the world and the problem than you had the day before.

The only way you totally immerse in working with a challenge is when you have an opportunity to get away from the mundane; to step away from the habits, thought patterns, and tools we use during our standard days; to see a wide variety of viewpoints.

The long hours give you enough time to try out, use up, exhaust, and discard habits and standard ways of doing things that haven't been capable of solving the problem. The long hours give you the time to move into trying out new, experimental forms of problem-solving. You can even use the long hours as a way to relax self-imposed rules that are holding you back—you can try out an idea without being so nervous about the listener's response. You can break taboos with excuse of fatigue, relax with fatigue, become more open to information, including information from your unconscious.

Dissolving old structures and reformulating new ones is part of the creative process. It is, quite literally, the chemistry of a solution.

From an interpersonal perspective, the long hours give the time needed to get comfortable with the people around you—get to know the new ones, and get to know the familiar ones in a deeper way.

Vantage Points Model
http://www.mgtaylor.com/
mgtaylor/glasbead/vantgpts.htm

Christopher Fuller, an artist providing visual interpretations and graphic support for DesignShop participants, says, "I first thought, Why the long hours? Then I realized that with human conflict, this is how you reach agreement. With short hours, people can leave mad and come back refreshed to fight again tomorrow. Long hours make you stay until you find a solution. You can keep working to a resolution if you have to find an answer."

In a time when managers are trying to increase their productivity by making meetings shorter, DesignShops are getting longer, stretching into more days rather than fewer. Two key factors driving the trend to longer DesignShops are increasing numbers of participants and increasing environmental complexity. The greater external complexity means you have to take more time to gather relevant data—there are more resources to be considered, more complexity regarding competitors and markets. To capture the complexity of the environment, managers include more and more stakeholders in the meeting. DesignShop sessions now routinely run with fifty to eighty participants, and the process therefore takes longer.

Frances Gillard, former Center Master for a AEDC's Gossick Leadership Center which offers an ongoing DesignShop capability for the organization, notes: "When people have had several DesignShops, they can productively do a one-day follow-up design session to work on smaller problems or follow-up problems. By then the participants know how to use the new tools, move quickly into the mental warm-up processes, don't waste time and energy fighting to revive an exhausted solution or use an inappropriate tool. Instead they buckle down to the creativity of generating new options, and get a lot out of a short session."

Why would anyone spend a lot of time and energy fighting to hang on to a particular management tool? It doesn't seem reasonable when your company's life is on the line, but people do. We saw it—especially with time management tools like schedules and agendas.

Schedules and agendas are standard, useful ways of moving efficiently through the business of a meeting or a seminar. They seem to be merely time-structuring devices, and yet have major consequences on brain function and creativity. They are also a major emotional hot button.

Freeing Time & Attention

We watched the buttons go off for every person for whom a DesignShop was a new experience. It started with Lynn Galida from the Wharton Graduate School of Business, attending a DesignShop for the first time. She is here on behalf of her boss—who, although a sponsor, will also be attending a DesignShop for the first time.

The day before the DesignShop activity starts, the entire facilitation team and the sponsors are deep in fine tuning and crafting the proposed schedule for the event. Lynn says very matter-of-factly that her people will, of course, want copies of the schedules and agendas, and could they have them in advance? The equally matter-of-fact reply comes back—don't worry about the "in advance" part, because we don't hand out schedules or agendas for a DesignShop session.

The explanation: The schedule now being crafted by the sponsors and the DesignShop staffers lays out a proposed route through different information exercises, in order to bring the participant group to the goal of a productive problem solution. As in theater, where actors, musicians, lighting technicians, and property managers must all coordinate their activities, the staff lays out action tracks for furniture and space preparation, toys, props, music, and video recording equipment needed for each planned exercise. Just as the audience concentrates on the play, DesignShop participants concentrate on the work—not on the schedule. The schedule is hidden. It is not displayed to participants.

The job of clock watching is handled by the staff, but even their monitoring is hidden. Break-out spaces may have been made smaller, made larger, set with table, chairs, and utensils for lunch or books updated with transcripts of the last module's work, but these events will have happened quietly, invisibly, without taking participants' attention from the current work, without letting them wonder what the title of the next exercise means.

As the hours pass, the schedule will be modified to tailor the future steps to the progress of the group. The facilitation team will make the judgment call to prolong a session if the group is working well and productively, or to redirect an exercise if, in their judgment, circumstances warrant. If, as the work goes along, the participants need something radically different than what has been planned in order to reach their goals, then the plan is tossed out wholesale and the entire event is redesigned at that moment. Think of it as being similar to improvisational theatre. A very experienced sponsor of DesignShops said he had seen it often: "With other consultants it's all done by the book, from A to B to C until you reach Z. Here, the book goes in the trash. The theme is never lost, the goal is never lost, but the plan undergoes continual and sweeping changes."

The explanation to Lynn about the schedule is given, and people turn back to the business of preparation.

But Lynn is frozen in place. It's as if she has "no schedules or agendas" going through Instant Replay mode and still can't believe what she heard. So she gives it another try. "Excuse me, but my people expect schedules." Her voice gets louder, "They want schedules!" Then with real passion and a little bit of panic, "They need schedules! I have to give them schedules!"

At this point, Lynn looks a wee bit high-strung. She's talking as if these professional adults are going to stress out or suffer major trauma if they don't get a sheet of paper with times and topics written on it. And guess what—she's right. When these people show up for the DesignShop, it's clear that they want those schedules. They need those schedules. They even get a little testy. "No schedules! Where's my schedule!" "What do you mean 'participants in the DesignShop aren't given a schedule'!" Some reactions aren't much different than a dedicated heroin addict being told he was going "cold turkey," eyes probing left and right, searching for a hidden stash of schedules.

What must be going through their minds?
- What kind of place is this, that doesn't have a schedule?
- How do I know if I want to be here or somewhere else if I don't have the schedule?
- How can I figure out what to pay attention to without a schedule?
- If something even more interesting is coming up later in the day, I need to prepare my comments for it instead of paying attention now.
- How can I coordinate the talks with my own schedule, so I can zip out and make phone calls?

Three Cat Model
http://www.mgtaylor.com/mgtaylor/glasbead/3catmod.htm

Freeing Time & Attention

- Where is the agenda? I need to know where we are going. I need to monitor my time and my content so that I do not bring up a big issue for debate when we have only a minute left for this topic.

We are so accustomed to certain ways of operating in the business world that we cannot properly evaluate their true costs, their subtle consequences, or their inappropriateness to certain situations.

Over time, after our first DesignShop event, the impact of an openly-announced schedule or the lack of it became clear to us. The openly-announced schedule creates a series of paradoxes. It lets one person tune out on the present conversation because the official topic "isn't my responsibility, and I don't need to pay attention until Item 4." Conversely, for others it places a tremendous intellectual burden of self-monitoring and self-suppression. Instead of paying attention to dealing with the problem, we are now paying attention to meeting a time budget. The one way you can have the freedom to engage fully at the present moment and not worry about the clock is if someone else is monitoring the clock and making the judgments about moving on or continuing to closure. The purpose of a schedule or agenda is not lost, but the burden or cost of handling it has been delegated away from people who should be doing other work. The DesignShop facilitation team provides this as part of logistical support to the intellectual process.

Other supports to the intellectual process include creative time techniques, called Time Compression and Time Travel, to help participants jettison other restrictive rules that have been encumbering their insight and creativity. The DesignShop starts with a quote from the poet Rilke: "Unless you've got a thousand year perspective backwards and forwards, you are trapped in the present."

With Time Compression, participants have a brief time—one or two hours—to come back and report a solution on a really complex problem. This is most useful for groups that have found themselves stalled back home. "Stalled" may be taking the form of arguing or endless thrashing as they search unsuccessfully for a "safe" or an obviously successful solution. Somehow, there needs to be a way to get these

What you see, yet can not see over, is as good as infinite.

—Thomas Carlyle

Even if you are on the right track, you'll get run over if you just sit there.

—Will Rogers

people off the starting block, to get them to stop the profitless worrying and start doing some designing and creating.

To take the pressure up further and to remind the group that the rest of the world isn't standing still, the time scale may be changed so that each minute of the time allotted for the exercise represents a week or a month passing. The next step in Time Compression is to announce that time is going by as they sit and stew. Suddenly, the group is handed a simulated headline from the *Wall Street Journal*, and someone notices, "Hey! This date is a year in the future and we haven't made a decision yet!" This often still isn't enough to prompt leaving the safety zone of thrashing mode. The next *Wall Street Journal* headline shows up, and it has your company's name blazoned across it with the comment: "Investors Becoming Shy. No Decisions Made in Eighteen Months." Now the reaction is "Oh, no! The market is reacting. We'd better start doing something!"

People respond to the information in the feedback loop. Under the challenge and stimulation of this high-compression, information-saturated, intense, demanding environment, people start to remember talent sets that they often haven't used since college. Their natural competitiveness drives them to do well rather than worrying about following the rules—the rules that won't work.

Time Travel, or what might be called the art of Backcasting, is another powerful technique related to time and perception. For whatever the reason, looking backward—Backcasting—to imagine events which have supposedly already happened is much easier for us than forecasting. When trying to work your way out of a current problem, it is more productive to leap into the future, imagine a successful end state, and then explain how you got there rather than getting lost in the myriad of current details and stumbling blocks. Psychologists note an empirically consistent and very different response when participants are asked to backcast instead of forecast.

Gail Taylor also has observed this consistency: "If you ask someone to forecast and hand them a problem which says: 'From today's date, describe the next twenty years,' people routinely say that they can't predict the future. Their written descriptions of the next twenty years are brief, not particularly rich, and are heavily

Freeing Time & Attention

weighted towards the content of today's newspaper headlines. But if you hand the same person a problem which says, 'Today is 2050; now describe the last twenty years,' people will write a great deal."

Maybe forecasting is less productive because the welter of current facts places a constricting barrier on our creative problem-solving ability. Maybe the fact that yesterday was very much like today, and today is very much like tomorrow, keeps problem-solving attention fixed on smooth trends rather than radical breakthroughs. Whatever the reason, forecasting is a weak technique.

The recognition of how powerful Backcasting is—of using it to create a common vision of the future, and then using that vision to let people achieve their maximum potential—was a gift of insight given to Matt Taylor by the novelist C.S. Forester. Forester was best known as the author of the *Horatio Hornblower* series, as well as the author of *The African Queen*. Here is Matt's story:

> When I was a boy, I loved the C.S. Forester *Hornblower* stories and reread them until I almost had them memorized. When I was about thirteen, my mother found that Forester was living nearby. She wrote him a letter and Forester invited us over for the morning. We came at 8:00 AM and stayed the whole day.
>
> We ended up in his living room at 5:00 at night, and he said, "Have you ever read *The African Queen*?"

Matt had seen the movie with Humphrey Bogart and Katherine Hepburn battling their way down the African river to single-handedly take on and sink a German warship, but—no—he hadn't read the book.

> "You really ought to read the book, because it's very important," Forester said. "Let me tell you how I wrote the book. I imagined two characters—people easily drawn from life, an old spinster and a drunken, irresponsible Cockney boat captain—and I imagined, what could they be at their maximum? I built that in my mind, then I wrote the entire plot of the book to give them the experiences necessary to become that."

"I knew," says Matt, "I had been told something really important. Of course it took a number of years to understand what I learned."

S'poze Model
http://www.mgtaylor.com/
mgtaylor/glasbead/spozemod.htm

Undoubtedly, we become what we envisage.

—Claude M. Bristorl

The first part of what Matt learned was "you don't get there from here, but you can get here from there"—you can't get to the desired future state by starting with your current vision of the present. What you need to do is envision the desired future state of what these people or this company could be at their maximum, and then you begin moving as much of that future state into the present as possible. That future vision will help to solve present problems, and keep you on course. Matt continues:

> What had to happen for the missionary and the Cockney was for them to come to an understanding—a mission, a goal. Now here was the vision: they are going to blow up a German warship.
>
> And then they had to solve the problems of getting their boat, the *African Queen*, down to Lake Victoria and doing it. At every problem they came to, for logical purposes, they were blocked, dead in the water—a broken propeller or impassable rapids.
>
> If they had not had the vision, the mission, they would have stopped. They brought "there," the vision of the future, to "here," the present problem with the busted propeller or getting through the weeds, to inform them how to proceed day to day. The vision provided the continuity and the wholeness. But the ability to take it day by day provided the capacity to deal with problems as they came. They applied the vision to each incremental challenge they faced, so that each incremental step took them closer to their vision.
>
> In the DesignShop, our job is to heal those diseases, the barriers, that stop people from reaching their maximum potential. How? Exactly the way I said. You take them down to the river and give them a boat and a goal and they go down through the swamps to blow up the German warship.

Treat people as if they were what they ought to be and you help them to become what they are capable of being.

—GOETHE

Forester did it with fictional characters. DesignShops do it with real people and organizations. An MG Taylor axiom states, "The future is rational only in hindsight." Client after client travels to the future and then discerns the rational path for having gotten there.

We have already implicitly seen one fairly simple Backcasting story when we talked about Carl Jr.'s creation of the plans for Store 2000. You'll recall that they asked themselves what they envisioned the store to be in the year 2000, not what they might want in 1994 when they were working the problem. They designed for what technologies and demands would be present in the future, but gave themselves the constraint that they would not include any technology which was not on the market within six months of their start-to-build date.

Avis Rent-A-Car

Gail Taylor gives an example: "We have told other problem solvers, 'You are so successful that *Fortune* magazine is coming to interview you. How did you do it?' And from there, people invent pathways that lead to the successful conclusion. We said to Avis: 'Picture this: you've got no central reservation center. How did you do it?'"

With business booming for Avis Rent-A-Car, their central reservation system was fast approaching overload. Operating costs in their Tulsa, Oklahoma, location had been rising, so expanding the existing center or building a second center in Tulsa was not appealing.

The planned solution—conventional and reasonable—was to open a second center in a geographic location with lower costs. The reservation load would be split between Tulsa and the new site. Cities had been evaluated, a new Virginia site for the second center selected, purchase of the property underway, the necessary funds committed, and building plans were being drawn up. Tulsa employees would be offered the opportunity to relocate to the new center.

Charlie Bell, the Vice President responsible for worldwide reservations, had been wrestling with the complexities of coordination between the two sites. With co-operation, he felt, everything would be fine. But with the employees as nervous as they were, as unhappy about the idea of relocating, cooperation could be scarce. To try for that smooth transition, to iron out problems, to soothe employees nervous about the change, Charlie decided to hold a DesignShop event.

The first task for the DesignShop session was to get everyone focused on requirements for continued success. Everyone knew Avis couldn't keep growing at the Tulsa location—just too expensive, something had to be done. Then they tried the radical Backcasting approach: "You've got no central reservation center, and things are running very well. The workload is way up, but costs are way down, and employee quality of life has improved. How did you do it?"

By Backcasting the question, the participants could find the solution. Instead of pouring money into a new building, instead of managing two geographically remote locations, instead of relocating people out of state, a very different picture began developing around telecommuting. Why not work in local neighborhood

Appropriate Response Model
http://www.mgtaylor.com/
mgtaylor/glasbead/appresp.htm

groups, use low-cost buildings scattered around the suburbs of Tulsa, keep all the jobs in Tulsa, but at a much lower cost of commuting to the workers, using cheaper space?

Working in the DesignShop context—while maintaining a focus on employee quality of life—had actually eliminated a variety of barriers, and in the process opened up possibilities which had not been previously visible or available to the Avis team. In the process of then bringing the future vision to the present, they worked through tactical solutions to the complexities and issues of the problem. It was hard work, just as the *African Queen's* journey through rapids and leech-infested swamp water was hard work.

For Avis, for Charlie, and for the employees, the results were great. They broadened their options beyond the conventional solution—the "pretty good" solution of building a second site—and moved to a great reservation system operating at lower cost and higher employee satisfaction through telecommuting and two additional mini-centers. Unexpected benefits kept accruing. They found they had greater flexibility, could add business without adding facilities, add new employees at lower overhead cost, and with the restructuring they gained better productivity at the central Tulsa location.

Innovations in time management played a role in getting this kind of breakthrough result, but they are only one part of the story. To see the others, we need to return to the Wharton event just now getting underway.

Challenge

1. As before, record impressions and questions upon finishing the chapter.

2. Very quickly compose a list of practices or systems that your company could not do without, but which seem to be limiting its development in some way. Choose one or two by circling them.

3. Before moving on to the next part of the challenge, pick a specific date somewhere seven to ten years in the future. Now put yourself into that date, in a specific environment—notice the season of the year, what you are wearing, the weather, what's happening around you. Once you're firmly, mentally established in that year and can envision it clearly, move on to the next part of this challenge.

4. For the last five years, your company has been operating without the practices and systems that you circled in your Journal almost a decade ago. Breaking free from these constraints once seemed impossible, but now it's all clear and so simple to see. You're on your way to have lunch with a friend you haven't seen for years, and she's very interested in hearing the story of how you broke free so she can apply it to her business. You pick up a pencil—a quaint tool from the last century, but you still like to use one—and draw a diagram that explains the whole story.

Exploring New Terrain...

All participants and staff are gathered in the radiant room, the largest space in the DesignShop environment, for the opening event. After a welcome from Wharton professor Jerry Wind, facilitators Matt and Gail Taylor give a whirlwind introduction to what is coming up, including:

- goals for the event, both for the overall group and for the individual organizations present,
- uses of models—a topic to be covered extensively throughout the session,
- resources available (the World Wide Web, library, the entire DesignShop facilitation team),
- ground rules, including confidentiality, fiduciary responsibility, and participants committing to working together for the full three days,
- a bare minimum about the schedule, and
- the underlying structure of what we'll be doing over the next three days: the Scan, Focus, Act sequence.

Scan, Focus, Act

In the Scan phase, participants reach out to explore ideas far outside their usual range of expertise. People will expand their usual time horizons, work with complex systems models, and learn rapid information-gathering techniques. They will look at the problem from a whole range of vantage points that they have never visited before. Just as important, everyone will get to know the skills and biases of fellow participants. During Scan, they are encouraged explicitly to avoid trying to draw direct connections with the problem that brought them here.

Only after a thorough Scan do you move into the Focus phase in which you formulate performance specs for the optimal solution to your problem. You are focusing on the problem, but you are also generating options for what that problem

In the Scan phase, participants reach out to explore ideas far outside their usual range of expertise. People will expand their usual time horizons, work with complex systems models, and learn rapid information-gathering techniques.

Scan Focus Act Model
http://www.mgtaylor.com/mgtaylor/glasbead/SFA.htm

SCAN

really is and, therefore, how it will be solved. These will range from no-risk to absolutely wacky. It's important to come at the problem many different times from many different angles. There is a saying at DesignShops that if you do seven iterations of coming at, looking at, and redesigning your problem, the results will be a thousand times better.

FOCUS

In doing so, the problem definition changes, often beyond recognition, from the one you originally brought with you—a sign that the Scan has been effective. Possible solutions undergo continuous reworking, with ideas that don't "fit" falling away naturally, until the strongest solution strategy is clear.

In Act, strategy is turned into tactics, and tactics into action steps which include target dates of completion. The DesignShop event is not over until there is an action plan in hand.

ACT

Scan is the longest phase, with Focus taking less time, and Act happening very quickly at the end—exactly the opposite of what normally happens back at the office. Normal procedure for just about everyone is to skip the Scan, zip through Focus, and spend almost all their effort on Act. The failure of that comfortable but ineffective sequence is what has brought everyone to the DesignShop.

But right now, at Wharton, there's no time to spend analyzing the sequence in advance. It's time to jump right into Scan.

Take-a-Panel, Share-a-Panel

Just as athletes and teams warm up before a game, everyone needs to warm up—as individuals and as a cooperating group—to prepare for solving our organization's problem.

A well-planned DesignShop session includes participants who are new to each other that may never meet again. As in the Carl's Jr. example, it can bring together dozens of people ranging from corporate executives to a typical fast-food customer. How can a large, varied group be most quickly brought into sync, performing at the highest possible level to address the key questions that called them together?

Exploring New Terrain...

In DesignShop sessions, as in sporting events, there will be some time before participants are directly tackling the problem that brings everyone together. First are warm-up exercises having multiple purposes: to stretch mental muscles, learn new information, get to know fellow participants and their skills, strengths, weaknesses, and biases, and develop new skills in collaboration and cooperation. This will happen quickly.

In a typical DesignShop, the first exercise—called Take-a-Panel—starts with questions which may range from provocative to very basic, such as "What do you want to get out of this DesignShop?" The questions act as a mental warm-up for each individual. Each person takes a large, writable wall panel and begins posting his or her responses to the specific questions assigned.

Why start this way? Why not have the groups just discuss the questions, with each person taking a turn, and someone serving as moderator?

The pragmatic answer—this kick-starting exercise has evolved over years, and it works. The longer answer requires analyzing human interaction patterns. In any sizable collection of people, some are extroverts, others shy, some articulate, others are not. Even in casual clothes, the "leaders" often stand out. Every move they make gives them away; their very tone of voice establishes their position within the group. If everyone is just thrown into a small group, all the standard patterns of interaction automatically kick in—the leader leads, the followers follow, the extroverts talk, the shy ones sit there nervously.

Is "being led" what everyone is here for? If the leaders had all the answers, nobody would need to be here to work on their organization's big challenge—you could just do as you're told, implementing the leaders' plan. Instead, the goal is to tap into everyone's skills and knowledge. In order to encourage this participation, it is wise to avoid triggering the status-related reactions that lead people to self-censor.

Instead of starting by sitting around, looking at, and judging each other, participants immediately start working individually on a problem: contributing, thinking, writing, moving. All are busy at their own panels—no one is watching— you can be as fast, slow, sure, or tentative as you want. There is a lot of room to write and draw, and mistakes are erasable. Over the next twenty minutes, a sense of momentum builds as ideas begin to flow onto the panels.

It is now time to share the results in an exercise called "Share-a-Panel." Participants divide into groups of about five—not randomly. The groups have been selected with care to provide diversity among the participants—different professions, different ages, and backgrounds, with as much mixing as possible.

But does everyone sit down and have each person present his or her work to the group for critiquing? No, this would break momentum. We're on a roll here and the last thing we need to do is revert to a standard meeting format where, once again, the usual leaders take over and everyone else shuts up, feeling dumb or dominated. Gail Taylor explains how the next part works:

> Now the participants search out each member of their small group and present their panels to each other, on a one-to-one basis. It's loud, lively, and chaotic: everyone is hunting for the people they've missed, introducing themselves, explaining their viewpoints, what their business is about, their challenges and desires — the focus is on the panels, with the explainer pointing to items there and the listener reading them.

It helps that what's being explained is now an external object—words on the wall—rather than a stand-alone verbal assertion. Again, as for the "Take-a-Panel" exercise, this is a clever mechanism: a technique to help us, as evolved primates, suppress our bad habits and nervousness and augment our intellects.

Ten-Step Knowledge Management Model
http://www.mgtaylor.com/mgtaylor/glasbead/tenstep.htm

Is this mechanism a key insight of amazing power? No, it's a relatively small thing. The reason that DesignShops work so well is not that they implement one major insight; instead, they incorporate a large number of strategies, tactics, processes, and tricks that combine to give high performance.

Physical movement is another tactic used during both the Take-a-Panel and Share-a-Panel exercises. Getting people up and moving is an eye-opener, and it gets the blood pumping—but what else is going on here? To answer this, consider your own experience. Where do you have your best ideas? For a lot of us, it is places like the shower, not at an office desk staring at the walls or at a computer screen. When you're mentally stalled, do you find it helpful to get up and take a walk? To tap into these poorly-understood benefits, the entire DesignShop process involves as much physical movement as possible—the exact opposite of the stifling, physically boring act of sitting at a desk in a cubicle.

As was explained in the ground rules given during the initial orientation at the start of the DesignShop event, participants have no need to make personal notes to preserve their insights during this (or any other) part of the event. While the participants are discussing their panels with other group members, facilitators are recording their work. By the time the panels need to be erased for reuse, all the information will have been captured.

Only now, after the individual panels have been explained, does the small group assemble and start some analysis. "The next exercise for the groups," explains Gail Taylor, "is to ask, 'Where are our agreements and disagreements? What have we learned as a set of five about our individual beliefs and our group beliefs?'"

Years of DesignShop experience have shown that giving the participants a common experience is even more important than achieving complete alignment or agreement. From the basis of shared reality, they will build the foundation from which they will ultimately solve their problems.

Note that, in this account, we have left vague the issue of exactly what these people are working on and what specific questions they are addressing on their panels, other than what their goals are for this meeting. That is deliberate for two reasons: first, it varies for each group, depending on what overall challenge their organization is working with at this DesignShop, and second, it's not critical at this stage that the questions be precisely relevant to the overall challenge. It is so early in the process that the immediate goals are different—getting to know each other, and, just as important, beginning to build a common experience base.

Creating a Common Experience

Years of DesignShop experience have shown that giving the participants a common experience is even more important than achieving complete alignment or agreement. From the basis of shared reality, they will build the foundation from which they will ultimately solve their problems.

"Creating a common experience base"? "Basis of shared reality"? These phrases may seem a bit—shall we say—touchy-feely. But shared experience, be it war, creative endeavor, or other life events, forges a strong bond between people and can form the basis of mutual understanding.

> *Not all experiences are equal. There is a hierarchy of experience. To the degree the human system is alerted, it will pay attention to some experiences more than others. This event is compressed, exciting, dense; they are in an environment of high alert. So this experience starts to outweigh all those other years of experiences.*
>
> — MATT TAYLOR

The exercises aren't motivated by what feels good to participants. In fact, exactly the opposite sometimes occurs. The value of the common experience holds regardless of whether a given participant enjoys, or even agrees with, the content. Matt Taylor explains:

> One of the canons of our work is that we try not to care whether people like the DesignShop process, or even whether they are all in alignment with the outcome. We would prefer that they are, of course, because that is a gentler and kinder experience, but the fact of the DesignShop is that thirty to seventy people all have a relatively common experience with the content of that DesignShop and each other. That is an undeniable fact that can never be taken away. That is now part of their experience base.
>
> Not all experiences are equal, obviously. There is a hierarchy of experience, and so to the degree that the human system is alerted, it will pay attention to some experiences more than others. This event is compressed, exciting, dense; they are in an environment of high alert. So this experience starts to outweigh all those other years of experiences.

If the situation requires even greater intensity, the staff designs a custom experience for a given DesignShop session. This can be extraordinarily powerful, bringing a feuding group to a powerful unity, guaranteeing that everyone present is on high alert, or adding a gut-level sense of realism to an issue that people aren't yet taking seriously enough.

Colorful Common Experiences

A series of colorful and memorable common experiences which generated loads of high alert was crafted over a number of years for Agency Group, a division of a complex insurance and financial services company with a diversity of corporate cultures due to a long series of acquisitions. These experiences provide examples of how—in modules structured to teach specific skills such as leadership or networking—the emotional strength of the experience helps anchor all participants into a common outlook.

DesignShops are often envisioned as discrete events, but Agency Group wanted to encourage people to use design process every day, bring "there" to here consistently, and thereby change the culture. They decided to do this by offering workshops in which people could learn about design work as part of a new way of working. The goal here was education, not producing a work product.

5 Es of Education Model
http://www.mgtaylor.com/mgtaylor/glasbead/5Esofed.htm

Exploring New Terrain...

Jon Foley, one of several who directed the workshops in cooperation with the company's visionary CEO and COO team, describes a common experience that served as a wake-up call:

> Understand where we are: We're in the conference room and our CEO comes over the videotape saying that the message we're about to see is being delivered throughout the organization. The news was that Agency Group had been purchased by Mitsubishi. Our CEO was on his way to the airport to become the president of Mitsubishi America. We would get a new CEO and learn new ways of working.
>
> Imagine what this did to the participants. A lot of them believed, a lot turned white. Many doubted, but suddenly everyone felt there was more significance to this when the staffers handing out packages of information, and a Japanese Gentleman dressed in a business suit walked around quietly accompanied by people dressed up as senior managers. The Japanese Gentleman would make quiet comments from time to time. People were freaking out.

Talk about a powerful common experience. For people who had worked in big organizations all their lives, this was probably the closest they'd ever come to facing what it would mean to have their comfortable jobs change overnight. This was now a group on high alert, a group that had a gut-level reminder that "Our huge, seemingly invulnerable fortress of a company is not invulnerable at all. And evidently our CEO would like us to try to keep that firmly in mind as we tackle the challenge that has brought us together."

In another exercise designed to encourage more leadership initiative by mid-level and high-level managers at the Agency Group, Jon led a team that designed a workshop modeled on an episode from the television series *Star Trek: The Next Generation*. At the time, the company was preparing to divide its unified structure into thirteen smaller business units. Each unit would have its own leadership team. The members of these teams had to wake up to the need to become self-directing, instead of awaiting leadership and direction to flow down to them from the top, as it always had. The danger for the new business units was that their management might not step up to the challenge in time to prevent damage.

In the television story that Jon used as a model, the captain of the Starship Enterprise has been kidnapped by a powerful and technically-advanced enemy—the

*Participants directly experienced—
with intensity
the need for them
to provide leadership,
to create new strategies
that would withstand
traitorous assault.
They felt and internalized
insights about responsibility and
accountability
in new and deeper ways.*

Borg (cyborgs). By linking the captain into their man/machine mental network, the Borg have complete access to all the captain's knowledge. Everything the captain knows about the Enterprise, the enemy now knows: technical vulnerabilities, assets, battle plans, secrets, top security computer access codes….and all the data contained in those computer files.

Back on the Enterprise, the remaining crew members realize that every bit of their existing knowledge is in the hands of the enemy. All the old plans are worthless. To defeat the Borg, they will need to replace the kidnapped captain with new leadership, create new answers and new fighting tactics that neither the old captain nor the computer know.

So, in the Agency Group exercise, Jon had the CEO similarly abandon the corporate ship taking with him the secrets of the company's future. They could no longer go forward executing someone else's plans; they needed to create their own, new answers. Participants directly experienced—with intensity—the need for them to provide leadership, to create new strategies that would withstand traitorous assault. They felt and internalized insights about responsibility and accountability in new and deeper ways.

S'poze Model
http://www.mgtaylor.com/
mgtaylor/glasbead/spozemod.htm

The simulation, fraught with the tension that comes from playing for high stakes, was both stressful and useful. Subsequently, many people asked to practice "thinking out of the box" using "real" scenarios more often.

Occasionally, a client will object to this kind of exercise, concerned about the intensity of the simulation. Gail Taylor observes, "In response to similar requests in the past, we have tried leaving out some part, but we don't get the same results." The DesignShop is an evolved procedure, having grown out of hundreds of cycles of design-and-test-and-redesign. We may or may not understand why each part adds to the whole, but it works whether we understand it in detail or not.

Another instance of success using a theatrical-style simulation to provide a common experience to build unity took place at the Arnold Engineering Development Center (AEDC), a military-affiliated test facility in Tennessee.

Burying the Hatchet at AEDC

While AEDC is owned by the Air Force, it is operated by civilian companies working as contractors and subcontractors, with very few military personnel on base. People who work at AEDC—whether military or civilian, management or union worker—are often the second or third generation in their family to do so. Frequently, both spouses work on the base, but that doesn't mean things always proceed smoothly. In this long and complex history of labor relations, there are no secrets. Everyone knows about everything in great and intimate detail.

Family fights are often the most vicious of feuds. One senior manager looked back at a particulary dark period:

> There had been a severe strike around Christmas of 1990—an evil battle, and probably unneeded. It had gone into a downward spiral, and it is hard to get out of those.
>
> From the point of view of many people, the bad blood wasn't about any substantive issue. It wasn't about whether you want $1 more or $2 more. Rather than working with each other, people took positions, and soon they couldn't get out of them. Things started going downhill. There was a new contract, but it didn't resolve the situation.

By now the problem was tearing the place apart. Labor and management had been at each other's throats for months. There had even been episodes of slashing tires and trashing offices.

Colonel William (Bill) Rutley, the Commander of AEDC, had a situation that could blow up in his face. He took a chance and decided to bring the two sides together in a three-day DesignShop. He explains:

> When we put the union representatives into a DesignShop with the management, we took a severe risk. You do not know exactly what will happen. I told the DesignShop staff that they were in this to try to drive a change. You can't drive a change and still be careful in this situation. You really have to put them into a room and start sucking the air out until that change happens. But I am convinced that organizations don't change unless you show them the abyss.

It was decided in advance that although he was the sponsor, Col. Rutley would stay out of the DesignShop event, letting the two sides interact without his mediation. On the front lines of the management side was John Poparad, who explains that—as in every DesignShop—the group doesn't start out confronting difficult issues immediately:

This was my first exposure to the DesignShop process. We did not start with the union/management relationship. We started working with the focus on AEDC. As the facilitator, Matt centered everyone on two essential tasks: Can we get everyone to build on a basic vision of the future for AEDC and then choose those parts that we can get everyone to agree on and start to implement them. Within that vision, what roles would people play? Now you have a vested interest in the success of AEDC because you are part of it and have helped to create it. It is a part of you.

To say that you "sign up for the big picture," or "have a common vision"—those words aren't good enough. Everyone works on modeling the organization. If Matt could get the warring sides to buy into the same model of AEDC, then they could work together.

Late in the second day, several people report, a moment of transformation occurred between the labor leader and the leader from management, with the rest of the participants looking on. The confrontation was heated. The labor leader demanded acknowledgment that labor had been put into a corner.

The management leader began moving toward the moment of clarity. He acknowledged, yes, labor had been boxed in, and he promised, he would never put labor in that position again. The room was quiet, awaiting the response from the labor leader. One attendee's memory of what the labor leader said: "Then we'll never need to strike again."

The room stayed silent. A facilitator recounts:

I don't know if anyone knew what had just happened! Or maybe they were all silent because they did understand: from that moment on, nothing was going to be as it had been.

Exploring New Terrain...

Colonel Rutley, though staying away deliberately, was monitoring the process:

> For the first couple of days of the event, the DesignShop staff would come up at night and tell me what was going on. I kept telling them they were in this to try to drive a change. After a couple of days, one of the facilitators said that this would break in the right direction tomorrow morning. They thought I should be there.

At 8 PM that evening, the staff members brainstormed on how to provide the right experience for the group in order to emotionally internalize the intellectual change that had been achieved. They had noted that participants had kept saying "we have to bury the hatchet," but didn't know how to get past the strong feelings and achieve closure. The inspiration struck to actually transform the symbolism of those words into action: "Let's do it! Let's actually bury the hatchet!"

The inspiration struck to actually transform the symbolism of those words into action: "Let's do it! Let's actually bury the hatchet!"

—Col. Rutley

Between 8:00 that evening and 8:00 the next morning, there was a massive amount of work to be done as they pulled together a complete set of funeral plans. The deceased hatchet would repose in a hand-crafted coffin: Frances Gillard, an AEDCer facilitating her first Design Shop, roped her husband into spending the night in his home woodworking shop building a coffin crafted to the hatchet's precise specifications. Black robes, veils, and other clothes had to be found for the hatchet's "wailing widow" and the knowledge workers who would act as mourners. They rounded up a car to act as a hearse, chose a burial site, got the death certificate drawn up, and got the death march music orchestrated. Then, the Grim Reaper made the rounds, and paid a visit to all to announce the death.

The next morning's session began with funeral music. The veiled widow and other mourners robed in black carried candles in a mournful procession.

John Poparad, a member of a contractor's management team, describes how it happened and the impact on the management/labor feud:

> On the third day I was sitting next to Barry, the union president, when the knowledge workers came in with a coffin. Inside the coffin was a hatchet.

A "minister" delivered the eulogy talking about the relationship that had just died. A funeral service, rich in opportunity for mourning, eulogy, burying the past, and establishing hope for the future followed.

Some people had been saying "we've got to bury the hatchet," and here it was. Barry looked at me and I looked at him. Certain people on both the union and management sides wanted a healing as well as a contractual resolution, and Barry was one of them. He said very quietly to me, "Some people are going to hang me if I do this." I said, "I'll do it if you'll do it." We both stood up together and went to the coffin.

The lid of the coffin was rimmed by exactly as many holes as there were workshop participants. Every single person would have to drive a nail home if the coffin and the dispute were to be sealed. John continues:

> Barry and I drove the first nails. Barry and I and all the attendees nailed it shut. We put it in a station wagon with the trunk open as a hearse. We followed it to a grave site and actually buried it. We went through a ceremony of literally burying the hatchet. If you come to the site, we can show you where we buried it. Some archeologist will go crazy when he finds it. But this was the commitment to stop this fighting.

It worked extremely well. Col. Rutley summarized the scenario.

> Attitudes did a 180-degree turn. The strike had been months before. Now, they settled the next contract six months ahead of schedule.
>
> Before the DesignShop, the union and management guys had been doing traditional things and were going to hurt each other. I had to use the process for transformation, for cultural change. It seems to work very, very well. It was an incredible change. I had not intended that. I was trying to solve a very specific problem. I did not know any other way than to throw them in there together and make them stare at the damn abyss and figure out where they were going.
>
> I still cannot believe it, but that one event has changed AEDC forever.

We'll be hearing a lot more about AEDC's subsequent achievements later.

There is no such thing as a problem without a gift for you in its hands.
You seek problems because you need their gifts.

—Richard Bach

Exploring New Terrain...

The "Burying the Hatchet" exercise worked as a common experience. It sent a clear message, both to those present and to those who heard about it later, that a total commitment had been made to end the conflict. But—as John Poparad explained—before this symbolic exercise was possible, much work had to be done first at the DesignShop. Specifically, the group needed to work collaboratively on their joint vision of AEDC. Only when a high degree of common ground had been established was it possible to move forward.

Working collaboratively is not common practice in most organizations—it is still mostly command-and-control, very top-down.

At a DesignShop, people come together for a short time to take on a major challenge for their organization. They need to work, to collaborate, at their highest capacity, taking advantage of the skills and knowledge of everyone present. If you don't operate this way routinely back at the office, how can the process cause everyone to start collaborating quickly, even those who've never worked this way before? These non-collaborators can be pretty hard-core—for example, many managers just don't operate that way. Many managers *think* they collaborate well, but often *do not* collaborate well when working with subordinates. Unfortunately, no one who works under them has the guts to tell them. The higher the manager is in the corporate pyramid, the more likely this is to be true.

The DesignShop process is literally that—a design process. People who attend come from many walks of life and expect to work in radically different ways. Getting them to change their way of working, their way of thinking—even for the short time it takes to do a DesignShop—isn't easy. Matt explains that many people have been specially trained in processes other than collaboration.

> Lawyers learn a process—largely an adversarial process. An adversarial process is very good at arriving at truths or understanding of some kinds but not of other kinds. Scientists learn the scientific process, which in its strictest sense, is very good at arriving at certain kinds of information and truth. In organizations, specialists use these different processes at different skill levels, but few of them have any awareness of what processes they're using.

> A design process is different yet again. At a DesignShop event, we have a problem to solve that is inherently so complex we have to bring people together from many different fields, different vantage points and life experi-

Working collaboratively is not common practice in most organizations—it is still mostly command-and-control, very top-down.

The Modern Attitude
http://www.mgtaylor.com/
mgtaylor/jotm/winter96/
modern.htm

ences, because it is simply impossible to have enough knowledge present otherwise. Suppose you somehow did solve it solo, you would not have the solution resulting from their interaction. Even if you somehow have that, you wouldn't have the buy-in—the approval from key players—once you have the solution.

So you have to bring these people together. They come in with different sets of assumptions and with different languages—literally, the same words can mean different things to them. But most important, they come in with different deeply embedded mental process structures that most of them are totally unaware that they have.

A person's own embedded deep process is often the most sensitive thing that they own, and the thing they will fight most about, usually without doing so explicitly. In a sense you are talking about their mind—their survival tool—and if you want to challenge someone on the level of their deeply embedded process, you are going to have an argument on your hands. It is an extremely sensitive subject.

Premises Regarding the Knowledge Economy
http://www.mgtaylor.com/mgtaylor/jotm/winter96/premises.htm

At a DesignShop event, time is at a premium. A large and talented group of employees and other stakeholders has gathered from far and wide—this is costing real money. Given the wide gaps in assumptions, languages, and embedded mental processes, how do you generate a fast way of learning new styles of working and using new types of embedded processes? Here's a story about achieving rapid learning through:
- managing information,
- discovering what the work really is about,
- using networks instead of relying on the familiar role of doing an assigned task for a supervisor,
- dealing effectively with emerging systems, rather than a static situation in which all the work is neatly defined up front.

At Agency Group, Jon Foley and his team, together with the MG Taylor team, created exercises to accomplish this by deliberately increasing (1) the complexity of the assigned task, (2) the richness of the information environment, and (3) the speed of change, until the group is thrown into chaos—and figures out how to operate in new ways. Jon described an exercise held during the Minding Our Business DesignShop.

Exploring New Terrain...

We had about forty people broken into teams working on various related assignments. One team—we'll call them the "InfoBroker team"—was the only team to get a copy of every team's task. The InfoBroker team's assignment is to design the infrastructure—How will the overall system work? How will tasks be assigned? How will people communicate?

At the beginning, the InfoBroker team spent some time trying to organize the initial work. They assume they have all day, so what's the rush? Then I start dropping by with extra assignments. At first, they don't know what to do with these. I come back again and again, and give them another two or three assignments.

Within an hour and a half, I've given them another ten assignments that they have to get distributed and done. At this point, some InfoBroker members get angry or walk out. Some start to break down the team barriers and pull people out of other teams. They just grab a person who can do a particular task—an individual assignment. It's all disconnected; it's chaotic. Tasks are getting done, but they aren't taking into account the whole system. Sometimes people on the InfoBroker team would break out and try running the other teams.

Ten-Step Knowledge Management Model
http://www.mgtaylor.com/mgtaylor/glasbead/tenstep.htm

We are always more comfortable when we know everything there is to know about a task or assignment before we begin to do it. This is a block to high productivity, because knowledge work is too complex for this. We can't know everything there is to know about our work. Somehow we must break through this barrier.

There were times when the InfoBroker team thought they were responsible for completing all ten or eleven assignments, without help from the other teams. Some of the more senior executives on the InfoBroker team were so good at managing the details that it took a huge information-and-task flow to reach their limits. My objective as a facilitator is to get them to the point where they realize they're in trouble; traditional processes of managing information are no longer working.

Most managers have lots of experience in directing others in their work, seeking to eliminate or reduce complexity. Some are very good at this. But this can also be a block to high performance, because generally this only leads to compliance from the workers. In this exercise, the InfoBroker team had to learn to let go of mental models of how work should be organized. They had to let an effective structure emerge through the interaction of the other participants. Part of this required the InfoBroker team to discover the difference between managing people and managing information.

The InfoBroker team finally pulled everyone into the same room and said that they had a problem with an organization in chaos. So each group would tell what they were doing on their assignment and then there would be between five and eight team reports on what the assignments were and at what point each team had reached in dealing with that assignment.

Gradually they would understand that if they would create a system of information management in which everyone could participate and everyone could volunteer, the tasks could be done. They would create a white-wall area where they would track each assignment. You would need seven or eight people to start a project, but after all of the ideas were out on the table, you would only need two or three to complete it. Then the others could work on something else.

No one team ever had "enough" resources, whether human or technical. The teams learned how to find and share those resources through networking between teams. How would they decide what to work on next? They needed access to the information and status of all projects. That's collaboration.

We are always more comfortable when we know everything there is to know about a task or assignment before we begin to do it. This is a block to high productivity, because knowledge work is too complex for this. We can't know everything there is to know about our work. Somehow we must break through this barrier. In this exercise, no one on the teams had experience with the assignment they were given. They had to start without knowing. Once they began, they discovered they knew much more about the work than they thought they did.

Exploring New Terrain...

Again, this doesn't sound like a fun process. But no one needs to like it for it to work. Going through this exercise gets people to realize that, at least for now, everyone is going to work as a collaborative team, sharing responsibility and—this is a tough one for management—information as well.

The complex, information-enriched, time-compression exercise sketched here forces participants to move to a different mode of work, sharing information. Sound easy and natural? Not for many managers, who are used to taking all of the responsibility and information upon themselves. An amazing example is one senior manager at Agency Group—an excellent manager otherwise—who in this exercise dashed around pulling information down off the walls: information that she thought other groups didn't need and shouldn't have. Don't laugh—there are probably people in your organization doing the equivalent of this right now.

The benefit sought in this exercise is gained if the current (expensive) group can now work effectively on the critical task at hand during the next few days at this DesignShop. Although not critical to DesignShop success, the hope is also that the experience has been sufficiently intense that some of these lessons will be brought back to their daily work.

The experience has been sufficiently intense that some of these lessons will be brought back to daily work.

Challenge

1. Let's continue our established pattern. Without looking back at the book, quickly record any impressions you have upon finishing the chapter. Also record questions that may have occurred to you.

2. Draw a diagram or create a list showing all of the tools, strategies, and techniques you use to solve problems in a high-performance, creative, and collaborative manner. Arrange or label your diagram, or sort your list according to which items fit under each of the three stages of the creative process: Scan, Focus, Act.

3. Take note of any gaps in the results from Challenge 2. Perhaps you have only one or two items under Scan, or use the same strategy whether you're in Scan, Focus, or Act. Where might you look to strengthen and broaden your tool kit?

...And Expanding Your Universe

"The first thing the facilitators do is explain the design process we were about to go through. It is a very powerful thing. The Scan/Focus/Act sequence is similar to Deming's 'plan, do, act, check, and act' but it gives you a broader perspective," says Elsa Porter, former U.S. Assistant Secretary of Commerce.

The first step—Scan—goes beyond "plan" in emphasizing learning as the creative foundation on which good decisions are made. Scan begins by looking very widely at the environment: scanning target markets, competition, economic and business trends, social and management trends, leading edge science and technology.

The creative process has a front half and a back half. In the front half of the process you do the work which will enable you to make a good decision. Learning is the nature of much of the work that is done in the front half. *Planning as Learning* by Swartz and Shelf shows that one of the major functions of planning and of design is as a learning tool.

Businesses are beginning to tolerate the time needed for learning—this first part of the design phase and creative process—although they say "it sure feels better when we get to engineering and building." Once a model emerges that the people involved hold in common, then they can move forward more comfortably to engineering, building, doing, acting.

Scanning, when uncertainty and therefore anxiety is high, is profoundly uncomfortable for most people. Yet staying in Scan a long time is exactly what is most needed to generate new solutions to challenging problems.

At Wharton, where Scan extends for almost two days—two thirds of the total time—the group challenge was designing the 21st century organization. All the

Seven Stages of the Creative Process Model
http://www.mgtaylor.com/mgtaylor/glasbead/7stagcrp.htm

Staying in Scan a long time is exactly what's most needed to generate new solutions to challenging problems.

work now going on is in some way relevant to that challenge, even though the actual problem has not been addressed and won't be for some time.

Participants are now assigned to completely new, five-person teams. The five people you came to know from Take-a-Panel have scattered. New team membership has again been determined for maximum diversity, combining people from different organizations or from very different parts of the same organization, with as wide a mix of age, gender, ethnicity, educational, and work experiences as possible. Also taken into account are the different books read in preparation for attending the DesignShop. The groups are provisioned with a diversity of leading-edge theory including information theory, systems science, and change management. Each team is joined by a facilitator who is there to scribe for them, provide insights, ask provocative questions, challenge assumptions, encourage collaboration, or support in any way needed.

The first task is understanding the environment and the demands of the 21st century. Each group has been given a different Backcasting cut on this question. Some focus on social questions, others have questions about technology and processes. When these groups reassemble, they will represent in-depth thinking about highly different parts of the same question. Viewing the same issue from different vantage points is a reliable way to get powerful insights. Carl's Jr. received valuable insights when they worked with the different stakeholder vantage points—customers, suppliers, franchisees. The teams here at Wharton are working with different theoretical vantage points.

Envisioning the Future
http://www.mgtaylor.com/mgtaylor/jotm/spring97/wsr_model2.htm

All the questions channel thinking away from the details of today and into "big picture" abstract issues. Compare the questions put to just two of the different groups. One group's question places them in the present looking backward to 1895. Here is the challenge handed them:

> Looking Back: As the millennium approaches, your team has been asked to provide a synopsis of the last century for the history channel. Important discoveries and innovations were made during this period. What were the processes, tools, and environments that led to these innovations and discoveries? What were the basic assumptions and paradigms? What did we learn to take for granted? What principles were employed in designing all organizations? What did we learn to be reality and, from that perspective, what accumulated baggage did we take with us into the next century?

...And Expanding Your Universe 63

The next group's question places them in 2095, looking backward—a very different perspective.

> Looking Back: The year is 2095. The virtual history channel is planning a major retrospective of the last century. Your team has been asked to identify the major threads to be covered in the program. Specifically, you've been asked to consider the following questions: What was the character of the century? The theme(s)? The style(s)? What did it feel like to live then? Look like? Sound like? What did we learn? What were the major drivers of change, the innovations and discoveries in all areas of human experience, and how did they change the way we understood, planned and lived our lives?

Every man takes the limits of his own field of vision for the limits of the world.

—Arthur Schopenhauer

Groups get right down to work—time is deliberately tight and there is a lot of ground to cover. Resources include books and articles located in the portable library, computer search capability on the Web, and an ever-changing body of information going up on the Knowledge Wall. The most valuable resources are the ideas and experiences of the team members. As they work on these questions, the teams learn about the others on their team: their knowledge, how they think, what they think is important, what they get worked up about. Because of our practice in the Share-a-Panel exercise, the process is active and participatory, with each person jumping up to talk or to write on the whitewalls to express points.

If "major drivers of change," "basic assumptions and paradigms" sounds pretty theoretical and just the stuff for an afternoon tea party, think again. It gets hot and lively right away. One participant states with certainty that the major threads looking back from 2095 will be pollution, overpopulation, starvation, disease, and war. Just as certain is the participant who tells her that the Club of Rome projections of doom and gloom are analytic nonsense, and that it is much more likely that things will be lush, green, and fruitful. The diverse nature of the groups is bringing people smack up against completely different points of view, different experiences, and different knowledge. Not tea party kind of stuff at all. In the limited time available, how will they ever come to an agreement?

Report-Out

When everyone regroups, the curving work walls are now labeled in segments for each decade from 1920 to 2020, a chunk of space for after 2020, and a chunk of space for before 1920. This next exercise will be a Report-Out on the work they have just been doing. Matt, acting as facilitator, defines how that reporting will happen:

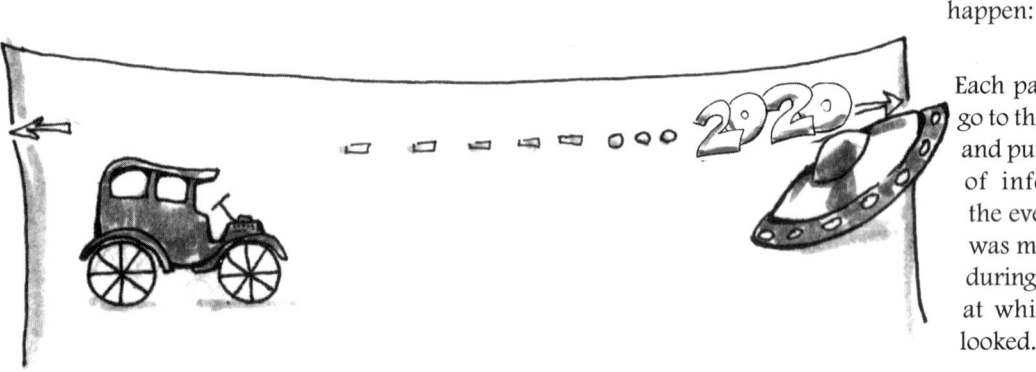

Each participant will go to the radiant wall and put up one piece of information on the event they think was most important during the 100 years at which they have looked.

They also use the opportunity for introducing themselves, giving their names, company affiliation, the kind of work they do (but not job title), and making a statement about the importance of the event they selected.

This exercise suddenly and deliberately shifts from the abstract, team-created points of view of the previous exercise to a specific event presented in each participant's personal voice. The results are fascinating. Because it is still early in the first day of the session, when new people take their turn at the work walls, most fellow participants are meeting them for the first time. You are getting to know this person in a very different way than if you had been conventionally introduced. Instead, in a moment, you get a glimpse of their unique knowledge, the details and the systems that they think in and recognize as important, their individual history, values, emotions, and their discomfort in struggling with future issues.

In an information economy, made up of knowledge workers, the most valuable resources are what other people know. Their most valuable skills, talents, decision-making abilities, or areas of creativity may not be defined by either their job titles or by their degrees. So how do you find out what someone has learned from a hobby, from a different culture, even from an accident? Gail Taylor: "We tell participants to go find out what they don't know about each other."

This information now emerges in a riveting way, presented as personal insight merged with history by people who are older than you, or younger—people whose lives were profoundly changed by something that you've always regarded as a minor or distant event…until now.

A man with silver hair and intense eyes talks passionately about the advent of the jet engine in the 1940s and how it has made the world smaller through international travel, commerce, and war. His description provides context and meaning. Personal revelation—bringing your personal passion and insight to explaining an event—is combined with the historical, objective timeline.

Gary, who works with Orlando Regional Health Care System, chooses 1980 and the work of Deming: "Deming's theories showed how important it was to drive out fear. When people are fearful, they spend all their time defending their current position."

How interesting: when manufacturing people or computer industry people talk about Deming, this has not been the main message that they have extracted. Moments ago, Gary was a stranger. Now you want to know who he is, and what experiences and knowledge have led him to focus so clearly on the impact of fear. Even a long-time co-worker would learn something valuable here because this exercise makes the implicit into the explicit, makes it visible, makes the abstract concrete—so *that's* why he's so adamant about that point. *Now* I see.

As each new person explains, as he or she searches for the words and images, the speaker is clearly learning as well. In reviewing experiences, stories, and principles, they are further articulating and understanding what their experience meant.

In 2002, says a co-worker of Gary's who did his assignment from the perspective of 2095 looking backward, the trust fund set up for Medicare and Medicaid goes

The Difference Between Night and Day
http://www.mgtaylor.com/ mgtaylor/jotm/winter96/ nightday.htm

No sensible man watches his feet hit ground. He looks ahead to see what kind of ground they'll hit next.

—Ernest Haycox

bankrupt. "Remember," says Gail Taylor. "We're talking about the past. Did you, as a health care provider, go bankrupt too?" He thinks it over for a few seconds. "Yes," he says. "We did."

From the Air Force, a very young-looking man (who turns out to be a Major) was also looking back from the year 2095. He talks about how he was influenced by the riots in 1960s. He worries about civil unrest and rioting in the future if such large gaps between the haves and the have-nots continue. He marks riots on the calendar as having occurred in 2025.

Another Backcaster from the 2095 perspective says, "In 2005 the first company staffed entirely by kids under 16 went public due to their work on the Web, changing the labor laws forever."

One of the Air Force people writes up on the wall: In the year 2010, we changed the Air Force business to the facilitation business, facilitating peace around the world.

A most valuable function of the Scan is to allow patterns to become visible out of seeming chaos. From the information covering the walls, people identify patterns that they have been missing previously. Whether revealed during the Scan or later during Focus, this key pattern discovery is usually what is necessary for success in the ultimate problem-solving strategy.

A good Scan, of which this Scenario exercise is but the beginning, is designed to:

- include short-term and long-term educational goals, immersing your organization in the critical techniques, technologies, and facts it needs to learn to stay up to speed.

- build a real understanding of the environment—the markets, the technologies, the societies—in which your organization does and will operate.

Weak Signal Research
http://www.mgtaylor.com/mgtaylor/wsremerg.htm

- develop a real understanding of the talents and knowledge of different team members.

- get team members fired up into creating, focusing on solving problems, and not worrying about a bunch of extraneous issues.

- get vital information shared between participants.

- challenge the assumptions on which current actions rest.

- develop a rich set of options from which you can make selections and design decisions.

Throughout the entire Scan, more information is continually brought forward, worked with, challenged, and learned. Working over the big walls, with lots of people providing insight—and taking advantage of lots of support and lots of time—a richer, more complex picture of reality builds up than you ever get to see during daily life. Some disagreements or confusions simply go away. Old falsehoods are abandoned, and new patterns are identified.

Staying Focused on the Objectives

The goal of the exercise is to build a complex pattern of information and perception, to open a rich dialogue between participants, and to create a common experience. And because these were the design goals, competing priorities—such as agreement or even accuracy—receive lower priority in a given exercise.

Therefore, as wonderful as these exercises were, they were also incredibly irritating, especially for people attending their first DesignShop event. Their difficulty was in trying to stay focused on the goals set for the first few exercises, and not find themselves swept away by competing priorities, such as correcting errors in what others are saying. When similar errors or misconceptions occur in other settings, it always bodes ill. No wonder alarm bells are going off.

For example, consider yours truly, Gayle and Chris. Our areas of expertise are future technologies and economic issues. We have spent many years thinking, researching, writing about, and running businesses involved with such issues.

During this Report-Out, we listened while some people repeated today's technology headlines, extrapolating from ideas that didn't make sense even when a journalist first wrote them. Gayle described her frustration:

The process was driving me wild. I loved it, but I hated it.

I'd think, "Oh, no! This person doesn't understand a thing about technology, about economics, about logic. Their interpretation of the past is flawed and now they're moving on to make a terminally stupid prediction about the future. And no one is correcting it! Someone—anyone—has got to stand up and set this person straight.

My training and experience tell me that everything should come to a halt until these incorrect ideas about economics and technology have been put right. I feel sure it is going to mess things up further downstream.

Previously I looked calmly (OK—smugly) at those people whose Hot Buttons were triggered about the issue of "no visible schedule"—but now every Hot Button I own is flashing. I can't believe I'm listening to this. We'll never get anywhere with this work; I'm wasting three days; maybe I should leave now. I want to get off the boat.

There are other newcomers to the DesignShop process who are feeling the same way. Their body language is clearly saying: "Why am I wasting my time doing this? What does this have to do with solving my organization's problems? I came here to work hard, not fool around." Three men sitting in a row, whom we later learned were all from Ernst & Young, had particularly fierce body language. Another E&Yer told us that Lee Sage, the senior E&Y partner in that row, had learned from an early career in pro baseball with a Yankee farm team how to wear the same kind of facial expression as an umpire: "If he looks at you hard enough, your face will break." Right now with just a view of his back, you really didn't want to see what was happening on his face. Any minute now, Matt and anyone else standing up front was surely going to disintegrate into a heap of rumble under that glare.

In contrast, DesignShop veterans are taking everything in stride. Accustomed to the design process and its priorities, they know that these issues tend to be sorted out later in small group exercises; many fallacies disappear. Now, they are being flushed out into the open—so you know what you're dealing with. As

...And Expanding Your Universe 69

exercises proceed, the big mistakes go away, the views—including the understandings of economics and future technologies — become more sophisticated. Not all differences and disagreements go away. But everyone comes out with a much richer, more accurate vision of past, present, and future. And everyone has had the common experience of working together.

Think of this "holding fast to a new set of priorities" as similar to what happens in starting an exercise program after years as a committed couch potato. The goal is to get out there walking or jogging, but you are distracted because the car needs a tune-up, or because you need to decide how to vote in next month's election. Granted, civic responsibilities and automobile maintenance are important, but if you want to get the exercise program rolling you set them aside long enough to get the program underway. Similarly, with the DesignShop process, the goals of the design process must be brought front and center, with other valid, critical concerns treated secondarily.

There are other common reasons for feeling frustration during one's first Scan. Scanning or learning doesn't feel like action directed toward solving the organization's problem. People say, "We've been trying to solve this problem for a year, and we need to come to a decision, we need to act *now*. We don't have time to learn."

As part of business, learning has a bad reputation. Here's why.

The belief held by science, educators, management, and society in general for the first part of the 20th century was that Adults Cannot Learn. "Adult" meant set in your ways, inflexible, not capable of learning. You can't teach old dogs new tricks.

Not until the 1940s, when World War II veterans returned to college on the GI Bill, did academics recognize that, in fact, adults could learn. Not just be trained—learn.

In times of change, learners inherit the earth; while the learned find themselves beautifully equipped to live in a world that no longer exists.

—Eric Hoffer

In the mid-1970s, a Fortune 100 CEO could still ask Gail Taylor in all sincerity whether adults could learn. Neither business nor the education establishment in the 1970s had yet adapted to the notion of adult learning.

5 Es of Educational Model
http://www.mgtaylor.com/mgtaylor/glasbead/5Esofed.htm

Traditionally, education has been excluded from action-oriented organizations. The notion that learning or thinking was unneeded by most workers derives from our Industrial Age heritage in which humans became part of the manufacturing process. Hands were needed, not minds. Creativity reduced the big prize of the early Industrial Age: standardization.

Added to the assumption that "only a few people at the top need to think," was the next dangerous notion: the people at the top are done learning or they wouldn't be at the top. They got to the top because they know something valuable which they are now expected to implement. So nobody here needs learning—which is a good thing, because adults can't learn anyway.

Matt Taylor recounts a DesignShop event which successfully merged two insurance companies. "The executives were very happy with the results, and we were going on to do additional work for them. Discussing an aspect of the plan I said, 'By the way, there's a good book about that. Here's the author and title.' One executive leaned forward and said 'You don't understand. We don't read here.'"

Fortune magazine estimates that, on average, CEOs read only three books per year. Think about your own acquaintences— if you know a senior executive that seems creative, innovative, and a strong leader, does he or she admit to reading and still learning? And what about the link between not reading, not learning, and lack of creativity in executives you know? Linda Vetter, a senior technology executive, has no question about the correlation. Over her career, she says, "the creative and successful executives were always reading and learning."

Businesses lack and very much need techniques that let everyone, effectively, quickly, and economically include learning as part of their job. One of the benefits of the Scan process is that by practicing it, your organization can acquire just such a technique and tradition.

Speed It Up

People think individual learning or change takes a long time—years of back-to-school or psychotherapy. People also believe that organizations change slowly, saying, "We will take the next fifteen years to transform." And, if you set up a fifteen-year plan for change, it becomes a self-fulfilling prophecy.

Does it all really take that long? Many psychologists now use "brief therapy," lasting a few weeks rather than years.

The DesignShop process proposes that learning and change, for both individuals and organizations, can be rapid. Gail Taylor brings the insight from her experience in elementary education. "I learned that with kids, you speed up the information—you don't slow it down." Accelerated learning and immersion learning techniques are powerful.

This insight and practice of Gail's was not uncontroversial.

> I used to fight with my colleagues all the time when we would work on our curriculum in development. The pace would be so slow!
>
> Even today, when we run programs for schools, teachers warn us, "We want you to come to the school, but don't use big words, no more than fifteen minutes at a time, the attention span is thirteen-and-a-half minutes." We say "thank you" and proceed. We work with the students for the whole day, from the first bell to the last bell, non-stop. We use the same language we use with executives, the same concepts, the same simulations. Teachers go nuts because the students will be hanging in all the way through the long hours, the vocabulary, the concepts. And teachers ask, "Why is it?" We say, because at the standard rate that formal education allows, you were boring them.

That's why business meetings are so boring. The datastream is so slow you can't pay attention and you go right to sleep.

The solution: Make it rich. Compress it. Use models to help people hold more content in their minds. Use all the ways people learn: visually, kinesthetically, auditorily. Take proper advantage of our ability to learn both consciously and unconsciously. Make learning as experiential as possible.

There it is. Simple.

Explore the Models
http://www.mgtaylor.com/
mgtaylor/glasbead/expmodel.htm

The time when "information" seems like noise is when it's jumbled, with little pattern to it. You can hold onto a lot of information when you've got a metaphor or framework or pattern on which to hang it. Use a model to give yourself some abstraction, and you can deal with a lot of complexity.

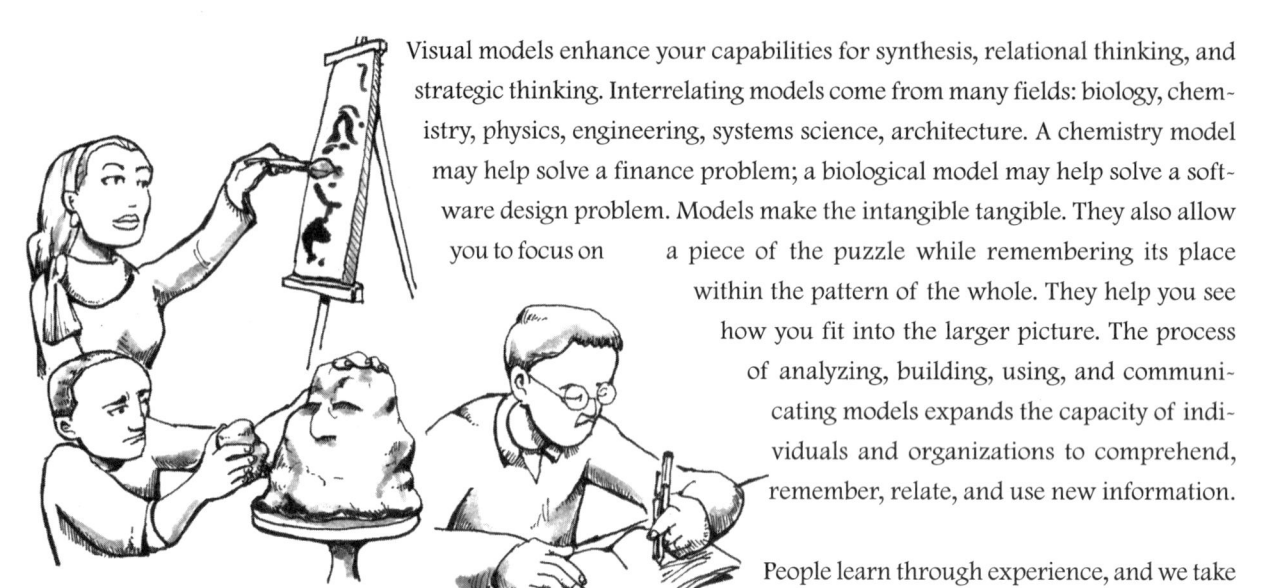

Visual models enhance your capabilities for synthesis, relational thinking, and strategic thinking. Interrelating models come from many fields: biology, chemistry, physics, engineering, systems science, architecture. A chemistry model may help solve a finance problem; a biological model may help solve a software design problem. Models make the intangible tangible. They also allow you to focus on a piece of the puzzle while remembering its place within the pattern of the whole. They help you see how you fit into the larger picture. The process of analyzing, building, using, and communicating models expands the capacity of individuals and organizations to comprehend, remember, relate, and use new information.

People learn through experience, and we take it in through our favorite sense modality.

Cognitive Styles

People vary as to which cognitive or sensory modality they find easiest to use: visual (or graphic), kinesthetic, or verbal. Some people are Visuals—"Give me a quick sketch" and "Now, I see what you mean"—and need information presented graphically or visually to learn it. Still other people need to touch it, feel it, or work with it physically in order to nail it down. Other people need the words—to hear it or talk about it or see it in black and white—before they get the message.

Of the population as a whole, over 30% are graphically or visually oriented, over 30% are kinesthetically oriented, and less than 30% are verbal/writing oriented. Less than one-third of the population is primarily oriented toward verbal and written communication, yet typically nearly all business information goes solely through this one channel.

...And Expanding Your Universe

While the selection effect of the verbal/written education process has probably raised the proportion of Verbals in the business world, there are still a whopping percentage of Visuals and Kinesthetics in your company. By incorporating visual language, pictures, and graphic display of information into communication, and by encouraging work processes that involve more physical movement, more people can engage more completely in the process of learning and working effectively. But—it rarely happens.

Most "training" or "education" in American business is still a one-way verbal experience, a lecture in which a speaker explains the subject matter. Sometimes a weak dose of "experience" is tossed in, where four people do a case study for a few hours. Explanation is necessary so that you can intellectually understand the material. But you can discover the ineffectiveness of explanation unsupported by experience when you return home, find little or no success in transferring or connecting your workshop data to the people in the office, and never apply the knowledge.

So where does business use visual and kinesthetic communication heavily, every single day?—In advertising and in marketing information. The direct feedback channel of customers inquiring or not inquiring, buying or not buying rewards us for effective communication, and punishes us—with lower sales—for ineffective communication.

Some facts or concepts only came to life when supported by an illustration, chart, or map. As people were speaking during the Report-Out, artists from the support team were continually illustrating the discussion using cartoon-style art and salient words on the walls. They would draw connections between related ideas with arrows. Word pictures and maps evolved.

Body language and symbolism are other ways humans actually communicate, ways in which people package information for transfer to others and to learn it for ourselves. Instead of stripping them out of the process, include them in the educational design as carriers of information. People learn by doing. During the Scan, even when addressing an intellectual question, people are writing on walls, moving around, engaging their bodies. Learning is physical as well as abstract. They are building into the body/mind on a neurological level. Actions relate to the concepts. The knowledge becomes acquired by the body and fixed in the mind.

Success of a Scan

Elsa Porter recounts an example of a Scan that created a problem-solving breakthrough for the Hispanic Chamber of Commerce.

Elsa's work, both previously in government and today as a management consultant in partnership with Michael Maccoby, centers on the quest for human productivity: how people grow and develop, or shrink and decline. "This has been my life's work," she says. "What I really wanted to do was to understand what happens to the human spirit in large companies."

Beginning with the Kennedy administration, she had seen situations that began full of hope, but then "produced no results, no real change in society. Inside huge organizations like the Department of Health, Education, and Welfare, I was seeing what happened to people who were trying to make a difference. They got stuck in boxes not of their own making. They began to get frustrated. Their spirits began to be extinguished. You saw a phenomenon of greatness becoming mediocrity."

President Carter appointed Elsa to the Commerce Department.

Before I became Assistant Secretary, I had directed the Civil Service Commission's Clearinghouse on Productivity and Organizational Effectiveness. My job was to look at innovations around the country to see what might help government to work better. That is where I encountered Michael Maccoby and his pioneering work on the Quality of Work Life. I brought him into the Department of Commerce where we began to study what motivated people to grow and develop.

Later, someone told me that MG Taylor was doing interesting work; it stimulated my curiosity. They arranged for me to be part of a DesignShop. A California Congressman had gotten grant money for the Hispanic Community, and they had a DesignShop run for them. This Hispanic Chamber of Commerce event was just amazing.

"Going into the Scan," recalls facilitator Bryan Coffman, "there was a feeling of despair. Asian immigrants were entering California and doing extremely well in establishing themselves in business, taking places in the university system. The Hispanic DesignShop participants were asking, 'Why can't we compete with these people?' The group's feeling was that the Pacific Rim was invading California and outcompeting the Hispanic community on their home ground."

It was during the Scan, creating maps of language and population, that things changed for the Hispanic community participants.

> During the Scan, they kept looking at the bigger world—at the Pacific Rim rising in power. It was noted that Hispanics would soon be a majority of California, and what would that mean for them? They looked at the language mix around the Pacific, and then the shift came—hey! most of the Pacific Rim speaks Spanish. We *are* the Pacific Rim. *We* could be the future.

The old pattern, unconsciously learned, had taught the community to see themselves as stationary, isolated, under assault by arriving immigrants, outcompeted in a zero-sum game in which the only resources available were those fixed in California.

By looking at a much larger picture, enough maneuvering room developed to find a new perspective. New patterns emerged, and perceptions changed dramatically. Spanish was a valuable asset. Spanish/English bilingual ability put them competitively ahead. Elsa continued the story.

> Before, when one young man had said, with a certain bravado, that he was going to be President of the United States, everyone hooted and hollered at him. But now, a spirit of hope had developed!

Bryan explained that, "Coming out of the Scan, the perception and the sentiment had changed to: 'Not only can we compete with them here, we can go over there and compete with them in Japan, in China, and in Korea.'"

Issues that previously may have been too touchy to address before, suddenly became things that could be freely discussed and dealt with.

This time, like all times, is a good one if we know what to do with it.

—RALPH WALDO EMERSON

"During Focus,[the step following Scan]," Elsa explained, "they listed the barriers to their achievement. The barriers were all internal: lack of self-esteem, education, courage, putting down of women, macho culture of the man. They knew it was internal information that they put out there. But for them to acknowledge it and own it was momentous. The Act day [the third step, focused on action planning] was wonderful. They were in clusters working with the planning software, laying out what they were going to do on their projects to inspire, to collectively work on the self esteem of the community. They were going to be the majority. They were full of pride."

Everyone leaves a DesignShop session with a wider range of options than when they walked in. They also leave with something in their hands that they created—tangible evidence of the experience, the work they did, and a reminder that something about the environment was different.

> When we left later that day, we had the documentation. It was marvelous. The documentation is something you can walk away with. It stays with you. To me, it was very powerful.

Regarding long-term results, Bryan explains: "A year later, I met one of the Hispanic leaders who had attended the DesignShop event. He had just returned from China, where he had been establishing business contacts—putting the new vision and plan that they had created into action."

Why should "discovering" this data during a Scan exercise make a profound difference in people's ability to make strategic and tactical plans for themselves? The language statistics of the Pacific Rim aren't secret. Everybody in the room had already known which countries on the Pacific Rim were Spanish speaking.

Experience as Learning

When C.S. Forester was talking about creating *The African Queen*, he said something with profound implications: "What experience can I give that person to make them reach their full potential?"

Embedded here is the notion that you learn best by experiencing something yourself, not by having someone try to transfer knowledge to you by telling you the answer. Why didn't someone go up to the Cockney and just tell him he was an

Nobody knows what is the best he can do.

—Arturo Toscanini

alcoholic and he needed to stop the drinking to reach his potential? Why didn't someone tell the spinster missionary she needed to relax and become less judgmental? Would that have worked? These opinions were expressed clearly between the two characters. Neither character was transformed by the mere transfer of this information.

They were transformed by experience.

The participants in the Hispanic DesignShop event had passively received this information many times before via newspaper, television, classroom lecture. The difference this time was learning within the context of an experience.

According to Gail Taylor, "Participants already know a solution to the problem—they have to learn to recognize it."

True enough, but discovery is very hard work. Some of it can be made easier. People all learn best by doing, so let them learn and discover through experience. Some of the difficulty of discovery can't be avoided—the anxiety that comes with ambiguity.

Tolerance of Ambiguity

You really are lost in the 21st century. You are lost in the change process. Being lost in a swirl of complexity can be an anxious time. You have cast off from the shores of the known, and are heading out to sea with the hope—but no proof—that there is land on the other side. Back home, in the old world, you knew who you were and what you did every day. Granted, you weren't happy with it, but it was known and safe. Now, you are feeling all the risk associated with the future state that you desire. The ambiguity even extends to the question of your identity: what kind of person will you be when you step off the boat?

Risk avoidance and shunning of change, ambiguity, and uncertainty have been bred into us by the long centuries of our agricultural past. Look at any agricultural society to clearly see our global heritage of risk-avoidance. There is nothing like a peasant farmer for resistance to innovation. Innovation is a dangerous thing: you might lose the whole crop and face starvation. Better to stick to the old, safe ways. That heritage stays with us today. We run away from risk, from innovation.

I hear and I forget
I see and I remember
I do and I understand.

—Lao Tsu

Transition Manager's Creed
http://www.mgtaylor.com/
mgtaylor/jotm/fall96/
trnmgrcr.htm

We try to banish the things that go with it: variety and ambiguity.

If we can't make the variety and ambiguity go away, we ignore it. If we can't ignore it, we medicate it away, or use some soothing substitute to drive it out of our minds: an immediate dive into work activity.

Placing yourself in a state of ambiguity is stressful. Everyone has heard of "writer's block." Not just writers, but creative people of all sorts—artists, musicians, film makers, sculptors, architects—who do not know how to deal with the ambiguity and anxiety end up miserably "blocked," often for years. Creative people who are producing effectively in their craft still experience the different types of anxiety and stress associated with each stage of the creative process, but they have figured out ways to work with and through the anxiety to produce a product.

What the DesignShop process offers is a known path through the anxiety and ambiguity. If you have the courage to show up, the anxiety will be limited. People hit the creative breakthrough with high reliability within forty-eight hours. The facilitation team manages the risk, and focuses on giving you what you need for the creative process to occur. You can reliably make it to your destination carried forward by the entire structure of the whole experience—like passengers in a boat traveling down a river.

Never kid yourself that business isn't creative work. It is just as creative as what an artist does with brush and paint. It is, however, even more complex, and the process less subject to control than that of an individual artist. The discovery process for a business is as much agony and ecstasy as for a Michelangelo. The works of art created in business can be as brilliant as those in any other field.

Seven Stages of the Creative Process Model
http://www.mgtaylor.com/mgtaylor/glasbead/7stagcrp.htm

Challenge

1. What were your discoveries from the chapter concerning scanning, building scenarios, and education? Record them here along with any questions.

2. Build a model of education as it currently is in your company, your family, or your life. How rich and diverse is it? When was the last time you learned something entirely out of your field of expertise or zone of comfort?

3. Now build a model of the richest, most diverse, experiential, and exploratory education system that you could build into your company or your daily life. How could you work to increase variety, ambiguity, and risk, and help people understand that? What experience can you give yourself and those around you to help them reach their full potential?

Using the Power of Space and Place

Louisville, Kentucky, October 1991, Agency Group: Everyone is packed into the same old lecture room. Standard rows of tables, standard chairs, styrofoam cups of cooling coffee, pads of paper, and a pen can be found at each place. Jon Foley, the trainer, starts taking roll.

At least Jon has let everyone dress casually—even though Jon himself is wearing a suit and tie.

Jon is droning on about how the course is going to be from 8 to 8 today, and 8 to 5 tomorrow. Rifling his stack of lecture papers, he says this has been a successful lecture before in the organization and you should like it. He says you can't afford to know just your job, so we are going to spend the next two days here understanding the marketing plan and what other parts of the company are doing. The overhead projector starts whirring. Up goes the first transparency accompanied by the silent moans and groans.

Five minutes into this, people's eyes are glazing over. Everyone thinks this is normal. After all, this is what a training class is like.

Then, a hand goes up. It's Bob Grannan, vice president in charge of transformation for the organization. Bob says, "Could I ask a couple of questions? I thought we were going to become a learning organization, but I'm not learning anything." So it's question, answer, question, answer, and then Foley starts reading from the overhead transparencies again.

Bob Grannan's hand goes up again, "I don't mean to be obnoxious, but I don't understand why we're doing this. You're talking about a marketing plan that was developed five years ago." So it's question, answer, question, answer, and Foley starts reading again.

Suddenly Grannan's hand is back up there. "But what is the point of this?" he wants to know. "What has this got to do with my work? Is the whole day going to be like this? We're just going to sit and listen to you talk?"

Everyone in the room is now extremely nervous. No one is saying a word, but everyone is very wide awake. After all, it's a senior vice president asking these pointed questions.

Finally, Jon says to Bob, "You clearly have a different idea of what is going to happen these next two days than I do. Why don't you come up here and tell us what your expectations are?"

Bob says politely, "I don't want to step on your toes."

Jon says, "Bob, why don't you come up front and teach this?"

No one says a word. Some people want to defend the lecture format, and some people want to defend Jon, but a senior vice president is...well, a senior vice president. Silence. A few people even start crying at the idea of confrontation.

Bob Grannan walks up to the front of the room. Jon Foley steps aside, walks down the aisle and out the door.

"Look," Bob says "I don't expect to sit here and listen to them talk about a marketing plan that was developed five years ago. What's that got to do with my work? And what about you?" he asks the people in the classroom. "Why did you come here today?"

"Because I wanted to learn about teams." "I wanted to know more about how the company worked." "Well, my boss said I had to." Bob writes down all these concerns, mainly future-oriented issues.

Using the Power of Space and Place

Bob says, "Great. I think we now know why we're here. Perhaps Jon can help us with these things we came to learn."

Jon Foley is back in the room and dressed in jeans like everyone else.

Jon looks at the list of future-oriented concerns that Bob has written up on the wall and shakes his head. "We can't learn that. Not the way we have everything set up. We cannot learn about the future from the past. We can't even learn about it from the present. We have to go into the future in order to learn about this, so pick up everything you've got and follow me. We're going to do some time traveling."

By now, people are ready for something new and different. OK—we'll go time traveling. The whole group walks out of the classroom, and Jon leads them out onto the street, into another building, and then into the Time Warp Machine.

The tunnel of the Time Warp Machine has flashing lights, blasts of turbulent air, silver streamers floating in the wind, and music from Star Wars pulsating in the background. "The Time Warp Machine," Jon tells everyone, "is a travel tunnel into a new world—into the future. On the other side of the tunnel is a Design Center which exists five years in the future. In walking through the Time Warp, the group is traveling into the future to see how the company's problems were successfully solved. When you return to the present, you'll return with a plan that tells us how to get back to the future and what our assignments are." And with that, Jon steps into the Time Warp Machine and walks into the future.

The group is about to move themselves conceptually into a future where they have already solved their problems. They also made a physical move: from a standard classroom environment, through a tunnel that signaled "this is a different kind of experience," and into a DesignShop environment.

The DesignShop process, in addition to its emphasis on rich information content and processes designed to enhance learning and creativity, is also a supportive *physical* environment. Just walking into the DesignShop setting makes us realize that of all aspects of our working life, the physical environment is perhaps the most ignored. (Most of us can make this evaluation by comparing our work envi-

The DesignShop, in addition to its emphasis on rich information content and processes designed to enhance learning and creativity, is also a supportive physical *environment. Just walking into the DesignShop setting makes us realize that of all aspects of our working life, the physical environment is perhaps the most ignored.*

Philosophy and Practice of Architecture
http://www.mgtaylor.com/mgtaylor/jotm/spring97/architec.htm

ronments to our home environments, and noting what elements we tolerate at work, but would never allow at home.)

The nature of the physical space people inhabit and their ability to move, see, breathe, and hear in that space are critical to their full mental and physiological function. Kinesthetic movement—positions and actions—are strongly linked to the mind's ability to perceive, function, and respond. You can induce or change a mood by how you move your body. If you are sad, make yourself dance, sing, or smile, and you will feel happier. The act of positioning facial muscles into a smile prompts a hard-wired endocrine response that floods you with chemicals which make you feel better. So, it's not just "I'm happy, so I smile." It is also "I smile, and so I become happy." It's not just "I am humble, so I kneel." It's also "I kneel, and so I become humble." These effects work internationally, universally for humans, with only minor cultural variations.

Architecture is often used intentionally to force people into patterns of movements, with the aim of instilling moods or attitudes, or coaxing us into taking certain kinds of action. The tsukubai, or water basin, in a Japanese garden is deliberately low: only 20-30 cm tall or even placed flush with the ground. Bending low to wash your hands before beginning the tea ceremony, like kneeling in church or bowing before a monarch, helps to induce humility.

Important government buildings and impressive cathedrals share the architecture of front steps: many steps with very short risers and very long treads. The architecture of the steps shapes your body movements, and through the body movements—your attitude. Next time you walk up steps like these, notice your mood. Unless you run or take the steps two or three at a time, you'll find the steps force you to move in a cadence of reverence. Watch other people going up the steps. By the time they have reached the top, there's a mood of reverence, respect, solemnity. When they walk into the high space of the cathedral itself, the architecture tells them to stop talking, and they fall silent.

The most infamous architectural team of all time was Adolph Hitler (the failed painter and architect) and Adolph Speer. They built with deliberate attention to the psychological consequences. Here is one of the more benign architectural statements from Speer's *Inside the Third Reich*: "Our happiest concept, comparatively speaking, was the central railroad station... The idea was that as soon as they (state visitors), as well as ordinary travelers, stepped out of the station they would be overwhelmed, or rather stunned by the urban scene and thus the power of the Reich."

Moving

Here's an example of how something as minor as not quite enough ability to move, to engage in kinesthetic action, can make the difference. In the Taylor's first permanent facility for holding DesignShop sessions, one little breakout room was always the low productivity area. There didn't seem to be any reason why the spot should cause low productivity—10' x 10' space back in the corner, a couple of stationary work walls, two moving work panels, a little round table, chairs, and just enough room to get four or five people in there. But because of this correlation with low productivity, it was the last place that they chose to put people for breakouts.

One day they happened to substitute four tall captain's chairs and a tall table in the low productivity corner. From then on every team working there produced fabulous results.

What was the difference? Because the space was tight and people had been sitting down low, it was too much trouble getting up to write on the walls. The Taylors had learned if people don't write on the walls, they don't share the information. If people don't write on the walls, learning doesn't become kinesthetic and neurally integrated.

Even though they were teaching the importance of moving, no one ever noticed that people using that space had not been moving. When the environment was changed, the behavior of those using the space changed. Now, because they were already almost standing in those tall captain's chairs, it was easy to pop up and down and write on the walls. Productivity soared.

Of the many elements that make a difference, one of the simplest is size—the volume of the physical space, how high or low the ceiling, and our proximity to other people in the space.

Dick Tuck, the political trickster who had Richard Nixon in his satiric sights, used the effect of physical space as the mechanism for one of his pranks. During a presidential campaign, Tuck had the responsibility for booking a hall for a Nixon speech. Nixon's folks expected around 250 people to attend. Tuck cunningly booked a hall which would accommodate three times that number. When the 250 expected attendees did show up, they were rattling around in a huge, empty room. The message conveyed by the wide spacing of bodies: no one showed up. The message that would have been conveyed by a crowded room of densely-packed bodies: wow! this is exciting and successful! In each case, the number of attendees is the same, only their proximity is different.

The architecture of imposing size and distance confers status, for example, in a CEO's office. When you walk in, it's a long way—sometimes 30 feet—to the desk. The desk is 52" deep, well outside of North Americans' interpersonal space—remote and distant. The CEO's chair is high; your chair is so low, your chin is sitting on the desk. If the CEO graciously comes around and says, "Come sit over here at a little round table for a cup of coffee," you think, what a nice person.

Structure wins. In her classic book, *The Death and Life of Great American Cities,* Jane Jacobs showed incisively how the physical structure of buildings and layout of the street determined the destiny of the neighborhood and the city. It didn't matter if the district was designed as "poor" or "upper class"; ultimately, the destiny of the neighborhood was driven by the physical structure. The environment actually caused people to function a certain way.

Perversely, when people try to squeeze better functioning from themselves and others, they turn automatically to self-modification, trying to change themselves through an act of will rather than changing a constraining environment. Perhaps there is difficulty taking seriously the notion that the details of architecture, lighting, or furnishings can significantly impact human performance. Perhaps it feels like an abandonment of the principles of self-reliance, responsibility, strength of

Using the Power of Space and Place

will or purpose: an admission of weakness or submission to biology, biochemistry, or the influence of environment.

If it's sometimes hard to accept that the environment affects your own performance, let's acknowledge that the environment can powerfully affect *other* people—your customers, coworkers, and employees—and deal appropriately with it for that reason alone.

If physical surroundings influence mood and behavior, surely everyone carefully designs offices, schools, and homes to help people focus attention and release their powers of productivity and cooperation. Surely the bottom line has already been driving everyone in this direction.

Evidently not strongly enough. Office layout, industrial plant interiors, and schools are generally not designed to generate maximum productivity. Architecture has been occasionally used well, often abused, but mostly ignored. People are accustomed to poor work environments. They even think of them as "practical" or "economic," because of the inability to capture the information about true costs and put a dollar figure on loss of productivity into an accounting system. While there has been more recent attention to "ergonomics," this has almost exclusively focused on physical, not mental or even sensual aspects of the environment.

The bad designs that are easiest to identify come from misplaced incentives. Matt Taylor points out that, ironically, janitors and lawyers control the design of schools and office buildings more than educational or business theory ever imagined possible. Much of school and office design revolves around the logistics of allowing the janitors to easily keep the rooms clean. Administrative worries about insurance and lawsuits further drive the creation of a low-variety, attenuated space environment, which is not ideal for the official business of schools—producing learning—or of offices—producing value.

Noise is the most impertinent of all forms of interruption. It is not only an interruption, but also a disruption of thought.

—Arthur Schopenhauer

Defining a Good Space

A space designed for enhancing human productivity would be a high-variety space. People thrive in high variety spaces, which is why they select high-variety environments for vacations as this is their opportunity to renew. Mountains, forests, or beaches—"simple" environments—are actually high in acoustic, kinesthetic, and visual variety. Leaves have multiple hues of blue, green, and yellow. Shade and shadow cause colors to change. Over the course of the day, the angle of the sun and the nature of the cloud cover modifies colors. An artist would blend more than fifteen shades of green, blue, and yellow to start approximating the color complexity you see in a single moment in the leaves of a tree.

Think about both tactile feel and acoustical quality of surfaces in different forests—an aspen grove in the mountains, a redwood forest in a cool valley, a cluster of palm trees at the ocean's edge. Each has unique and rich acoustic and tactile qualities. You experience variation everywhere in nature.

Usually the natural environment also causes you to engage in physical activity, and we find movement invigorating and restorative. Even sitting on the beach, your eye is continually changing focus: looking far away, then close up, then into the distance again, dealing with shifting light and shadow. Your skin senses the changing temperature, shifts in the direction and mood of the wind. Your ear notes the variations in the noise of the surf and sea birds calling.

The more living patterns there are in a place, a room, a building, or a town the more it comes to life as an entity, the more it glows, the more it has that self-maintaining fire which is the quality without a name.

—Christopher Alexander,
A Timeless Way of Building

But when you go to work, you find all of those qualities removed from your environment. In this artificial environment, colors and variations are designed out until it mimics a low-quality rendering of a space, eliminating all the qualities of a real environment. It is as if the complexity of a forest had been replaced by a crude drawing of trees as brown sticks supporting balloons colored one constant, unremitting shade of green.

The simplistic argument for utility says that all parts of a person's workstation should be together. But it is not healthy to sit at one place for eight hours. Doesn't it make more sense to create a situation in which you have to move as part of the work? This is not inefficient—on the contrary, it is more efficient, because if you can't move as part of the work, you will manufacture other excuses to move, or take a hidden reduction in productivity.

Using the Power of Space and Place

People often work in a space where they sit for hours in a glaring, highlighted environment. What often makes business spaces feel so sick—and gives 17% of the workforce headaches—is the lighting. Technicians say that, for "utility's sake," the entire room should have uniform lighting. But uniform lights produce glare. You lose the resting points the eye finds amid the variety of high and low light levels found outdoors in nature. People use tools that keep their eyes riveted on a single point of focus. Opthalmologists remind them to look up from work frequently and focus on a distant object, but they succumb to the structural combination of tools and environment.

Architecture should help the building fulfill its mission. But based on the appearance of most buildings, you'd say the purpose of the corporate environment is to enable manufacturing and to project "corporate identity" by looking prettily uniform to visiting outsiders. What about supporting the mission to be productive and create value?

Innovation in Group Work Environments

One of the most powerfully effective innovations is the mobile DesignShop environment: custom-designed walls, furniture, lighting, and equipment. It's analogous to the way that emergency crews bring equipment, personnel, structures, and supplies to set up a self-contained field hospital and deliver appropriate medical services near a battlefield or in an earthquake-ravaged city. Over the course of three days before the arrival of participants, the facilitation team rapidly deploys an entire, traveling DesignShop environment, setting up a portable, creative workplace in any type of setting: warehouses, auditoriums, hotel ballrooms.

Rapid Deployment Systems
http://www.mgtaylor.com/ai/airds.htm

They start with the same disadvantages that everyone else routinely deals with—carpeting over a cement slab, flat overhead fluorescent lighting, wonky air-conditioning, the sound of repairs on the roof. They replace it, to the greatest extent possible, with fresh air, natural light, variable and complex lighting, controlled temperature, a good sound system, artwork, and plants. As much as possible, every distraction and discomfort is done away with, and every environmental support needed for your mind to function at its best is provided.

Walking into the DesignShop environment, you are immediately flooded with the message that this place is for action, for rolling up your sleeves—not a sit-around-

*Gold-collar workers,
like supercomputers,
are a precious corporate resource.
If they are left to stagnate
in a setting that inhibits
their creativity,
they are being wasted.*

—Robert E. Kelley

Premises Regarding the Knowledge Economy
http://www.mgtaylor.com/
mgtaylor/jotm/spring97/
premises.htm

and-talk-about-the-same-old-stuff space. Rather than a formal, "is my suit right?" environment, it is an environment of tools, of stimulation. This is a place to store, retrieve, compare, create, and recreate knowledge and information. The environment tells you this as a unified message that comes on all levels: visual, intellectual, visceral, the way you are led—and allowed—to move.

Designing for the Knowledge Worker

In a Knowledge Economy, organize the environment around the work, don't force the work or the worker into accommodating the environment.

A knowledge worker or executive has approximately twenty distinct activities or sets of functions. A typical office design is either optimized for one or two tasks, or is a compromise to support four or five of those functions. The rest of the functions are just not recognized. The office does not adjust itself to the work. Far from supporting the range of the work of a knowledge worker, the environment actually introduces blocks.

The creative process is complex. It involves multiple stages, multiple modes of work, multiple tooling setups, and multiple engagements with different sizes of groups of people. At times, what is wanted is a quiet niche in which to concentrate. At other times, you may have to be engaged with twenty other people in a highly-interactive relationship.

Ideally, you would create a space for standing, sitting, and working that enables people to see each other. Make it informal, relaxed, adaptable, tactile, and resizable. Make it possible for people to move around and share common experiences—which may be drawing on work walls together or building models. Enable people to easily get up and down and move. Don't put physical barriers in their way. Create work walls, writing spaces, and furniture that are easy to move so people will start to grab walls and resize the rooms, or pull in light, adaptable furniture and tools and use things the way they want. Let the whole environment say that this is adaptable and collaborative where people can see one another and engage with one another.

This is exactly what has been implemented in the MG Taylor working environment. All the custom-designed furniture and structures are…unusual. None of it

Using the Power of Space and Place

is recognizable from a standard office supply catalogue. Furniture colors are light, soft—soft gray for the wallboards instead of the harsh, reflective glare of whiteboards. There are natural wood surfaces, textiles with texture. Everything carries the faint echo of Frank Lloyd Wright's design aesthetic.

Everything is fluid, alterable. You can move walls, increase or decrease the size of displays, or juxtapose overlapping displays, as you fit the environment to the work instead of the absolute tyranny of fitting the work to the environment.

Walls are all on wheels and easily moved. Their surfaces are writable, postable. "Hypertiles"—11" X 17" writable panels that stick on and peel off the gray writing walls—allow you to peel off your ideas and stick them up in new locations or in new combinations. Complete work setups—including easel, drafting board, grayboard, desktop, and file cabinet—are on wheels and can be brought along behind you—like a dog on a leash.

Throughout the environment, walls, tables, and chairs move easily to transform spaces from eating areas to conversation areas to writing or model-building areas. Spaces are enlarged or pulled to intimate compactness, depending on the size of the group.

All around this central work space, movable walls form a simple maze—a warren of differently-sized spaces where individual groups can work. Some of the spaces are set up for use as workgroup breakout spaces; others have interesting things in them inviting exploration: computers displaying the World Wide Web, online search capabilities, changing art. Varying background lighting within the spaces adds tone and visual variety, making each space unique and enriching the flat, even overhead lighting of the hotel convention center. The layout is complex enough to stimulate curiosity about what is around the next corner, but not so complex as to confuse.

It's an environment that easily stimulates the imagination. The design is simple, but full of variety. It is rich in the architectural qualities of prospect and refuge: *Prospect* is the introduction of visual uncertainty, of possibility. Looking over there, you can see there is something around the corner: it goes up over here, around over there; there's a background, a foreground, a tremendous amount of prospect

The task decides, not the name, the age, or the budget of the discipline, or the rank of the individual plying for it. Knowledge, therefore, has to be organized as a team in which the task decides who is in charge, when, for what, and for how long.

—Peter Drucker

in this DesignShop environment. It also has a lot of *refuge*—places for the eye to dwell, little nooks and niches, varying textures. The environment participates in the deliberate creation of an information-enriched situation.

Prospect, refuge, and visual ambiguity are physical qualities in the environment. Our eyes respond by wandering, looking, seeking, resting. As the eye moves, the mind is asking questions, being curious, moving into a mode of exploration and creativity.

Sources of information, inspiration, perspective, and practical advice are placed in inviting locations. At one junction between breakout areas is a tall, triangular information kiosk offering custom compendiums of articles found in online computer searches on relevant topics. In a niche on a popular pathway into the largest space, a sticky wall—a wall with a surface like Post-it Note™ adhesive — is covered with individual articles of the most immediate value. Fluorescent yellow, green, and orange highlighting makes relevant words jump out for easy scan. The keywords are tantalizing, provocative, urging "You've just got to take a quick peek and see what this says." And when you decide that it's great information that you really need, you can take the article with you.

As you walk along the outside rim of the big semicircle wall, an ever-changing display of articles, photos, comic strips, and book jackets clings to its adhesive surface—capturing your eye. The information on this wall and in all display areas constantly evolves. On the Scan day, the articles on display are thought-provoking ideas from outside the DesignShop session. Over the Focus and Act days, the work, models, and key concepts used or created by participants start augmenting the display. It is a direct reflection of the changing thinking of the participants. Every day the information becomes more structured. The most important themes emerge more clearly. Somewhere on that wall is the pattern which will become the answer to the problem. This is a Knowledge Wall.

Using the Power of Space and Place

The physical environment should be a tool for the creation, display, storage, retrieval, re-display, and mixing of information and knowledge or pieces of knowledge—lots of knowledge all needing to be simultaneously accessible at a glance. You just can't do that adequately in traditional office arrangements. The amount of information you need to be able to work with at one time is greater than you can provide with slide projectors, a bulletin board, some networking software, and a few software packages sharing a 17" display. So your information is segmented, fragmented, displayed only in very small glimpses of the whole picture. You almost never see information juxtaposed to itself.

Notice that creativity often comes when you juxtapose unexpected or different pieces of information and are able to combine them in new, interesting, and exciting ways that spark you. Unfortunately, there's usually not a big enough wall with enough information displayed to enable this to happen. But here there is a lot of room for real perspective. Hundreds of concepts can be easily accommodated, and this is only the start of the information-supporting aspects of this furniture and environment.

Books help make it a very rich environment. The portable DesignShop environment includes a portable library. Out of MG Taylor's 5,000-book collection, a selection of the 350 most useful and provocative titles for this DesignShop event fills four mobile bookcases. If inspiration is needed, you walk over and scan titles, pick up a book and forage for ideas.

The books are in constant motion as people browse and replace them in new locations. The new location calls a book to your attention that you'd missed when you were looking at the shelf before. It's next to a new set of titles—a new juxtaposition of information to consider.

As part of a "cognitively expanded" environment, there are tables filled with every kind of 3D modeling equipment—from Legos, to miniature models, modeling clay, chemistry modeling kits—all of which come into play for designing a model, explaining a solution, depicting an interaction or a business relationship. Arrays of colored markers, pastel crayons, paints, brushes, colored pencils, computer drawing packages, colored paper—anything you might need to spark your creativity and express your idea—invite their use.

Employing the Environment in Support of the Creative Process
http://www.mgtaylor.com/mgtaylor/jotm/spring97/envir_creative.htm

The new emerging industries, therefore, embody a new economic reality: Knowledge has become the central economic resource. The systematic acquisition of knowledge has replaced experience as the foundation for productive capacity and performance.

—Peter Drucker, 1968
The Age of Discontinuity

If you can't have fun with the problem, you'll never solve it.

—MG Taylor Axiom

These tools provide the ability for all sensory and cognitive types to learn and express ideas beyond the normal confines of time, materials, or venues allotted in the standard office. There are times and places where the requirement is to summarize in a one-page, bulleted memo or a five-minute verbal summary. This is not one of them.

The 3D models allow kinetic learning and expression and different modes of visual learning. Using the models lets you apply other areas of knowledge to solving your problem. Perhaps it's been defined as a "finance" problem, but now that it's been modeled out in 3D, you suddenly start seeing connections from your physics background, chemistry training, or mechanical engineering experience that suggest solutions.

Throughout the entire DesignShop environment are scattered toys, games, stuffed animals, balloons. As we first looked at the environment for the Wharton DesignShop we thought: "OK, we can see how a business person *might* use the 3D modeling equipment to capture a complex issue, but no serious executive is *ever* going to pick up the toys, the stuffed animals, or any of this other stuff!" Wrong.

Over the hours and days of the DesignShop, the mood and behavior of participants change. Someone begins toying with a Slinky™ as he works on a problem. Someone else assembles a quick 3-D model to bring home her point about a business relationship.

A stuffed dinosaur, rabbit, and giraffe appear at a table. When you walk by some hours later, they've started playing cards. Now a pile of coins forms a pot in the center of the table. Over the days, a little poker drama plays out, with the giraffe proving to be a foolish player, the rabbit a card cheat. No one had "responsibility" for the dinosaur-poker diorama, it just evolved, just happened, done by—whom? The Air Force brass? The hard-driving management consultants? The intense business school professors? Yes.

By this point in the event, the focus on learning, creativity, inventing, and problem-solving has taken firm hold. Many DesignShop activities are deliberately designed to put people into a

Using the Power of Space and Place

playful mode. Play, the psychology of play, humor and its closeness to creativity are known to theoretical psychologists, but ignored in our society as a whole—especially business. DesignShop events have as an axiom: "If you can't have fun with the problem, you'll never solve it."

Axioms
http://www.mgtaylor.com/mgtaylor/glasbead/axioms.htm

The DesignShop environment has succeeded in transmitting its message. The power of architecture and environment to shape a way of life, help or hinder you in fulfilling your mission, was something Matt Taylor learned from Frank Lloyd Wright. Matt was an apprentice to Wright and worked in the heady, creative Taliesin community that was home, workplace, and playground for Wright, his team, and a visiting stream of artistic, musical, and literary talent. Matt explains:

> Architecture expresses and facilitates a life style, a way of life, a concept of life. When you are in that architecture, the architecture facilitates you down that path and actually will fight you down other paths.
>
> The power of Wright's work was that he built architecture around a unique way of life for a particular family. The life lived in the house was the artistic expression. Wright was creating a way of life based on what he thought was their potential.
>
> Despite the legends to the contrary, Wright never ruled a client. But he would redesign and redesign until he and the client together arrived at a fit. It was a beautiful and effective synthesis of his view and that of his clients.
>
> Ten years after Wright's death, a book on his existing buildings showed that over 60% built during an almost 100-year span were still in the hands of the original owners or their descendants. You couldn't blast those people out of there. There is no other domestic architect in the history of the world who can claim such a successful record with his customers.
>
> I've driven around the country interviewing families who lived in Wright houses for 30 to 50 years and the story is always consistent—like Mrs. John C. Pew. She was living in a minimalist and extremely simple house: beautiful and variegated, but simple. The first four or five years she fought the house.

She thought the house was totally foreign to her life style. I suspect that if she was able to build a conventional house in the early '30s or '40s, it would have been a very solidly middle-class house, something a little more opulent. She came to the conclusion that before she sold it she would spend a year being totally non-combative, stop trying to make the house work in the way she thought she ought to live, and let it instruct her in her life style. When she stopped fighting, she discovered that Wright had designed the house to her future, not to her past. After she had been in the house 20 years and raised her family, she said she could not imagine being without the house.

A client commissioning a Wright house would ask for an arrangement of space and utilities, but it also had to be an expression of human values—explicitly an expression of knowledge work. If you refuse to accept traditional separation of function—this element is for structure; this element is for utility; this element is for beauty—but instead say each element has to serve all those purposes, then your decorative elements become the tools of your work. This is the rule that has been applied to the DesignShop environment.

Wright's designs worked to support the potential of a particular family. The DesignShop environment works to support the potential—the future—of organizations.

Back during his architect days, Matt tells of designing new offices for a family business that was moving from the old building that had housed them for decades. In their old building, the family members' offices were side by side, running down a long, narrow shotgun hallway in a grim, echoing warehouse. Matt observed that they'd stand out in this hallway and argue for hours each day. This was how they communicated.

In the new building, Matt designed custom office arrangements and furniture to suit the personalities of each family member. The shy, reserved son got an office layout that built his confidence and power.

Behind that individual fine-tuning lay an overall architecture combined with details to help change the family dynamics. Finish details were designed to promote harmony: several hundred gradations and shades of colors, banks of plants, and proper acoustic design created a high-variety, low-stress environment. The family members' offices were all on one floor, but on different sides of the building. Paths led from the offices and all met in a central, plant-surrounded gazebo.

Using the Power of Space and Place

"The gazebo," Matt said, "is where they were supposed to come to meet and talk."

One very forceful brother objected to the layout: there was a pillar and plants—obstacles—between his doorway and that of the more reticent brother. "I can't go directly to his office, I've got to go to the gazebo and then to his office," complained Mr. Big.

"Exactly," said Matt, "that's why it's there. To stop you from running right into his office."

After they'd been in the building a month, the shy brother said to Matt, "We haven't had a fight in a month. We're working well together—better than ever. Does the building have something to do with it?"

"The building," said Matt, "has everything to do with it. That's why I designed it the way I did."

The power of the environment to shape behavior can be seen by observing people who are infamous in their organizations as "uncooperative," "unmotivated," "uncreative," or "difficult." Gail Taylor describes the phenomenon:

> We have sponsors warn us, "Wait until Mr. Difficult gets to the DesignShop session, he will drive you nuts, he will never participate in this exercise, he is going to be horrid, there is no way to motivate this person." And then Mr. Difficult comes to the DesignShop, cruises through it, has a fabulous time, loves the interaction, contributes, cooperates, loves the results. And the sponsor says, "I don't understand this!"

What happens in the DesignShop environment? People become spontaneously creative, productive, and cooperative.

And then Mr. Difficult goes back to the company's standard environment with its built-in structure and consequences, and he returns to his old, horrid pattern of behavior.

Why is the behavior so different? Because in the DesignShop, says Matt, "We are paying attention to the complete environment. What is the message? Manage the total environment. Have you ever thought about putting Mr. Difficult in a DesignShop-like environment back in the office? Try that."

It is amazing how something that seems so "small" as environment could make such a huge difference in how people interact. But even a small change in environment can make a large difference in creativity, cooperation, and the bottom line of productivity.

Buckminster Fuller said, "Change the environment, not the person." The Taylors' thesis is "properly manage the environment, and people will spontaneously become creative, productive, and cooperative."

Buckminster Fuller said, "Change the environment, not the person." The Taylors' thesis is "properly manage the environment, and people will spontaneously become creative, productive, and cooperative."

Design and implement an environment that systematically and thoroughly supports creativity and cooperation, and you have created a structure—a pathway—that leads to this very complex behavior. What is going to happen? Gail Taylor says, "People come in there and behave, act, function, think, feel in ways that are a total mystery to them." They become more creative, cooperative, intelligent, and productive. They solve problems that have bedeviled them for years. They have energy and enthusiasm that they may not have felt for decades. The source of their tranformation remains a mystery to them because—after all—environment can't possibly make that much of a difference, can it?

Challenge

You've already addressed your environment in the assignment following Chapter 2. Now, with new information from Chapter 6, it's time to iterate your design. Iteration is one of the keys to success in the application of the creative process. Seven iterations of a design improves it 1000%.

1. What did you pick up from Chapter 6 that was new or intriguing? Summarize these items as general principles that could be applied to make any environment a more healthy, stimulating, and supportive place to work and live in. Also list any new questions you have concerning environment.

2. Take a few days or weeks to really observe how environment affects behavior. You'll have to watch for things you're not used to noticing. Keep a journal of your findings. Draw your workspace as a living organism. What organs, limbs, size, mobility, functionality will it have? What kind of organism is it: a tree, an amoeba, a tiger, a dog, a coral reef, a genie, what?

3. Living systems need be flexible to respond to changes in their environment. How flexible are the environments you live and work in? How quickly can you adapt them to a change of use? What are the changes you could make to radically increase the flexibility? Chances are some of these changes will be prohibitive but others will involve only a shift in thinking: "Oh, we could use that room for such-and-such." Watch out for culturally-burdened words related to environments. Why think of a house in terms of living room, bedroom, family room, den? Think instead of how a house should support what you want to do in life. This also goes for corporate terms: reception, board room, bullpen, cubicle (who on earth really wants to work in something called a cubicle?), conference room (is "conferring" the only essential part of the creative process, and does a big table really facilitate it?).

4. Compose a new iteration of your vision for various environments that takes into account the design of high-variety spaces having both prospect and refuge, and the performance specifications you uncovered in question 1. Be sure to include the tools necessary to promote collaboration and creativity.

Facing the Abyss

If you want a surprise in the way people change when placed in an environment that supports creativity and cooperation, you'd be hard pressed to find a better example than what happened to Arnold Engineering and Development Center (AEDC). Even though AEDC is a government facility, issues of relevance to any business come through loud and clear. So, we are telling the AEDC story as if AEDC were in fact a for-profit, private sector business. This lets us translate military and government-style operations into business equivalents that have more meaning for most of us.

By sketching the AEDC story in business-oriented terms, we've converted it into an allegory rather than the complex and detailed process it had to be to succeed. So, forgive us as we cite our Literary License to let us omit a host of laws and military procedures which dictated how AEDC, the Air Force, and related personnel had to operate, and which all parties involved faithfully followed.

Whatever civilian conception there might be about rigidity or lack of complexity in a CEO who is "a military man," a visit with Colonel Bill Rutley shows that his job isn't all that much different from that of CEOs in aerospace companies. We had heard from others that Col. Bill has been wooed by the private sector, with no success to date despite the large financial incentive for him. By the time we finished chatting with Col. Bill, we wanted to buy stock in whatever company finally succeeds in recruiting him.

As an organization that had done outstanding seminal work for decades, but to many were questioning in 1991, AEDC was not especially productive or cooperative enough for the challenge that they now faced. In over 22 months of DesignShop process work, they went from feeling like victims of reduced Department of Defense funding, to helping create the game. By the time we saw them in action at the Wharton DesignShop event, they had transformed almost beyond recognition.

AEDC is located close to the middle of nowhere—near the town of Tullahoma, Tennessee. In Tullahoma—in fact, in the entire area known as Middle Tennessee—getting a job at AEDC is the biggest game in town.

Founded soon after World War II, AEDC was so thoroughly modeled after German aircraft test facilities that initial designs even included a rathskeller. It has 40-year-old facilities, some of which are on a 24-hour-a-day duty cycle, 7 days a week, 365 days per year. Says one engineer: "We have electric motors and other equipment from World War II Germany still operating that are more than half a century old. We just rebuild them and rework them."

At AEDC, the employees test solid and liquid fueled rocket motors. They test the Peace Keeper, Minute Man, and Trident missiles. They operate wind tunnels, hyperballistic ranges, impact ranges, and arc heaters for ablation testing. They do environmental space simulation and wind tunnel design. They also do flight dynamics testing of aircraft at subsonic, transonic, and supersonic speeds.

They wrestle with the usual Environmental Pollution Agency issues of being an industrial-type plant using PCBs and cleaning fluids—ethyl chloride—plus the dangerous potentials of solid rocket fuels, the joys of corrosive, toxic, hypergolic liquid fuels, and the explosive uncertainty of what is tactfully called "uncontrolled combustion." Production, reliability, and aging equipment are problems.

Not just the equipment is old, cantankerous, and volatile at AEDC. The base is still staffed by many of the original workers. The first employee, a chauffeur for General Arnold, only recently retired and still appears at parties. By now, though, there are second and third generation employees. Entire families work at AEDC—one spouse working on the government side and the other on the contractor side. Of the approximately 3,400 people on the base, less than 300 are Air Force military and civilian personnel. The other 3,100 are local civilians on contract, which represents the majority of the working population of Tullahoma's 16,000-plus population.

Far from being a happy family, in 1991 the place was rife with disputes that rivaled the Hatfields and the McCoys for acrimony. A union/management battle was raging that included acts of vandalism. Even when things ran calmly, fragmentation problems were endemic, and cooperation and communication lacking. Things came together only on the commander's desk. Even within the Air Force, once it got out of the commander's office it was "mine" and "yours." There is a name for this type of complete compartmentalization: *stovepiping*. People ignored the work of the person at the next desk and the impact that their decision was going to have on the project that the person next door was working on.

In 1991, with peace breaking out all over the world and war business dropping off, the U.S. Congress said that the game for AEDC was going to face amputation through drastic cutbacks—a 30% to 40% budget cut.

Not that things had been in such great shape before that news arrived.

Enter Colonel Rutley

The base and all its varietal problems was about to be transferred to its new Commander: Colonel William Rutley.

With multiple advanced engineering and business degrees, he had started out flying as an F-4 crewmember back in the Vietnam days and had grown into a specialist in project management, orchestrating complex teams for operations, planning, research, development, and production of complex weapon systems. Most recently, he had been the Director of the F-16 International Program where he headed developing, delivering, and supporting airplanes to seventeen countries plus the United Nations.

Col. Bill elaborated on the situation. "The F-16 work was wild and wonderful. Some of the program participants are normally very hostile to each other, like the Greeks and Turks, the Egyptians and Israelis, and the Japanese and Koreans. We had to work very hard at understanding cultures and figuring ways to get people together into a common place to get things done. So it was quite fascinating."

The brass decided that a guy who had done just fine dealing with centuries-long enmities like Greece and Turkey, or Japan and Korea, was the right one to handle difficulties at Arnold.

John Poparad, Program Director of OAO Corporation, observes: "You will never meet another guy like Col. Rutley. He is an outstanding leader. He runs a very disciplined military organization. Rutley was an equal opportunity order-giver; he didn't care if you were contractor, civilian, or military."

Col. Bill quickly evaluated the situation:

> When I arrived there, I was briefed by everyone in the place. A lot of Total Quality Management and other good things were happening.
>
> But there was a general belief in a continued downsizing into less activity and fewer people. An analysis revealed we were on a downhill slide. Either we had to accept this as inevitable and for the public good—the public having decided they wanted less of us. Then perhaps that would be how we would go—a way to fade away gracefully.
>
> The other alternative was to offer a higher level of good to our customers and the nation. It was also obvious that our activities were too scattered, and there was really not enough identity-building being done.

Col. Bill had substantial personal control of AEDC—more than the typical corporate CEO. He could operate autonomously as long as he got things done, and he answered only to one person in the Air Force, a four-star general. He could ignore anyone else if he wanted to. He didn't.

His challenge to AEDC was "What will the situation be at AEDC after the year 2000?" Col. Bill recalls the reluctant response:

> We had dialogue on that. First, they said, we are too busy. It's hard to take time off from doing the work to pay attention to this question.
>
> I said that we were going to have to decide what we were going to be in forty years. We were going to have a tough time doing that while at the same time we were trying to serve our customers every day. But we were going to do it.
>
> Second, we did not have anything that resembled a change agent. I said I wanted to bring in someone who didn't know us, but who could understand us and partner with us.
>
> Until now AEDC's change agents had been consultants who came in once per year and did surveys. That was of very little value and the changes were minor. As part of my Master's degree, I had done work on organizational change.

The safest road to Hell is the gradual one — the gentle slope, soft underfoot, without sudden turnings, without milestones, without signposts.

—C.S. Lewis

Facing the Abyss

I realized that intensity and long-term involvement were critical.

I had longitudinal data on the impact of brief consulting visits, and had said to my base commander, "You need to stop this. You are wasting time and money. You look at the written comments on each survey, the drop-off in the surveys, the indicators. You are hurting the organization more than helping it when other people are not involved or committed. Get a consultant to come in and do it right or not at all." They were only spending $25,000 per year. This consultant comes in and does a couple of seminars with a few people and then we sent out a survey. I suggested they just stop it, and they did. It would be better to spend $100,000 and get some intensity. I said they should just figure out what they want to be and go get that done—make a commitment.

But Col. Bill found that there was one type of short-term consulting work that had achieved interesting results prior to his arrival. In January 1991, based on a personal recommendation, an AEDC group had gone down to Orlando to an MG Taylor management center and spent three days creating a strategic plan.

The plan got all kinds of accolades. It looked like a neat plan. I asked what they had done with it, and they said "absolutely zero."

Col. Bill's predecessor had said to the staff, "Now, here's the plan. Let's go get it done." But, there was no follow-up. To Col. Bill, it was clear why the plan had not produced results:

First of all, AEDC didn't change anything when they came back. They tried to stuff a square peg in a round hole. If we're going to do something like this we needed to change the whole organization by constant association with a certain level of intensity.

I went through a complete study of the whole DesignShop process. I came back and said, "I think this has value." It was a combination I had never seen before. I had seen consultants who were good in areas, but I had never seen anyone who could assemble the architecture, light, music, sound, models, learning, iteration, food — everything. They have taken Drucker's ideas and a number of other folks' ideas on similar things and gotten them to coalesce. They are very good at that. I had never seen anyone assemble all that in that way.

I felt it had utility, but we would need a long-term commitment from our organization. We had to have a series of engagements over a full two years. We laid out a series of DesignShops every ninety days and started a broad base of participation.

One of the folks at AEDC said, "Why can't we do this ourselves?" I said that my reading and experience tells me that would be an exercise in frustration. The facilitator is a professional change agent. If you are a facilitator working from the inside, you are no longer a change agent. You really need someone from the outside.

Another said "They don't know us." I said that was the very reason I wanted them. I did not want them to know us. I wanted them to start out with a blank sheet of paper, and what they knew about renewal and transformation, and as we work with them together as partners we will both have more that will emerge. It worked beautifully.

The Transition Manager's Creed
http://www.mgtaylor.com/mgtaylor/jotm/fall96/trnmgrcr.htm

AEDC's First DesignShop Event: Welcome to the Abyss

MG Taylor was brought in to help AEDC transform. When they led participants through the center's first DesignShop session, there was no team, just factions. All the stakeholders were present—the customers, union members, labor leaders, management, contract civilians, Air Force—and it was not a happy crowd.

Some employees were apprehensive, thinking that closing or downsizing AEDC was a certainty. These folks walked in the door to the first DesignShop event with the certain belief that they were going to downsize. If the seminar or conference or workshop they were attending could offer any assistance, many felt, it was going to help them decide where to make the cuts and, perhaps, how to do them as humanely as possible. Maybe it would help those present be the ones to hang on to their jobs. By their own description, they were frozen "in the defensive crouch position."

Doug Cantrell, who in 1991 was staff manager for a bogglingly complex range of technical support services at AEDC, had been wrestling with the lack of vision in his daily work. He now saw the same problem among the incoming DesignShop participants. Charged with defining and instituting Total Quality Management (TQM), Doug said:

I saw there were things we were doing that did not make any sense. I was not sure what the real objectives were in the TQM effort. It was as if we were implementing some kind of program, but the object was to implement the program, not to get the results.

Going into the DesignShop session, everyone knew there wasn't enough business to keep AEDC going. We were thinking, "How in the world will we preserve the organization and institution?" There is often not a lot of vision beyond protecting the organization itself. People are thinking, "How do we protect the organization, hold on to the bodies, and budget?" Not, "What is the service we are expected to perform? What is it we are doing now, and what is it we are going to need to do out here in the future?"

It is not because things are difficult that we do not dare; it is because we do not dare that they are difficult.

—Seneca

Others coming into the DesignShop thought no problems existed and that holding yet another meeting was a waste of time. One participant relates: "We were brought in, and people's attitude the first day was: We were ordered to be here, and we will sit through it." But that was all.

Customers and prospective customers were there, too, just as nervous and uncomfortable as everyone else. There were the government entities, such as the Air Force, and commercial folk such as Boeing, General Electric, Pratt & Whitney—all the big aircraft and rocket engine builders sitting in the same room with their competition. In the beginning, they sat in little clumps—all the GE guys together, all the Pratt & Whitney guys together—with lots of distance between them and the competition. Col. Bill described the scene:

> The commercial customers wanted to go off and have personal breakouts so they could talk about this. It made them nervous—the adversarial issues and vulnerability. Pratt & Whitney was having a tough time trying to put things out on the table. When we originally had suggested that GE was going to show up, they really hit the ceiling."

Every time a touchy issue was raised—and there were lots of touchy issues—the room would erupt into a mass of little football huddles. Union guys whispered to union guys. Contractor management whispered with other contractor management guys.

John Poparad explained: "On the Meyers/Briggs inventory of cognitive types, 98% of the people at AEDC are Sensory-Thinking types: action-oriented individuals. They love to go from data to decision with little thinking in between: 'Don't slow me down because I have things to do.'"

Colonel Bill puts it even more bluntly:

In the Air Force, it is even worse. We are trained to attack. If there is a problem, kill it. Instead of looking at things from seven angles, the attitude is to blow it away and not think about it.

You have to fight that, and it frustrates people, especially some of the young officers. They come up and say, "Let's make a decision. Tell us what you want us to do, and we will go do it."

I tell them that I will not tell them what to do. The fact is I don't know the answers to all the problems, and that is why we are here. I tell them I will sit with them and work it out, but I will not tell them the answers. They want the old command and control—'Hop To It, Major.' Most of the guys who did business that way are not here any more. I do not know all of the answers. I am not sure I know the right questions. I am still forming the problem.

They get frustrated and will ask why they have to talk about something they talked about yesterday. The facilitator will tell them, "You talked about it for one hour yesterday, and you have to go back to it." They don't want to define the problem; they want to decide what the solution is. Having a decision done and made is where humans are comfortable. That is where they want to go, whether or not it is appropriate.

The discomfort attending Scan—the fog of uncertainty, the ambiguity and paradoxes—causes anxiety that makes people yearn for a decision, any decision, as long as it puts an end to that uncomfortable feeling. John Poparad describes how people repeatedly drove toward premature closure:

During the DesignShop process, people would drive to decisions, and Rutley would get up and say, "No." This was much to the frustration of the group. Rutley said his purpose was to keep us uncomfortable, because in that way we could have a chance to make changes. As long as we were comfortable doing things the old way, we would not change.

And then, to make it worse, there were the AEDC staffers assigned to work during the event. Yes, MG Taylor brought an experienced team with them, but the support team for DesignShop sessions normally includes personnel from the sponsoring organization.

Michael Kaufman, a specialist in the Deming Management Method, "Learning How to Learn" models, and the MG Taylor DesignShop process, was part of the MG Taylor staff who worked with AEDC from the start. Michael recounts the experience:

> There were horror stories from the beginning. Fifteen to twenty AEDC people were told—ordered—to come to be knowledge worker staff with us. None of them really wanted to be there. They hated the whole thing.
>
> You can ask Frances Gillard, who later became a permanent staffer of AEDC's management facility offering DesignShop capability on a daily basis. She remembers hearing about me: that I was a big ogre—a terrible person to work with.
>
> The whole DesignShop experience was so contrary to the past experience of the people at AEDC. The fact that we asked them to stay beyond five o'clock in the evening was a problem. The facilitation team works until midnight or whatever is required for success. At 5:01 it was too much for them.

None of these people seemed to realize that they were all in the AEDC boat together—and that the boat was sinking. Granted, there were some people who thought that "your end of the boat is sinking," but that was as far as it got. The only common experience they were having so far was, with the exception of Colonel Rutley, no one wanted to be there.

DesignShop events begin with two statements: one from the sponsor, one from the facilitator. Before the facilitator explains *how* the session will proceed, the sponsor—the hosting manager—explains *what* the group will focus on and *why* that is important. Col. Bill's plan for his message was to show them the abyss.

> Like Covey, of *The 7 Habits of Highly Effective People* fame, I get a lot of things from movies. I was watching *Wall Street*, an interesting film about the junk bond traders. At the end of the film, the young guy had gotten into trouble and is about to be arrested for insider trading. A senior partner came into his office and told him there comes a time in your life when you walk to the edge of the abyss and stare in and nothing stares back. At that moment your character is defined, and this is what keeps you out of the abyss. That has stayed with me for a long time.

In the middle of difficulty, lies opportunity.

—Albert Einstein

Guidelines for
DesignShop Krew
http://www.mgtaylor.com/
mgtaylor/jotm/winter96/
krwguid1.htm

Guidelines for DesignShop
Sponsors and Participants
http://www.mgtaylor.com/
mgtaylor/jotm/winter96/
partguid.htm

A force like that is a catalyst for change. I used that as a metaphor and said we had to walk this organization to the edge of the abyss and stare in. Especially those who think they are really nowhere near the edge of the abyss. At AEDC they thought they were doing pretty good. They knew there was this downsizing, but that did not look like an abyss. You are going to shed 25 people this year and 50 next. They are small numbers, and you don't add them up. But we look down into the black hole and define our character and what we want to be…I like that.

I told them, "We are getting a signal from the customer and taxpayers that they don't want more of what we have been doing."

Dr. Keith Kushman, Chief of Plans and Requirements for AEDC, put it dryly: "It was unfortunate that it took being brought to our knees because of budget restraints to get our attention."

Says John Poparad: "Rutley is a guy who doesn't mess around."

The AEDC DesignShop event followed the sequence of Scan/Focus/Act. It's not hard to see that the Scan phase, tailored to the needs of AEDC, was desperately needed. They needed to learn what was going on in the outside environment and how their organization related to it. They needed to build the base of a common experience if they were going to be able to talk to each other, to trust each other, to work cooperatively for the good of AEDC, to jointly understand their past, to create a unified vision of the future.

Scan Focus Act Model
http://www.mgtaylor.com/mgtaylor/glasbead/SFA.htm

Everyone learned surprising things during Scan. Ralph Graham, a strategic manager who works with Keith Kushman, talks about just how out of touch they were:

We couldn't even add up our assets. At that time we thought we had $3 billion in assets, and it was actually $6 billion.

Matt said to us, "If I had this industrial plant out here with these highly skilled people, I would not be in a crouch mode. I would be going out there and grabbing me something. It's out there, guys."

Facing the Abyss

But it wasn't a message that people could hear easily. At this point, they couldn't see $6 billion in assets, and they couldn't see what Matt was pointing to "out there."

Jon Foley, working as part of the MG Taylor faciliation team, recalls when the perception of what was "out there" started to change:

> At some point, there was an exercise with eight teams all working different assignments. Each team had an assignment to Backcast a successful alliance with an organization outside AEDC, such as Boeing. Their job was to describe why the alliance was a win-win situation, what obstacles had been encountered and how they were overcome, and what the historical development had been of this successful working relationship. They all entered this assignment and for the first half hour all you could hear was, "Man, this isn't real! What are we doing here wasting our time?"
>
> About two hours into the assignment, we were hearing, "You know, these alliances have possibilities." By the time they were through with the assignment, they were engaged in the process, and they were so excited.

A shift was starting to take place, and the momentum kept building. Col. Bill:

> We did an Inventions workshop where they take a pile of junk and have to make a fairly complicated invention. I love to watch their ingenuity. It blows them away every time. At first they are appalled.
>
> First, you have the Type A's. Then you have the Tinkerers: they have already figured out how to attack the sucker, and they are ready to roll. We maliciously put the teams together to make the maximum chaos. I have never seen a team not engage. Some of them engage at a more trivial level than others or find ways to work around the instructions—which is innovative itself.
>
> Basically, it is a great barrier breaker. It teaches them to play and the ability to use play is a constructive way to learn. When they walk out wondering why in the world they did that, they realize that it was really fun and they really did enjoy themselves, but they do not really realize what they learned. You would not realize unless you sit down and ask yourself why it is important. Some of them will come back and say later that they understand and suggest doing it again. It is great.
>
> What is really cute is to stand there before and after the DesignShop and watch the participants. They will try to walk past the toys. Sooner or later they have to go play. You watch them—they start to play with the stuff. You

The ability to use play is a constructive way to learn.

—Col. Bill Rutley

can watch them work with the puzzles. They have the little rake and the sand, and they will sit there for half an hour doing that. They will make different things, stick their hands up the dinosaur's butt and make a little puppet. These are people who make fairly crucial decisions about the national defense. The fact is they are getting outside of the box. They are being kids again. The important part of being a kid is the ability to explore and extend.

You have to be an extraordinarily strong individual to keep the DesignShop process away from you for three days. I have seen people keep it away for one time, but the second time they will not make it. It just does not allow it. I love the way it produces chaos and keeps people off balance. It teaches our folks to not always anticipate a very rigid agenda. Not that they don't get stuck.

The first time you don't do anything. You get a piece of paper that says you will be there for three days, and don't bring a briefcase. It drives them nuts. They are not used to books and background papers—the military especially. I have seen workshops with a huge book, and there is no way you have read that. This creates chaos, and this is the way the world really is. Everything else is just constraining the real world.

I think the fact that in the very first day you get people off center and put them into groups is wonderful. It is a marvelous way to break barriers. It is hard to keep the barriers up when you are sitting on the floor or on a bench together with the VP of Pratt & Whitney. The barriers fell. I actually believed those barriers would not fall, but it happened within a relatively short period of time—within my time span at AEDC.

AEDC Decides to Live

The DesignShop session turned to focus on the problem. Should AEDC fade gracefully away, or somehow reinvent itself? People were now capable of focusing on the issue in a way that simply hadn't been possible when they first walked in the door. They had moved past both the denial that AEDC had problems and the fear-based focus on saving their own jobs.

Eventually, we said there was a choice. AEDC was an over six-billion dollar investment. We could close down and let the work go out to the commercial world and NASA—throwing away the enormous assets of AEDC—or we could offer a value-added alternative that is better than the other alternatives.

Facing the Abyss

We started to ask, is death of the base the pre-determined end? We decided the only answer that was rational to us was to create a higher order path. We looked at the original charter and asked, "Why was AEDC created over forty years ago?"

What they had to do was discover themselves, their mission, and a reason for being. It turned out to be a voyage of rediscovery. The answer was there in the charter, and also in the memories of the original employees who first created AEDC.

General Hap Arnold had come back after World War II vowing that the United States would never again be caught behind the technological curve as it had with German air superiority. He had been faced with fighting an air war in Germany in which the Messerschmidt 262, a jet engine-driven aircraft, and the rocket-driven 163 aircraft began to attack his bombers. He did not have the technological advantage. He had the quantitative advantage, but it was an unpleasant situation to have to deal with. His feeling was that never again should the U.S. be in a position where the technology of the opposition was greater than ours.

A team of aerospace notables such as Theodore von Karmen from Jet Propulsion Lab joined Arnold to return to Europe to look at the German facilities. The story is told that their recommendation to establish a special U.S. center was written in the airplane flying back home across the Atlantic. The base, named after General Arnold, was created by two special Acts of Congress to serve as a national economic and technological asset in fulfillment of Arnold's goal, contributing to the security of the nation.

Through time, the vision had faded. Col. Bill explains:

> Over the decades, the base's work had become narrower and narrower, until it was pretty much only doing Air Force work. But, we said, that was not what it was created for! It was created for *national* defense work. AEDC was created as a center of excellence and as a national facility. A national facility, not just an Air Force facility.
>
> Coming out of World War II, the generation of aeronautical technology and national defense had been essentially the same thing; almost everything came out of the fighting. But over time, commercial and military aviation got going on parallel but separate tracks. Aeronautical technology was no longer solely

What they had to do was discover themselves, their mission, and a reason for being. It turned out to be a voyage of rediscovery.

*In a dark time,
the eye begins to see.*

—THEODORE ROETHKE

Vantage Points Model
http://www.mgtaylor.com/
mgtaylor/glasbead/vantgpts.htm

a military province. And although administered by the Air Force, AEDC was supposed to be an independent entity.

According to Ralph Graham, "The DesignShop experience broke our paradigm—that we were part of the Air Force—and broke our paradigm that we were locked into doing only military testing. It changed to—we are self-sufficient. We can test military and commercial systems and must take action."

Keith Kushman explained, "We had to take action, become vision-driven. We had lost the vision. We restored it. It was compelling enough to cause us to want to go that way. I have to give a lot of credit to Matt as a facilitator, for shifting our attitude of how you live your life as a government employee at AEDC."

In a remarkably short time—"It worked much more rapidly than I expected," said Col. Bill—they had unified behind a common vision of the future. It went far beyond just providing a vision: "The original DesignShop sessions resulted in overall strategies, individual strategies, tactics, and the feedback of an interactive system."

Creative Problem Solving: Getting Out of the Box

But the problem of implementing the vision of an independent AEDC serving the national interest looked flatly impossible. There were still an enormous number of tactical problems that stood between the vision and AEDC's current situation as a government organization. Col. Bill:

> We had to show American and international organizations that we could change and bring value to AEDC. We had to figure out what a real cost is and what a real business looks like. We had to prove that we could operate in a way that makes everybody a part, and not just be an Air Force operation.
>
> The solution didn't come, though, without a lot of iteration on the problem. We went around and around. You don't get yourself jammed in a corner without there being multiple sides to the box.

Doug Cantrell, the quality expert, vividly remembers going around and around on this particular problem:

Facing the Abyss

During early discussions and for a long time after, I noticed the question would be brought up about whether we could move into commercial testing. The next thing someone would say would be "constraints—we discourage commercial testing because of regulatory constraints. We are required to add outrageous surcharges to our prices for commercial companies."

Matt would say, "Well, what if that weren't the law?" and it was as if he had not said it. The conversation would go on, and later the subject would come up again.

It was as if they could not hear the question. It was as if we had equated social systems to physical systems. As if someone was proposing the law of gravity be changed. It never happens, so why think about it?

That is why the breaking of barriers and habits is so important. You have to break down the barriers, break the forms. You have to unleash your creativity by breaking down the forms you are used to.

The federal law, this fact of nature, had been a condition of life for AEDC from the beginning. Under the law, a government organization like AEDC was told how to schedule and charge customers. Military customers were to receive priority scheduling and bargain basement pricing. If the customer was another government agency or a commercial organization, their schedule could always be disrupted to accommodate the military customer. For a commercial customer, almost prohibitive rates were charged—twice the rates charged to a military customer.

How would it be possible to work with commercial companies if AEDC couldn't operate in a business-like manner? Col. Bill knew the extent of the problem:

> We knew we had to figure a way to charge and work with commercial customers. We were not competitively priced, and the commercial customers were just not going to come. At NASA, a commercial customer can be charged either nothing or $1000 an hour to use a wind tunnel facility. This makes no sense at all.

S'poze Model
http://www.mgtaylor.com/mgtaylor/glasbead/spozemod.htm

Boeing told us that, say, if they needed to get into the wind tunnel on 17 April and be there for two weeks, that is what must happen. Hundreds of millions of dollars hang in the balance. NASA, as a provider of wind tunnel services, will say they might be able to fit Boeing in during April. On the other hand, it might be September. NASA is research-oriented, while AEDC is more production test-oriented. An organization like Boeing cannot stand the uncertainty. For basic aerodynamic research, Boeing could use NASA; for design decisions driving production, Boeing needed AEDC.

Under the law existing at the time, standard commercial practices—like giving someone a place on the schedule and then keeping the promised date, or charging all customers the same price—were not possible. Commercial customers were being charged so much that AEDC was non-competitive. In order to work with commercial customers fairly, either this federal law would have to be changed…or AEDC would somehow need to move into a realm where this law didn't apply.

In a sense, AEDC was already in a realm of its own. Col. Bill elaborated: "AEDC was unique. It had been created by two specific laws. What was needed was a modification of the original 1949 arrangement. We wanted a fundamental change in how AEDC viewed itself as an asset and in how we priced our services. The old pricing rules were not letting AEDC fulfill its mission as a center for excellence and as a truly national facility."

There was only one problem with pursuing this change—it was illegal for AEDC itself to take steps to modify its own legal charter, its own pricing structure. AEDC and the Air Force officers who run the base cannot go to Congress to request changes, even if the changes were believed to be in the taxpayer's interest and for the good of the country. "Don't even think about it. We're all going to jail if you even think about it," the lawyers said.

Business of Enterprise Model
http://www.mgtaylor.com/
mgtaylor/glasbead/busofent.htm

But by now, the people thinking about AEDC were no longer just those within AEDC proper. All the stakeholders were participating in the DesignShop—existing military customers, potential commercial customers, suppliers, civilians—people who wanted to keep AEDC alive—people for whom it was not forbidden to think or act or talk to Congress about laws affecting AEDC. These folks held a one-day DesignShop session to figure out what kind of change was necessary in the AEDC charter, and launched the effort to get it made.

Watching from the sidelines, Col. Bill observed the reaction to the proposed changes for AEDC in pursuit of the higher-order good:

> If you stay on the high road, people will cooperate. They will say, "Let me see. Do I want to see a $650 million propulsion test facility sit idle, go down the drain? Or should we sell time for whatever we can get, even if it means charging this commercial guy less than we have been? Why charge the commercial customer this artificially high price? Here is a guy who, if we give him reasonable pricing, will come in and spend $150 million per year with AEDC, plus pay to put in equipment test cells which could then also be used by others. Is it better for the American taxpayer to let the facility sit idle with its overhead being paid out every day?

In every case, we walked to the edge of the abyss and then walked away and found a better approach. It worked.

—Col. Bill Rutley

Less than six months from the DesignShop session, an equitable pricing and access bill was signed into public law.

DesignShop Sessions on a Daily Basis

Col. Bill acted on his perception that intensity was needed to drive change. They created a "management center" at AEDC, an environment for DesignShop activities and other collaborative events. At this new Gossick Leadership Center, AEDC conducted scores of DesignShop sessions and other events—seventy in the first year of operations.

Nav Center Emergent Node
http://www.mgtaylor.com/mgtaylor/navctr_emerg_nod.htm

Colonel Bill describes the expansion:

> The tactical action backed with strategy got more and more people involved in the Center at every level, down to where the work actually took place. We started to use the "management center" approach for everything down to negotiations—for everything. We took an incredible risk that could have blown up in our faces. In every case, we walked to the edge of the abyss and then walked away and found a better approach. It worked.

The Management Center as Information Factory
http://www.mgtaylor.com/mgtaylor/jotm/winter96/infofact.htm

John Poparad was closely involved with using the DesignShop process and Management Center for a range of critical business issues at AEDC:

> A lot of work starts in the DesignShop event and goes into work sessions afterward. Major alliances, strategic plans, big decisions—those are created in the DesignShop evemt and then followed up in work sessions.

The list of benefits that have come out of DesignShop events goes on and on: radically reduced testing times; early approval of the 777 engine for intercontinental flight, based on setting a world record for running an engine in a tunnel continuously for 52 hours; new, validation testing of icing on turbine engines; simulation of flight testing of engines on the aircraft in the wind tunnel.

Boeing, at one time, was looking very seriously at building their own wind tunnel. We had a DesignShop session to prepare to meet with the Boeing people. In our subsequent meeting they were surprised that we knew something about their business. They eventually decided, for various reasons, not to build a wind tunnel; now they are a commercial customer and an alliance partner.

Pratt & Whitney decided to take a chance with us, again through DesignShop activity. They test their engines here and had come to several DesignShop events. They decided to take the risk of developing the commercial 4084 engine series at AEDC. They signed an alliance with AEDC to do all of the development work—outside of that done in their own good test facilities—for this engine, and for the 4000 engine family at AEDC. You are talking about up to twenty years of work.

Results at AEDC

Col. Bill summarizes the bottom line:

> I do not believe that AEDC would be where it is today—facing the future with a better understanding, using that understanding to change strategy and tactics—without the DesignShop process. I would hope that if the DesignShop process did not exist, I would have done other things to try to help that, but this was beyond belief.
>
> The process as it has evolved in the last four years—and I think it will continue to evolve—gives the freedom to put people at ease and to let down the barriers, build trust, and expect trust to be there. Nothing has a guarantee. The bottom line is—it works.
>
> The bottom line for AEDC is $750 million dollars in business added for the next twenty years. A loss of government funds was compensated by a gain in commercial funds.

There are the tens of millions of dollars that came from commercial contractors for facilities, such as the $10 million from Pratt & Whitney for the big propulsion test cell used to test the GE, Rolls Royce, and Pratt & Whitney engines for the Boeing 777. These engines could not be tested without specific hardware. Pratt & Whitney paid $10 million of their own money to put that hardware in there, at no cost to the American taxpayer. Rolls Royce and GE have used it, and paid Pratt some to cover their costs. The net result is that the U.S. government gets it free.

That kind of alliance and partnership were really pioneered at AEDC. We can do these things together if we change.

Other partnerships have also developed. Boeing said they were not in the technology development business, but in product development and production. Technology development is what AEDC was built to do. We started to work as a team.

We got other results from change and working together. Like having the Navy come on board, not just to do their testing but as a full partner.

We got rid of the NASA versus AEDC hostility. There were things we sent people to NASA to do because they had time and were better suited to do it at that point. And they were sending people to us. We also made NASA a partner because AEDC is production-oriented; NASA is laboratory-oriented. It was helpful to all of the customers—both military and civilian—not to be in the middle of hostility anymore. NASA and AEDC are natural partners.

> *We got rid of the NASA versus AEDC hostility. There were things we sent people to NASA to do because they had time and were better suited to do it at that point. And they were sending people to us. We also made NASA a partner because AEDC is production-oriented; NASA is laboratory-oriented.*
>
> —Col. Bill Rutley

More AEDC Results: The Mystery of the Missing Complaints

Where is AEDC today as a result of this work? Col. Bill:

> AEDC is not even close to where they were four years ago. I used to have a chemistry teacher who would come in with a beaker of very, very heavy liquid and throw one crystal in there, and crystals would be shooting up all over the place and in a matter of seconds the thing would go solid. That is what it is like at AEDC. You get fifty people here, plus ten there, five here and it spreads rapidly. AEDC, in a very short period of time, was engulfed by a very different way of thinking and feeling. And the culture of AEDC suddenly took a leap forward into the 21st century.
>
> Using this process, I have seen people change dramatically in how they do business and react to situations. I don't think they are aware that they have changed. I have watched people who were extremely rigid become much more flexible, perceptive—more effective leaders.

Stages of an Enterprise Model
http://www.mgtaylor.com/mgtaylor/glasbead/stagent.htm

> I have watched some people change tremendously—people who had been in the civil service for a lot of years at one place—they changed a great deal in just twenty-two months. Their productivity is up; they felt better about things; they became proactive; they had a much more dynamic, rich view of what was going on. Our rate of innovation was clearly up. We were getting inundated with good ideas.

John Poparad's work had been strongly affected by the frictions and the endemic stovepiping:

> I believe that Rutley used the DesignShop methods to work on the stovepiping problem. Matt did a vision/empowering thing where everyone knew what everyone else was up to, because of what was happening in the DesignShop sessions. He held them accountable. By going through the DesignShop process, you got to know each other. If I have worked with someone for three days in a DesignShop event and am now sitting next to him at a desk, it is harder to ignore him than it used to be. It's not so easy to 'slip it to' the person you've been working with in a DesignShop event. Now people could call each other up and talk, and call each other by first name.

Col. Bill evaluates the degree of change:

> The stovepiping is still there to some degree. We had to really drive home the "Team AEDC" concept as the higher-order good.
>
> I saw some amusing things. You can tell a lot by watching the number and types of complaints people make. The vice commander came to me about a year after we instituted the complaint system and said, "I don't know if we are doing this right, but the complaint system has gone dead."
>
> It turned out that a lot of the trivial things people had been complaining about still hadn't been fixed. But with the DesignShop process, we found something that worked. They were engaged in something they felt was important. They were involved. There was activity and suddenly minor things—like a pothole, the grass, or a light bulb—were not important. Complaints just dropped off the face of the earth. I would still get a complaint here and there as I walked around getting input. But 3,500 people and only one or two complaints...this was a major change and a major signal.
>
> I really love people and put them first above all else. That is what I care about. I feel my job is to turn them loose.
>
> Within less than twenty-two months, all I had to do was work the environment, focus on people, help them grow, and stand back and unbelievable

things happened. That is true. Unbelievable things happened. I wish I could take credit for some of the things they did—like going off and forming these alliances, not taking "no" for an answer, and creating a law. They did all of that themselves. I merely created an environment that allowed that to take place.

DesignShop Techniques and Other Management Tools

DesignShop techniques weren't the only management tool Col. Bill brought to bear. He continued the Total Quality Management, Covey's *7 Habits of Highly Effective People*, and expanded the selection even further. Col. Bill:

> Our toolkit contained many tools to meet the overall requirement for change and renewal of the organization. We used Covey, which we thought was underpinning the foundational things. We used reengineering— good stuff but with limits. Juran's stuff is excellent. Lots of TQM was productive.
>
> All these tools were synergistic—none replacing the others and in some cases dovetailing and overlapping. I would argue that the success was all of it together.
>
> The fact is that not any single tool will do everything. Although for this process, if I had to drop every other tool but one, the DesignShop process would be the one I would keep. I would dump all of the rest. I can reengineer through it. I can drive the TQM through it. I can drive the Juran, drive education, cultural evolution—all those things through the DesignShop process.
>
> We consciously drove all our management methods using the DesignShop process. People began to see the connections. They would say they understood how this would help them in their quality circles. Covey gave me some personal growth and principles that I can operate with whether I am in quality circles, working with reengineering or TQM, or in a DesignShop activity, or am on my immediate work team. All of that seems to gather together into a nice synergistic system.
>
> Now the challenge to the Leadership Center is to figure out what's next for AEDC in using the DesignShop processes. They overdid it and got through the first five years' work in two years. Everyone thought it was going to be a long two years. It was incredible. I wanted to stay another year. I hated leaving the place.

However difficult it may have been to hammer home the Team AEDC concept back at the beginning, Team AEDC came together during Col. Bill's stay. By the time of the Wharton DesignShop event, he had moved on to the F-15 program, but AEDC is still strong, seamless, and flourishing. The dynamics were obvious when watching the participants from AEDC at the Wharton DesignShop session.

Individually, AEDC folks were among the most active, effective, and insightful at the Wharton event. The contrast between AEDCers and first-time attendees was most obvious during the first and second days. Even comparing them to the management consultants and business school professors who participated, the AEDC personnel walked in the door more mentally "in shape," more creative, mentally nimble, and accustomed to using a larger and more sophisticated mental toolkit.

Later, when participants broke into groups to focus on each company's individual challenge, AEDC teamwork had the kind of passion, energy, and intelligence that made them a brainstorming DreamTeam. A facilitator pointed out two participants, both working intensely on AEDC problem solving. One was the new contractor who had just won a bid for some AEDC work; he was learning how to become a part of AEDC. Sitting beside him—and working just as enthusiastically—was the previous contractor who had lost the bid and was being replaced. He was still a member of Team AEDC, still committed to its success.

Now, as the next exercises of the Scan started, the AEDCers were distributed throughout the workgroups, sharing their mental skills and knowledge of collaborative work with the rest of the participants.

Challenge

1. Diagram, list, or describe your impressions and questions after reading the AEDC story. Describe the key elements involved in the success of the transformation process.

2. Sometimes we need to make clear what we know and what we know we don't know. Imagine employing the key elements you just described in your business or other personal situation. Now, for each element, what do you know about delivering it, and what do you know that you don't know. One DesignShop axiom reads: Discovering that you don't know something is the first step to knowing it. You may wish to refer back to previous challenges to increase your list. Recall that in each challenge you were asked to record any questions that you had. These questions help define things that you know you don't know.

3. Develop some ideas for tackling your areas of potential learning. Chances are these areas can be chunked into groups or systems that will reinforce and relate to one another as you proceed.

Leveraging Complexity

Back at the Wharton event, it's late afternoon on Wednesday, the first of the three days. It's been a very full day, but there's one more exercise before breaking for the night: Metaphors. This will also be the last exercise before turning attention and energy to the organizational problem that has brought everyone here—so it had better be good.

What's the purpose of this episode in the adventure ride of the DesignShop process? The Metaphor exercise has been designed to load participants' heads with new concepts of complex systems, use the night's sleep to assist integration of the knowledge, come back in the morning, and begin using the difference in people's problem-solving abilities. At that point, everyone needs to be operating at the very highest level of performance that can be reached, both individually and as a team.

The problems that have brought everyone here involve their organizations—each a system embedded in a larger external system. Therefore, each problem is a systems problem. Almost by definition, it is a *complex* systems problem. If it weren't complex, so many people and so much time would not be needed to deal with it.

Complex systems problems are among the hardest things that people ever think about. Just holding such a problem in its entirety in your head is difficult. Add to this the challenges of seeing how all the parts fit together and affect each other as well as how to make a change in one part that will accomplish the goal without bringing down the whole system.

Ironically, as hunters and gatherers, we evolved by living within complex systems. Our brains can, with effort, address this task.

An Introduction to Complexity Theory
http://www.mgtaylor.com/
mgtaylor/mgtaylor/jotm/
summer97/complexity.htm

*It may still be
one of the most important tasks
of our intelligence
to discover the significance of rules
we never deliberately made,
and the obedience to which
builds more complex orders
than we can understand.*

—F.A. Hayek,
Nobel Laureate in Economics

Creative Process Model
http://www.mgtaylor.com/
mgtaylor/glasbead/7stagcrp.htm

*Genius, in truth,
means little more than
the faculty of perceiving
in an unhabitual way.*

—William James,
The Principles of Psychology

However, we have also acquired a strong tradition of linear thinking which, for all its benefits, now stands in our way. Aristotle, Descartes, many of the people providing the basis of our historical way of working, liked to take things apart and understand the pieces in detail. The Industrial Revolution, the rise of engineering practices, and the Saint Simon Engineering School of France showed the tremendous power of linearity applied to the final stages of the creative cycle: building in a controlled and linear fashion. The assembly line is the golden grandchild.

Out of the success of building roads and bridges, many disciplines, such as philosophy, economics, and political theory, became carried away with over-inflated notions of what linear processes could and should be used for. Many of the disasters of 20th century politics and history, such as the rise of Communism—which had its roots in the Saint Simon school—stem directly from this error.

American management owes its foundation to two champions of linearity, a husband and wife team: (yes, it's ironic) the Taylors. This first Taylor revolution produced "scientific management," which completely swept the country at the turn of the 20th century and produced the first generations of young managers and technocrats. The approach dominated industry, the military, government—the works. Most famous for its time-and-motion studies, there was nothing that couldn't be Taylorized, and so everything was. You could even Taylorize your home—and people did. Today, when a real estate salesman or an architect points out how wonderfully few steps there are between stove and sink and fridge, you are living the kitchen legacy of the first generation of Taylorizing.

But how about linearity for designing and tweaking complex systems comprised of employees, customers, suppliers, regulators, and the physical systems that support all the related activity? Nope. Wrong tool. It is insisting on using a hammer—a fine and noble tool for driving nails and prying them out again—for absolutely everything else.

Even in the best of circumstances, with smart people and lots of computers and tons of training and mental conditioning, linearity is not going to solve your problem. (See the collapse of communism in the late 20th century for a long-term experiment.) Linearity, from which we have all reaped benefits, will only take you so far before the complexity of reality stops you cold.

Leveraging Complexity

The most intelligent thing to do is to optimize the circumstances to provide every possible advantage. This means allowing our brains—evolved for dealing with complex patterns—to do what they do best and work with complex systems metaphorically.

Matt explains that the purpose of this next exercise is to provide "strategies that add value for us as we think about complexity." Throughout the day everyone has been learning. This involves looking at analogies, making new connections, picking up new factual information we didn't have before, as well as continuing the ongoing task of getting to know each participant's skills, strengths, and weaknesses. For the next couple of hours, it is time to do some high-level, abstract learning of new systems models in the Metaphor exercise.

For this exercise, the facilitation team has selected eight complex systems to serve as metaphors for human organizations, one to be studied by each of eight participant teams: the ant colony, the river, the rainforest, the ship, the beehive, the ocean, the human body, and the garden. While these systems are different in important ways—there is a mix of planned vs. unplanned, natural vs. manmade, single entity vs. community vs. entire ecosystem—they are all complex systems with enough depth to lead to insights about human organizations.

New teams are formed and each group receives one of the complex systems as its object of investigation. This marks the fourth new group formation today. By the end of this exercise, each participant will have had the experience of meeting and working intimately with almost half of the other participants.

Groups are asked to look at (1) the organizational requirements for success in this metaphorical environment, and (2) what would a 21st century organization based on this metaphor look like, in terms of strategy and specifications. Each team needs to do quick learning to extract the high level concepts and defining details about, for example, ant colony organization, and then use that knowledge in thinking about the future of organizations.

When each group goes to its own break-out space, they find that the facilitators have already stocked each space with a rich collection of the best books and other resources on the appropriate topic. In addition, the facilitators are available to assist the group's library research or in surfing the Internet, especially the World Wide Web.

Work continues on into the evening. Hunger is not a problem as dinner is served and people return from the buffet to their work areas, everything continuing in a seamless fashion. Empty plates disappear as if by magic, unnoticed, as the teams concentrate on the task at hand.

As usual with the DesignShop activities, you need not like it for it to fulfill its purpose, but this particular part is enjoyed by almost everyone. Some people can get downright crabby, especially first-time participants. Explains one veteran of many facilitation teams: "The first-time participants have found the thinking to be very hard work, they're exhausted, and by five or six o'clock when you come around with one more thing to do, they can get downright hostile."

Weak Signal Research
http://www.mgtaylor.com/
mgtaylor/mgtaylor/wsremerg.htm

However, the experienced DesignShop participants are loving it. Gail Taylor points out that the reason participants love this accelerated learning task is that they so rarely get to immerse themselves in a rich new topic, discover fascinating and sometimes bizarre new information, and share it immediately with interested others.

This joyful exploration is playful yet intense. One woman smiles and says, "I'm starting to float." This state has been termed "flow"—it happens when people become so engrossed with an activity, moving smoothly and almost effortlessly from task to task, that they lose track of time.

The rainforest group gets blocked about 20 minutes into the session. The reason for their misfortune is instructive: one member already knows quite a bit about the rainforest, so initially they're relying on that resource instead of doing their own research, their own learning, and firing up their brains in the process.

This problem is spotted by one of the support staff and a facilitator steps in to redirect the team. Participant Dorothy Zeviar from AEDC explains:

> What impressed me in working with my team is that when we had spent about 20 minutes, Matt came around and challenged us to "push the limits of the box" in applying the metaphor to our organization. We stayed until 8:30

PM going over the details, until we reached a deeper level of insight and understanding.

The ant colony team is also doing something odd: instead of working on ants, they're talking about themselves, getting to know each other better. The staff notices this too, but in this case, the facilitators don't intervene—it's a good development. In fact, the team decides on their own to come in an hour early the next morning, at 7 AM, to work on the main task.

Meanwhile, the team thinking about ships was having a difficult time getting started. Participant Elsa Porter describes the process:

> Our instructions were to use the ship as a metaphor of the 21st century and explore how the ship can be the metaphor for organizations of the 21st century. We took it seriously and tried to think of how ships run and work. We were putting up ideas and struggling. Then John Poparad looked at me—he had been silent throughout this first part. He was sitting there letting us do all the work. That was my first impression. Then it became clear that he had an idea. He said, "I think it's the wrong question. The real question is how can a ship survive in the 21st century?" Then you have to think about the environment. From then on, it was just wonderful. It was a very different assignment: principles of how to survive in the future.

What the group was doing was struggling with the problem, making it their own. From outside the group, this reformulation may not seem like a major change, but it served to galvanize this group's work. The group extracted a tremendous amount of learning from their session. Although, as we found out later, it was not at all the interpretation that the designers of this exercise intended. Value was created through merging the designer's direction and the participants' interest.

At 8 PM it's time to break for the night, but despite the long day, some groups and individuals are in the flow of their work and choose to keep going...and do. This break has been deliberately timed so that participants have twelve hours off and a night's sleep to integrate their new knowledge before making their teams' reports to the larger group.

Long after the participants reluctantly left for bed, the staff is still going full tilt, capturing the work of each team from the breakout room walls, getting this latest round of discussions into the computer, and printing it out for the team break-out

Creative Thinking Guidelines
http://www.mgtaylor.com/mgtaylor/jotm/spring97/creative.htm

*Towering genius disdains
a beaten path.
It seeks regions
hitherto unexplored.*

—Abraham Lincoln

**Anatomy of the Stages of the
Creative Process Model**
http://www.mgtaylor.com/
mgtaylor/jotm/fall96/7stanat.htm

books which will be awaiting the participants when they reassemble at 8 AM the next morning.

The Second Day Begins

By 7 AM—an hour before things are supposed to start—participants start showing up. The support team, of course, is already there working on today's events. Some participants are there to peruse library shelves or other information that intrigued them yesterday. Other participants grab some breakfast and then head off to their work group. The ant colony group, says Colonel Bill as he heads off to join them, is fulfilling its 7 AM meeting time to complete the assignment postponed from yesterday.

By 8 AM all participants and staff have finished breakfast and are gathered as a large group for the Metaphor team reports. Matt greets everyone with an overview of the structure for the day, and a comment from yesterday:

> The best remark yesterday was when someone came up here around ten or eleven and he said he was more confused than he had been before. That is the true test of scanning. If you do not go out far enough in the design process to get upset, confused, and lost, you have not gone into new territory.

> The theme of today is "forming the problem." The question is to form the right problem. If you form the wrong problem, then you solve the wrong problem. In our society we are good at solving the problem. We solve problems which are really conditions, and we get a result we did not want.

> First, we are going to put together the processes, tools, and environments for the future we want. We are not going to put ourselves in a system we do not want. We are going to report-out the metaphors. We'll look at the strategies nature produces, and the kinds of specifications that add value as we think about complexity. There is nothing wrong with the organizations we have today except they cannot handle the environments—internal or external. We will harvest what you did yesterday and then go into organization teams.

The ants are up first, and their report contains an astounding quality and quantity of work, replete with provocative insights. They have clearly done both real research on biology and real thinking about business. There is much more content than one would have expected. Even more amazing is that they've done the work—the ant-specific work, that is—in just one hour this morning.

Leveraging Complexity

Their comparison of an ant colony with a 21st century organization covered an amazing number of similarities and contrasts, including:

> Variation in sources of supply, adaptability, resistance to attack, robustness, division of labor, sacrificial activity (benefitting the group at the expense of the individual), balance, variety of internal communication methods, leadership and its succession, dedication level of team members, organizational size issues, life cycle issues, the problem of inbreeding, managing the social environment, learning strategies, teamwork, need for face-to-face contact compared to virtual contact.

Next, the ant colony group drew lessons for the 21st century organization based on these insights about similarities between human organizations and a complex, evolved system which has been successful for millions of years.

Robert Taylor, best known as the author of *How to Select and Use An Executive Search Firm* and with decades of experience as a senior executive for companies such as Mobil Oil and ITT in Europe, South America and the U.S. as well as the founding of a global executive search firm that became a worldwide success, looked back at the work done by his fellow ant colony team members with pleasant surprise:

> I would have expected that especially the hard-noses would, at least initially, have ridiculed the idea of spending serious, valuable time learning and thinking about ants. However, the prior five modules in this Scan phase of the DesignShop process had initiated a shift of minds that were already open to quite different ways of thinking. This enabled the group to achieve the purpose of the exercise—expanding thinking and stimulating creativity.

It was a virtuoso performance, presenting business-relevant insights of the highest quality, the kind of insights one expects to pay a high-priced consultant to get. Watching this process, the first thought that occurs is—"These were bright people before, but now they're top-notch. How did they get so much smarter overnight?" The answer is that they didn't; these are the same people, it's just that they have absorbed a great deal of useful information, and have run though a process that boosts them into a higher state of performance. There has been no real change in IQ, presumably—though it would be fascinating to test this—it is their effective IQ and an ability to apply what they know that has increased, at least short term.

The same observation of enhanced performance also held true for all the other groups. Not only their minds seem different. Physically, they have all dropped years. This can be seen in their postures, the way they are sitting or standing, the way they are talking and listening so intensely. The environment is being modified, furniture being moved around, lots of laughter is heard. There's more energy: some people choose to stand instead of needing to rest in a chair. They are paying rapt attention to the insights presented by the other groups. Someone starts to unconsciously play with a toy while intently listening about how a ship and a company each use and misuse a network of sensors to sense, measure, and process responses to its ever-changing environment. The ant colony group had mentioned the parallels between ants' succession plans and those for leaders in the 21st century organization; now the beehive group touches on how radically different bee succession planning is as well as their organizational vision and style. The metaphors, the analogies, the connections, parallels, contrasts, and implications are being drawn thickly, richly—productively.

Metaphoric Richness

What is telling about the richness of these metaphors, though, is how a very small change can make a huge difference. Change the participants working with a metaphor and different results emerge. Change the question you put regarding a metaphor and different results emerge. Change your understanding of what you mean by a "ship" and different results emerge.

The group working on the ship metaphor had made an unintentional change in how they worked their exercise. The design and writing team that had formulated this exercise had intended that "ship" refer to a masted sailing ship, a wind-driven ship. Maybe because of the presence of military folks in the group working the problem, the participants had thought of "ship" as one of the Navy's floating cities, bristling with radar and satellite dishes, tied in to weather satellites and international communication systems. What they extracted from this model was very useful...and very different from what they would have extracted from the metaphor of a sailing ship.

What richness had the DesignShop team intended to have the group draw from the sailing ship metaphor?

The same observation of enhanced performance also held true for all the other groups. Not only their minds seem different. Physically, they have all dropped years. This can be seen in their postures, the way they are sitting or standing, the way they are talking and listening so intensely.

In a sailing ship that is tacking, the wind is pulling the sails, not pushing them the way most people think. Minor corrections at the beginning of a sea journey made such a big difference at the end: a trim tab, just a small part of the rudder, controls the direction of the entire ship. You tack to make progress, you don't always sail directly toward your goal.

Now, how is your business like a sailing ship?

How It Works: Increase Complexity

Since the DesignShop session began, the activities assigned to the participants have asked them to handle more and more complexity. This is in preparation for the next stage, in which—for the first time—participants will split into groups based on their organizational affiliation and grapple with the specific business challenges facing that organization.

Usually when an organization faces a difficult decision or needs to make an important plan, a decision-maker drives a push for simplicity, wanting to identify the dominating factor or short list of main factors to consider. There is a lot of truth to the cliché of the manager who refuses to look at a proposal until it's boiled down to one piece of paper: "If you can't do that, you haven't thought it through." Requiring one person to do this eliminates the group input that would make it a much better proposal.

Bringing in more people takes time, because it adds complexity, as does bringing in more information. But the answer isn't to artificially screen out the real complexity of the situation. Instead, accept it and use it. Matt Taylor explains:

> The general principle is if you have trouble solving a problem, take it up an order of magnitude in complexity. Instead, people try to take it down to something simpler and somehow are supposed to aggregate that up. Wrong. If you are having trouble solving a design problem, it means that you do not have enough variety in the problem the way you posed it. It means that there is no material in the problem from which to get an answer. Instead, you add more to the problem, bring more content into the problem. You bring more content in and have complexity. Complexity leads to spontaneous order. It gives you more substance to deal with.

Design Build Use Model
http://www.mgtaylor.com/
mgtaylor/glasbead/dbumodel.htm

This increase in complexity requires that those participating all agree to reach for divergence, to tolerate ambiguity, in the ultimate quest to reach a goal. Matt gives an example from architecture:

> A master designer will pursue an idea in the first parts of a design without consideration of whether he knows how to do every part. He would say, for example, "The solution would be to cantilever this building 50 feet out over to the right." I might object: "No one has done that before." He replies, "That is irrelevant, and I will solve it tomorrow. If I can cantilever this out, that enables me to have all of this freedom up here. Then I have this roofing problem, and I have to deal with this roof. Gee, what if I come down here with this and suspend the roof. That is interesting. What if I suspend the floor? Then I have the solution to the first problem that I ignored. But I did not solve the problem that I ignored early on, instead I solved another problem."

Recall the earlier example of this kind of thinking back at AEDC when Matt kept saying, "What if it weren't illegal? What if it weren't the law?" This formed a perfect example of ignoring a problem and thereby giving yourself room to come up with a brilliant solution.

It highlights another aspect of the analogy we made back in the beginning to Gulliver tied down by a multitude of little threads. Each condition is a thread that limits your freedom of motion. If you are designing while tied down by one thread, you've still got a lot of flexibility. But imagine you are trying to move when you're tied by two ropes…or three…or four. It's not long before you're virtually immobilized. Getting rid of the constraints and increasing the complexity of possibilities actually gives you the freedom to go discover the solution that might be hiding behind and beyond the constraint. Matt:

> Through Scan, the divergent part of a DesignShop activity, there is actually more control over the process than later on. The reason we exercise control at this time is to drive divergence into greater complexity, because most people would not go for divergence. They try to force a decision too quickly.

Some people come into a DesignShop session saying that their problem is so complex that the only way they can get done is to consider just one or two alternatives. We say no, the problem is so complex that the only way to get it done is to consider *hundreds* of alternatives.

Part of the strategy is an awareness of when to give in to the problem, when to let it take you where it wants. We start off each DesignShop event with an extremely well-worked design of the event. There is a certain point where that slips, where you let it work on its own dynamic. You have to know where to let that go. We go through all of this DesignShop planning as if we know what the outcome should be. But we don't. So we design it as if we know what the outcome will be, but at some point the actual outcome reveals itself. Then you follow the outcome, not the original plan. It's the same in any design process.

One counterintuitive aspect of the divergence stage is that error is tolerated. Most of us have experienced this in traditional brainstorming sessions, when we're told that the goal is to generate ideas, not critique them. Mindy Bokser, a Director of R&D who has pulled off a string of technical breakthroughs in the field of optical character recognition, comments: "In brainstorming sessions, what appears at first as a bad idea, might in fact be good. It is just not fleshed out in the speaker's mind, or it's not understood by the listener. But later, you find that it has provided the tip of an important thread."

We had seen plenty of errors going up on the walls at this DesignShop session, but no one called a halt to the process to correct them. Over time, the quantity and severity of the errors had just seemed to magically diminish. Matt elaborates:

> The work had errors in it, but it was still useful. Most people would say that you have to straighten out all these false assumptions. But designers do not care. They are in the creative process. They observe reality. They build a model. Then they try building the real thing and they test it. Error is filtered out during that process. You do not have to argue about it. Erroneous things do not fly. You learn from them and repeat the process.
>
> Meanwhile, you document errors, improve your understanding of the principles, and add to the knowledge base, which makes future iterations quicker until your solution gets so good it actually works. But being systematically ignorant—pursuing ideas that are *prima facie* false—is an excellent technique for a designer. Designers manipulate information and ideas—they don't care about accuracy when designing. Is the idea interesting? Does it cause me to do something that I otherwise would not do—and as a result is useful? I am a designer and that is the way I use information when designing. When I *report* information, I try to be extremely accurate. But I *use* it, internally, in ways that many may view as criminal activity.

In brainstorming sessions, what appears at first as a bad idea, might in fact be good. It is just not fleshed out in the speaker's mind, or it's not understood by the listener. But later, you find that it has provided the tip of an important thread.

—Mindy Bokser

Three Cat Model
http://www.mgtaylor.com/
mgtaylor/glasbead/3catmod.htm

So—the design process is messy. When you present the final product formally, you don't present the messy process that gave you the result. Instead, you explain it in a clean, formal way that makes sense. This is unfortunate, in a way, because it confuses people about how the creative design process actually works. Then, when they try to do it themselves, they get into trouble. When they get into messes and don't realize that this is a natural stage of the successful process, they get scared or frustrated.

The NASA Example: Add Complexity to Reach a Solution

NASA Aeronautics headquarters held a DesignShop event when that organization was under intense pressure to downsize, and had been for some time. Morale was down. There was even reason for a certain amount of panic. Their response was to simplify. Matt Taylor sets the stage:

> They had to come up with a whole new organizational design for Aeronautics. They wanted to study only one white paper with the goal of implementing this white paper. The white paper was a "roles-and-missions" statement for the existing NASA Aeronautics centers.
>
> We said that the answer did not lie in the white paper. We talked to the sponsors about this for two-and-a-half days, and they finally agreed to widen the possibilities being considered. What emerged was an entirely new model.

Make the complexity of the design process match the complexity that your system actually faces.

What they came up with in the DesignShop session was—no center, roles driven by projects, a cluster organization, and an aerospace alliance—the opposite of the earlier plan. Before the DesignShop experience, the complexity that had been brought into the design process was not in proportion to the complexity the system actually faces. We were able to fix that. It is so basic. It is very simple.

They solved their problem by moving to a higher level of complexity. You can increase complexity in a number of different ways. You can become more abstract, thinking in conceptual terms. You can dive to depth and become more detailed on some aspect. You can add complexity horizontally, by including more aspects of the environment or more vantage points. Narrowing complexity has the same kind of logic as that of the drunk searching for his car keys under the lamp post "because that's where the light is." You need to broaden the search zone if the answer to a complex problem lies beyond the beam cast by the street lamp. Often, in the process, the original problem dis-

Leveraging Complexity

solves into the larger structure and is "solved" even though it is never specifically addressed.

The lesson is: add complexity, bathe in it, revel in it, and try to hold back the urge to narrow options and reach a decision. This is difficult to do for Type A people, but the exercises at the Wharton event seem to be working at broadening everyone's thinking. In Metaphors, they've been provided with complex paradigms from other aspects and artifacts of life. They've spent some time working to understand what those paradigms are and then carried them over to their present situations. As a result, they ended up transforming their insights into business theory.

The usual attitude in business is "make it simple so I can *do* something." But for complex problems, this is counterproductive. From the moment this DesignShop session began through now, just before the participants regroup with others from their own organizations, everyone has been immersed in sophisticated, evolutionary systems thinking.

The report-out on the Metaphors exercise has shown a clear and rapid transition from simple, linear thinking to complex, evolutionary systems thinking. You could take the insights from these Metaphor reports, polish them up, and make a book from them. You could then sell yourself as a management consultant on this material alone.

As people assemble to tackle their organizational problems, there are probably a few people who still think that only now are they beginning the "real work." But "real work" is a misleading term—everyone has been working hard since they got here. People are not just warmed-up, they are close to overheating. It's time to aim this mental energy at the key problems that brought each organization here, and start harvesting the value created since yesterday morning.

Challenge

1. Take a trip to the library and pick up a dozen books on one of these complex living systems with which you are unfamiliar:
    ocean and shoreline ecosystems and environments
    rain forests
    hive insects, such as bees
    ants and ant colonies
    the human body

   The books can range from children's picture books to highly technical scientific textbooks. Get some of both: the pictures will simplify things and the textbooks will challenge your understanding.

2. Immerse yourself in the books and compose several diagrams which illustrate the philosophies, policies, and strategies that the system uses to work as a whole system; to evolve, grow, and maintain itself. Do a thorough job: work until the degree of complexity pushes your ability to handle the ideas and connections. Then sleep on it, or do something else, and come back to it with fresh energy.

3. Now, how do those philosophies, policies, and strategies apply to your company or your department, or your life over the next three or four years?

4. Expect the unexpected.

Inventing the Problem

The Scan phase emphasized divergence. Now it is time to shift from Scan into Focus and begin to concentrate on each organization and its problems.

Scan emphasized reaching out, learning, and exploring ideas far outside our usual range of expertise, outside the usual time horizons, above the usual level of complexity. The fact that it was a goal-driven divergence with all parts contributing value in ultimately solving a problem was masked. There was an explicit avoidance in drawing direct connections with the problem that brought the different organizations here.

Now the challenge is to carry forward the acquired attitudes, skills, and information into Focus. If the Scan has been effective, participants will be able to view their businesses and their problems from completely new perspectives.

The goal of Focus is to generate options, from no risk options to wacky ones, and to explore the ways to decide which is the right one. Instead of zeroing in on the problem right at hand, everyone will construct big-picture views. They are able to do different takes, and come at the problem a couple of different times. The problems may look completely different than they did 48 hours previously. Many new possible solutions should emerge and become grist for new cycles of design-and-test iteration until the strongest solution strategy emerges. There is a quote floating around about this: "If you do seven iterations of coming at a problem, looking at it, and redesigning it, the results will be a thousand times better."

As everyone separates into organization-based groups, the physical space has once again been reconfigured to accommodate the new task. Individual break-out areas are set up for each company—a large area for the large AEDC group, a small one for the three-person team from Carl's Jr. Each area includes an informal semi-

---

Scan Focus Act Model
http://www.mgtaylor.com/
mgtaylor/glasbead/SFA.htm

The goal of Focus is to generate options, from no risk options to wacky ones, and to explore the ways to decide which is the right one. Instead of zeroing in on the problem right at hand, everyone will construct big-picture views.

AI Product Line:
Management Center
http://www.mgtaylor.com/
mgtaylor/ai/aimctr.htm

circle of chairs and is stocked with objects ranging from 3D modeling kits to extra writing space in the form of rolling portable whiteboards.

As the teams begin their work, we drifted in and out of hearing range, monitoring progress. Gayle taped her impressions:

> Every group has at least one facilitator in full-time attendance. What the staffer is doing changes, adapting his or her function to the needs of the group in order to move them forward in their task. Bryan is acting as a coach one minute, then a scribe, then an artist, then into Socratic questioner-mode to help the group clarify a point. All the facilitators are working intimately with groups in the same fashion: challenging participant assumptions, drawing individuals out, really understanding and addressing the most critical business issues. You cannot tell the difference between a facilitator and any other member of the business team based on commitment, involvement, or understanding.
>
> Despite the long hours of work they have been through, the participants are alert and refreshed. Physically, these folks look ten years younger. There is an intensity of concentration that can be seen.
>
> Over at the Ernst & Young group, they have four guys standing up and working on the board at one time. These formerly uptight, sophisticated, and stressed-out guys are now bouncy, squirting each other with the bottle of board-cleaning solution, and they are bursting with ideas and insights. Michael, their knowledge worker, is scribing vigorously. He has converted a bunch of their comments, scrawlings, and illustrations into neat models where he has really brought things into perspective. The E&Y guys look at this and said, "This is great. You should be a staff consultant at E&Y."
>
> E&Y has already come up with an idea on how to approach their business problem, and are ready to flesh it out into a real model. Michael asks them if they want to get into modeling their solution as a business *per se*, or as a presentation. Then he goes off to collect additional modeling tools to help them through designing. While he is gone, the E&Y team is revisiting solutions and cycling plans. They are iterating carefully between one and the other.
>
> Meanwhile over at the Carl Jr.'s team, the three hamburger guys have sketched out a diagram stretching from the customer, through multiple levels of information, and flowing back to the CEO. One of the guys has circled the middle level and said, "Look: I think we could eliminate this whole level and go from here to there." Now they are really working on restructuring the units. Jon, facilitating for the group, is in there pointing out that certain functions still need to be handled.

Bryan is acting as a coach one minute, then a scribe, then an artist, then into Socratic questioner-mode to help the group clarify a point. All the facilitators are working intimately with groups in the same fashion: challenging participant assumptions, drawing individuals out, really understanding and addressing the most critical business issues.

Inventing the Problem

At the F-15 jet fighter group, they have written up on their wall, "Downsizing is not a problem. It creates the opportunity." And "How do we make the F-15 needs match the taxpayer needs?" After working along for a while, this group is so pleased with their progress that they have asked for a tape recorder because they need to make sure everything is being recorded, not just what is written on the walls.

They have asked for some change models, and now models are coming in from Frances, their knowledge worker support. Frances has taken rough diagrams from the board and is creating second-generation models. There is a discussion of resources—designers, technical people, technology in hand, and new technologies needed.

Here at the AEDC group, they are talking intensely, swapping back and forth, really listening to each other. Absolutely everybody is writing and scribing and modeling with rapt attention. Some senior AEDC members are sitting on the floor with their markers, pen, and papers, working intently. There is a steady energy, a charge of vibrancy here. The atmosphere is supercharged.

The goal for this stage of the process is being met—the teams are addressing fundamental issues in their businesses, using models to help them think about complex problems, and getting hard work done fast. They are rethinking the problem they thought they had, and designing systems solutions to address the new problem statement made possible by a new, broader perspective on the businesses and the surrounding world.

The very title of this stage of the process encourages taking a radically new look at the original challenge—this segment is called "Inventing the Problem." They are to re-create each problem in a new way, and not design a solution until the next day.

Somehow during the jam-packed event schedule, Bryan Coffman found a moment to sit down and recount his first encounter with the DesignShop process, coming from the client side. It's a classic story of how concentrating first on "Inventing the Problem," rather than trying immediately to solve the problem, enables a group to achieve surprising benefits that go far beyond what was initially envisioned as the desired outcome:

> When I came into contact with MG Taylor, I was in the Army Corps of Engineer Captain Training Program. Our mission was to redesign the training for the captains. We worked with the University of Florida and designed a course with a huge flow chart, lasting 36 months.

The process encourages taking a radically new look at the original challenge during this segment of "Inventing the Problem." They are to re-create each problem in a new way, and not design a solution until the next day.

Creating the Problem
http://www.mgtaylor.com/
mgtaylor/glasbead/problem.htm

The commanding officer said that was nice, but we had to trim it to under 18 months. The guy in charge of the program had heard about MG Taylor in Colorado. So we went out to Boulder and redesigned the program. We did that in four days. Then we came back and implemented it in less than 18 months and under budget.

From Bryan's description so far, it sounds like what they did was in fact solve the problem with which they had walked in the door: how to get the training program done in half the time. How did "Inventing the Problem" enter into it? Were there additional benefits besides the improvement in the schedule?

That wasn't the main achievement. The big advance was that we changed the way the material was taught. The way they had been doing it was that you would sit and listen, and guys would talk at you and show you flip charts. Then you would take a test. And if you passed, you passed, and if you failed, you failed. It was just that modality of learning—stuff it in and fetch it up.

As we went into the DesignShop session, we knew we needed more than that, but we really did not know what. The achievement of the DesignShop process was to add the experiential side of learning—real-world learning. Basically it was like training you would get in the field. There would be a simulated war environment. This allowed you to be put under the stress of the real situation, and see how you would apply what you know and what you don't. You got to work together as teams and play different roles.

Of course, there was still classroom work—usually due to budget limitations—but we put in quite a bit more simulated wartime. For example, we would call you up at four in the morning and you would report and go and simulate war for a while. So if you were learning to build an airfield during combat, the situation was more real. There were two types of simulation: there was the "big picture" scenario in which you are the senior command, and the narrower scenario in which you are troops.

Or let's say you get stuck in a command vehicle and your only contact with the world is radio. We had messengers coming in delivering stuff to you as if you are getting radio communications. We simulated as much of the real situation as we could. Best of all, because we changed over to simulation, we could more rapidly change the curriculum in response to an actively-evolving understanding of America's place in the world.

Using simulations may not sound like a big deal today, but remember, this was over ten years ago. It was a very innovative program at the time. We were the first to develop an approach to training of this sort in the Army. It was a model program for other branches of the Army to use for their company-grade officer training programs.

---

5 Es of Education Model
http://www.mgtaylor.com/mgtaylor/glasbead/5Esofed.htm

Inventing the Problem

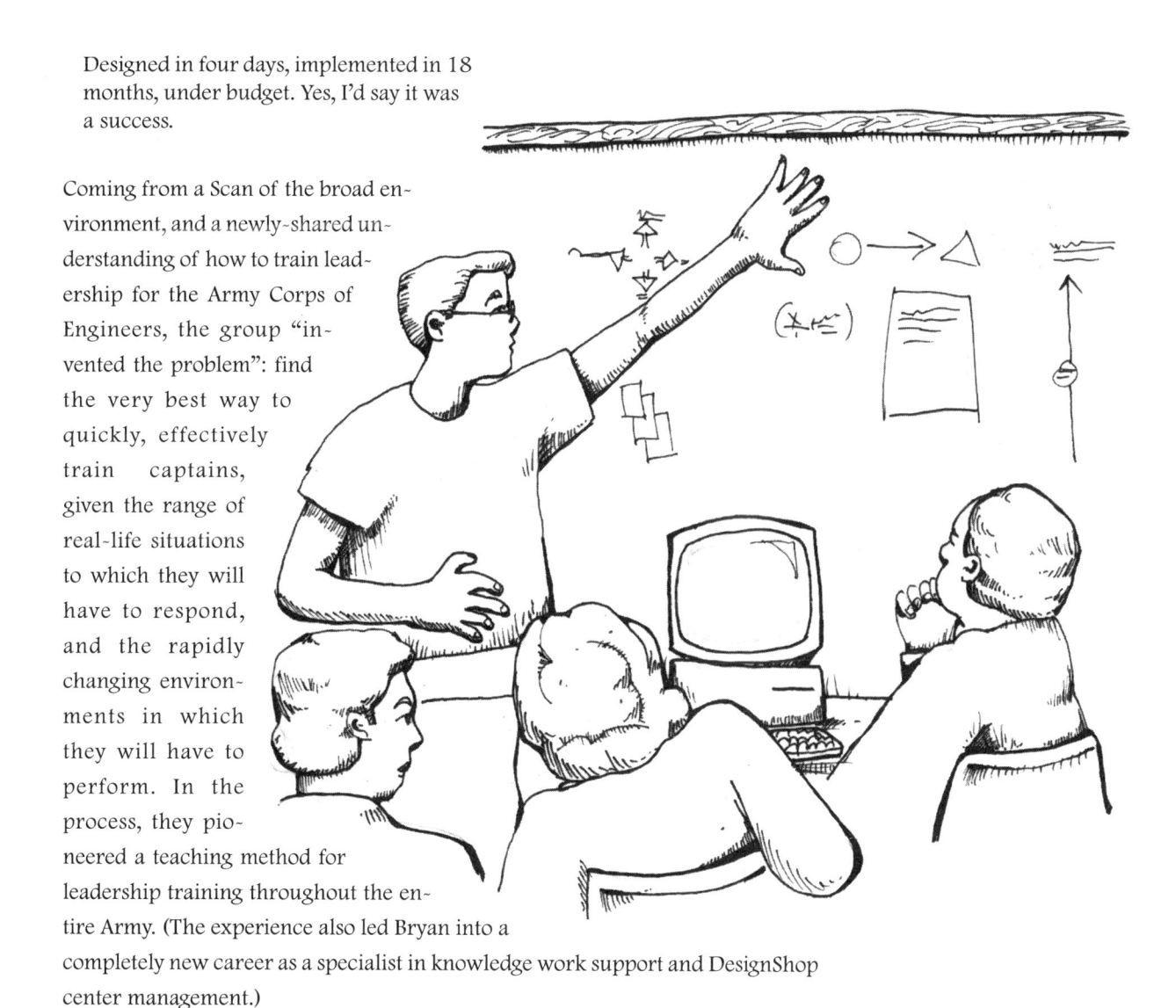

Designed in four days, implemented in 18 months, under budget. Yes, I'd say it was a success.

Coming from a Scan of the broad environment, and a newly-shared understanding of how to train leadership for the Army Corps of Engineers, the group "invented the problem": find the very best way to quickly, effectively train captains, given the range of real-life situations to which they will have to respond, and the rapidly changing environments in which they will have to perform. In the process, they pioneered a teaching method for leadership training throughout the entire Army. (The experience also led Bryan into a completely new career as a specialist in knowledge work support and DesignShop center management.)

Some of the innovations at this "Invent the Problem" stage of the process can be surprising, even shocking. "By now," says Gail Taylor, "people can often work comfortably at a high level of abstraction—the abstract thinking mode." They are able to put aside their emotions and look objectively at their organization—even to the point of considering the elimination of their own current positions. Jon Foley, who at various times has played the roles of sponsor, facilitator, and staffer, described an example.

We held a series of two DesignShop events for the same company—The Learning Organization—and at the end of these two activities, we had 45-50 participants acknowledge, accept, and embrace a concept in which they were going to give up their jobs. They had come together and decided that most of the structure that we currently had in the organization—most of the jobs—would not be useful to the organization the way we designed it.

They agreed that the work should be designed first. We should throw all of the jobs into a pool. Then, once the work was designed, we decided to have some sort of structure to support the work. Everyone in the room said, "Yes, I know I may not have a job, but this is the right thing to do." It was interesting to watch people recognize this fact—that they were designing themselves out of jobs. There would be an emotional burst when they would see they might be out of a job, but then they would decide it was the right thing to do. We were talking…I don't remember how many jobs. In essence, we agreed that five departments should be combined into two, and there would be only about half the number of people.

They came to understand that a job is not guaranteed, but the work is, and you structure to the work. Once they get that, they really *get* that.

Is this heartless—encouraging people to design themselves out of a job? It is just the opposite. Enabling individuals to take part in the redesign of their organization maximizes their chances of remaining employable, either there or elsewhere. Redesign will happen anyway—whether it is called "downsizing," "re-engineering," or "restructuring." The DesignShop process enables broader participation and a greater likelihood that whatever happens will at least make sense for the organization. That's more than can be said for many redesigns today.

DesignShop participants are much more likely to get a clear picture of what exactly it is that they bring to an organization, and to see how—and where—they can continue to contribute. As economists point out, one of the most valuable uses of our time is figuring out how we can make the best use of our talents—i.e., selecting a profession, looking for a job. A DesignShop experience is, among many other things, a crash course in giving participants the broader perspective they need to do this well.

But let's return to the recognition that these participants from The Learning Organization were willing to take—a profoundly radical perspective, which included the possibility that they would be left without a job in their organization. What we should pay attention to here—what is of significance—is that these people

---

Enabling individuals to take part in the redesign of their organization maximizes their chances of remaining employable, either there or elsewhere. Redesign will happen anyway whether it is called "downsizing," "re-engineering," or "restructuring." The DesignShop process enables broader participation and a greater likelihood that whatever happens will at least make sense for the organization.

Vantage Points Model
http://www.mgtaylor.com/mgtaylor/glasbead/vantgpts.htm

Inventing the Problem

were now capable of thinking and acting in a way that would have been impossible two days previously.

It's only now, halfway through the Wharton DesignShop, that participants are ready to deal with the really tough issues, such as revisiting the official areas of concern that brought them together. Why wait so long to address the problem? "If they 'invent the problem' too soon," says Gail Taylor, "they'll be blocked." These are bright, talented people— people who have often spent more than a year trying to solve their organizations' complex, virtually intractable problems. Whatever methods they have used to date haven't produced a satisfactory answer. If their pathway to a solution has been blocked for a year, why should they now be able to generate an answer in the two days remaining in this DesignShop session? Why is there reason to hope they can now avoid the traps that have blocked them previously?

This delay in tackling the problems head-on does not seem to fit with the action-oriented approach we've all been trained in, and it makes everybody nervous. Uncomfortable. Antsy. On the first day it was easy to see the gnawing impatience of many managers here, straining to attack their problems by the jugular vein, showing with the body language of folded arms and frowns that "Time is Money," and that metaphors about rivers weren't bringing them any closer to solutions.

As Gail Taylor says, "You don't solve a problem, you dissolve it." For the last day-and-a-half, these managers, engineers, and analysts have been resolutely held in an expanded information pool, undergoing accelerated learning, scanning their environment for new knowledge about co-workers, systems theory, the past and the present, and speculations on the different kinds of futures their organizations may face. They've been unforming and reforming a wide variety of paradigms, metaphors, and systems concepts. They have put these new tools to work to solve the various problems posed in the DesignShop work sessions. They still have their old tools, but they now have added a broad range of new ones. And by working together with people from whom they are normally separated, each group has access to a lot more intelligence, knowledge, and experience than they had when they first walked through the door. The names are still the same, but these people now make up very different teams than they did at the start of this event.

Without a shared language for dealing with complexity, team learning is limited. There is simply no more effective way to learn than through use, which is exactly what happens when a team starts to learn the language of systems thinking.

—Peter Senge
The Fifth Discipline

Creative Thinking Guidelines
http://www.mgtaylor.com/
mgtaylor/jotm/spring97/
creative.htm

They are now able to think about their organizations and themselves in new ways. Sparking this difference has been the Scan learning exercises.
Many participants are drawing from parts of their intellectual tool kits which haven't been touched in twenty years.
In other cases, participants are learning from outside sources.

Every person who has participated is now grounded in two important areas:

1. A commonly-constructed language of education, business, and process. They are now using the metaphors—high-level models from different disciplines—to think much more creatively about their own enterprises. They have been acquiring business insights in the course of learning about the rainforest, the garden, and so on—these complex, intricate biological models transfer directly to enterprise.

The importance of this language is hard to overemphasize. Our brains, our culture, and our professional tools aren't set up to handle the complexity we are dealing with in our present world, and most of us have not had formal training in complex systems theory. The metaphors are vital tools.

2. A broader awareness of issues—more sophisticated perceptions of the world surrounding their enterprise and how it could change in the future.

When many participants first arrived, they were working with conventional, negative visions of the future: massive unemployment, exhausted natural resources, and so on—simplistic ideas from the mass media. Today we are seeing the same people displaying a broader perspective on a more complex world. They are also displaying another payoff from looking into the future—they are now able to think about their organizations and themselves in new ways.

Sparking this difference has been the Scan learning exercises. Many participants are drawing from parts of their intellectual tool kits which haven't been touched in twenty years. In other cases, participants are learning from outside sources. Recall that every participant received a large pack of ReadAhead material selected to provide missing tools and data of value. Each participant also read one specific book, usually selected for the important paradigms presented. The small-group work during the early exercises, such as the Backcasting scenarios tracing the trends of the "past" century, brought much of that information out into the open and let people really get their hands around it in a working context.

Inventing the Problem 147

Iteration: Design and Test. Design and Test

By midafternoon on Thursday, each business team has taken a shot at inventing the problem facing their organization. Everyone now reconvenes in the larger group to hear and do a first critique of these initial results.

Design. Test. Redesign. Test. Redesign again. Test. This continued iteration, going from the drawing board, to stress-testing the solution, before heading back for another round of invention, is a key part of the design process. We first saw this iteration during Scan, when concepts of the future were designed, then critiqued, and then worked with again; these concepts of the future are being further refined as the groups continue to work on Reinventing the Problem. Now, the Problem is also entering the cycle of iterative design and testing.

The testing questions put out by other participants and facilitators are probing and razor sharp. Not surprisingly, the organizations at Wharton that are new to the process—such as Orlando Regional Hospital—are challenged with the most fundamental questions, and rightly so: "Are you sure this is your problem? Are you jumping too fast to your solution? Have you redone your mission statement?"

The newcomer groups share similar patterns of problems in their thinking: they have abandoned complexity, fled ambiguity and broad perspective, dropped down into an impoverished simplicity, limited their set of solutions, and set themselves up for difficulties. They tend to try to move directly to a solution; they haven't spent enough time in redefining the problem and searching the idea space. These were the people who during the Backcasting exercise had said, "Medicare goes bankrupt and so do we." Where is the redefinition of who they are and what they do that is going to let them survive the tsunami of change that they themselves described?

One group has quickly reverted to the definition of the problem which they brought with them from home. ("Of course we know what our problem is. That's why we're here!") In the process, they have identified one troubling symptom and want to insist that the symptom is the only problem. It's like a doctor noting that the patient has an elevated temperature and concentrating on making the reading go down by placing the patient in a bath of ice water, instead of doing a thorough

Design Build Use Model
http://www.mgtaylor.com/mgtaylor/glasbead/dbumodel.htm

When you get to it, and you can't do it, well, there you jolly well are, aren't you?

—Lord North

> *If one of my engineers can't describe the solution and model it out in detail, it's a sure sign that it's not understood yet and probably won't work.*
>
> —Mindy Bokser

evaluation and appropriate diagnosis of the medical problem. It's the newer groups that show this "thermometer fixation" instead of looking at the whole entity.

In this dogged insistence on holding on to their old problem definition, on defending this intellectual chunk of turf, something stands out clearly: the ego attachment to a particular agenda rather than the open, calm curiosity that marks other teams who have focused on working for the greater corporate good.

The group is questioning these folks because they are still trying to use the standard "jump to the bottom line," "cut to the chase" style of working. Previously, you would have called this "facing reality" or "business sense." Suddenly, these wanna-be business solutions sound glib, hollow. Although professionally delivered, the answers are unconvincing, a minor remodeling of conventional fixes. Clearly, the hospital team hasn't really dug into the complexities of their situation. The larger group is forcing a deeper exploration by asking the foundation questions of business, "Where are you delivering value? What are you building?"

Another newcomer group turns out to be unclear about who their customers are. One of them is stuck in the rut of focusing strictly on the short-term interests of their current stockholders. Here, the bottom line reigns to the point that breakthrough thinking is completely inhibited: "We have to show that this model is more profitable than the other model." Unless a fledgling idea can immediately show its numeric superiority, it is kicked out of the nest. By asking pointed questions, the larger group encourages them to break out of these mental ruts and dig deeper.

The key word in Inventing the Problem is *invent*. Inventing and designing are often messy. The experienced groups dive in and work broadly, stretching the definition of what is included in the problem. Even groups like AEDC, secure in their identity, with a clear vision of where they are heading, and with strong motivation and intent to fufill that vision, constantly cycle back to the fundamentals of their identity, their vision, their intent, and other key factors when testing out a new problem design. In contrast to the deep exploration that the more experienced groups are producing, it is clear that "cutting to the chase" and trying to keep the problem neat and controlled is not providing useful results.

Seven Stages of the Creative Process Model
http://www.mgtaylor.com/mgtaylor/glasbead/7stagcrp.htm

Testing Continues: Build a 3D Model

As the critiquing session wraps up in late afternoon, the participants split up into organization-based groups again, and are assigned the unusual task of building a three-dimensional model of the 21st century organization. They are to include features that deal with feedback, growth, and other characteristics we've been talking about in the past two days. Many of the groups have already been drawing 2D models on their work walls. But now they are told, "Make your model concrete, make it mechanical." Finally, everyone will see whether an organization based on this 3D model works to address the organizational problems defined in the previous session— a tricky and complex assignment.

Initial enthusiasm for this difficult task varies, with the organizations having the most DesignShop experience launching into it quickly, while some others are a bit intimidated by the 3D model kits—which look an awful lot like expensive, high-tech variations on Tinker Toys™ or Lego™ or Meccano™. Also, those old inhibitions have come bubbling back with thoughts of, "What does this have to do with real business? I've already done a 2D model. Besides, I don't know how to make 3D models. This is embarrassing."

But as usual, there is reason behind the task. This assignment is yet another cycle of design and test, and it gives a different insight into the solution than that of the last exercise. Then, the job was to design the problem in the abstract. Now, modeling with 3D parts gives the business problem or solution an actual physical shape and structure. Modeling in three dimensions suddenly gives people access to ideas from physics, architecture, chemistry, and mechanical engineering to generate solutions.

What do you use to represent the marketing department in your model: a wooden block? A Miss Piggy doll? A pair of giant spectacles? The inherent message in your choice of materials is quite different.

Modeling also serves as a physical test of the proposed solution: are there dangling strings? How does this part communicate with that part? The nature of the proposed solution becomes quite visible....and so do its gaps and errors. Eventually, with some support staff assistance, all of the groups were able to embody their ideas in a physical model of some kind.

The winning edge in planning is gained not through the science of charts, graphs, and computer models, but through the constant pulling apart of perceptions and putting them back together again in a new configuration.

—Edith Weiner

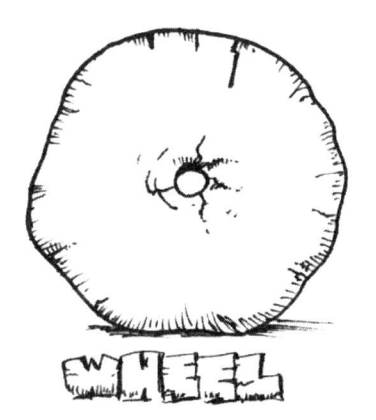

The modeling exercise makes plenty of sense: in order to come up with a new system, we *must* build and communicate some kind of model, either in our heads, on paper or wallboard (2D), or using a modeling kit (3D). Building the new system model only in our heads makes it hard to communicate, and 2D models have their limits as well for complex systems. In the following example, participants at a previous DesignShop built their model in two-dimensions, when the complexity of their system could have benefited from a 3D model.

National Car Rental

Matt Taylor tells the story of National Car Rental's experience with the DesignShop process:

As you probably know, rental car companies return most of their cars to the manufacturer for resale after they're through with them. When we started working with National in 1990, domestic car sales were very slow, and the manufacturers, like General Motors and Ford, were having trouble selling these used rental cars. There was some concern on the part of the rental companies that the manufacturers could even start resisting taking these cars back—it had happened before, somewhere around 1970. And although the rental companies had their own used car sales lots, they weren't positioned to effectively market the vast volume of automobiles that would be created by this change in their basic business. To put this in perspective, at that time a company like National would have in effect been the biggest car dealer in the world, because the number of cars that they buy, operate, and then sell in a year is enormous. So to be suddenly forced into this new, high-volume sales role was a potentially big problem for National.

Also, the rental car business was then—and still is—extremely competitive. The companies were racing to introduce new technology, new procedures for getting the car to the customer quickly, expensive new computers and reservation systems, and very competitive bids for big corporate accounts. This was not the environment for them to take on this new problem of how to dispose of the fleet.

A DesignShop session was held to deal with this problem, but what we ended up addressing was how to manage the asset of the automobile as a total system, from manufacturing the car right through to when it's a piece of junk. Traditionally, the rental companies tried to extract all the revenue possible from a car in the first 25,000 miles of its life—actually a small part of the useful life of an automobile. And they had no economic model of what it meant to get into the business of dealing with the car through other parts of its life cycle after those first 25,000 miles. Could you lease the car out long term? What else? No one had ever systematically thought their way through that: what it meant to deal with the asset from start to end.

We had people here from sales, from marketing, from operations, from corporate headquarters, we had people here that ran the lots. So we had a cross-section of people that probably, in their total experience, knew the total post-production car industry from one end to the other.

Usually, in a normal decision process or the day-to-day life of a business, all that information is competing against itself: someone says we ought to sell the cars afterwards, others say no, we ought to lease them, or no, we ought to send them back. Instead, we put everyone into an environment where all of these ideas were respected, honored, and needed to be brought up. We asked, "What can we do that we never thought of, or that we thought was impossible? How can we engineer a total systems response to our situation?"

I remember at one point we asked the team to go out and do a wiring diagram of the complete life cycle of an automobile, from beginning to end. And this thing came back that looked like spaghetti. We have the drawings to this day. It looked like a drawing of spaghetti. There were boxes with all these lines running back and forth between them, curving around and jumping over one another, and it was just a big spaghetti mess. This was a classic case of needing a 3D model.

In looking at the natural economic life cycle of a car, it turned out there were two places where the car was immensely profitable—once when it was brand new and then later when it had 75,000-80,000 miles on it but was still in extremely good shape. We then thought about what do the users want? What do the customers want? What does ownership really mean to them? And we developed a matrix in which there were multiple levels of utilization and service, so the user could say, for example, "I want a car, and I want you to wash it every week. I want you to change the oil. I want you to give me full service." In other words, the kind of service that they would get if they were renting the car short-term from a rental company—this would take advantage of National's immense installed capacity to take care of these fleets. Or the customer could say, "No, I want you to do only an annual check of the car." So there could be minimal levels of service, and in-between gradations of levels, affecting the cost of the car to the user.

We imagined that cars could come out of the fleet and be sold with the idea that after the owners drove the car for two or three years, they would sell it back and get a newer model. Meanwhile, the first car might go into another kind of rental, termed "replacement." There is a whole market where you rent cars to body shops that make them available to people when their car is being repaired. And then the car might come out of that fleet and get sold or leased again, and so on.

We then started looking at the cars themselves and what people really wanted. The net result of the concept is that the buyer or the user could come into these quasi-boutique sales offices and shopping centers, where there might be one or two cars on the floor, several display kiosks, and one or two people to help. They could go up to the kiosks and start looking through—using, say, a CD-ROM—pictures and descriptions of the various cars in the fleet that are going to be available. They could put in their own profile: their profile of what they wanted to pay, what kind of car they wanted, the color, and what level of service they wanted, and this package could be priced right there. And then the automobiles that fit into that price range, and overall profile, could be shown on the screen with a timetable and delivery schedule to meet customer requirements.

So what you have is the ability to totally customize to the buyers' preferences and offer the maximum number of alternatives that would be imaginable for them—in a relaxed, non-competitive, non-sales-focused environment.

From this, we developed a huge, comprehensive flowchart showing all the different ways to utilize and ultimately dispose of the car. This model changed the rental business from a business of just dealing with over-the-counter sales to the management of an entire asset—the fleet. It was immensely exciting stuff, very innovative—it would massively affect not only the car rental companies, but the manufacturers, dealerships, and the whole way people think about buying, managing, and maintaining the asset that is an automobile. In the experience of the participants—and there was a *lot* of experience in that room, with many people having worked for multiple rental companies—this was the most integrated, comprehensive, and totally optimized system to manage the value and leverage car rental assets.

We literally dissolved the original problem because, coming out of the DesignShop session, it didn't matter whether General Motors and the other manufacturers wanted to buy the rental cars back or not. Obviously, there would have been work to do to get ready to actually install a system to take on the volume of this kind of work, but the beautiful thing about it is that our solution was modular. In other words, to install a sales outlet in a shopping mall with this kiosk would be a relatively modest financial commitment. It could be tested on the level of one or two or three units. These kiosk sales outlets could be put right in the rental car companies' environments, they could be put in shopping centers, they could be put in hotels, they could be put in airports, they could be put in anywhere it makes sense to put one. You could grow the business by doing a series of modular enterprises. And you could stop at any point that made sense, or you could continue doing it until you were even taking over other car rental companies' used fleets.

This DesignShop experience showed us that answers emerge when people can share their ideas and develop a synergistic combination of their ideas,

This DesignShop experience showed us that answers emerge when people can share their ideas and develop a synergistic combination of their ideas, and when they start by looking at a problem from the necessary perspective, as a system.

and when they start by looking at a problem from the necessary perspective, as a system. Then their individual experiences and perspectives are no longer in conflict, because they are not trying to persuade each other in the context of a limited set of options, where one idea has to prevail over the other. They are in effect, as a unit, creating something new.

Before this plan could be implemented, National was bought out by General Motors, and the plan has never been implemented as a total system by a single company. But the plan has proved to be an accurate projection of the needs and direction of the industry. In 1994, Ford began leasing used cars through its Hertz subsidiary. In Japan, through a U.S./Japanese collaboration, you can order new and used cars by computer. In 1996, new independent businesses like Autonation, being described as "innovative," were beginning to adopt the restructured approach to selling used cars described in the DesignShop session: a low key, non-bartering atmosphere where consumers can select the year, model, and service level of a used car.

In formal logic, a contradiction is a signal of a defeat; but in the evolution of real knowledge, it marks the first step in a progress towards a victory.

—Alfred North Whitehead

As Matt pointed out, National's 2D model was good, but would have been better in 3D. Modeling in 3D is a strong form of testing for errors, oversights, and contradictions. It is applying the knowledge latent in mechanical objects to an intangible, to an idea. How do you connect two parts of your company—with a rubber band? with a steel rod? Whatever material you choose will have implications regarding communication, flexibility, and solidity of the attachment. When you look at what has been assembled and say "no, we need to do it differently," your discovery of the error is pushing you along on the path to the true solution.

Testing Continues: Authors

Back at the Wharton DesignShop session, it's late on Thursday and time for the final stage of testing each organization's problem concept: the Authors exercise. So far, participants have tested in a variety of ways—in their small groups, in presentations to the large group, by bumping up again physical reality with a 3D model. Now they are going to test their concepts against people who are specialists in a range of disciplines.

Weeks before the event, readings were assigned to all participants. From the Taylor library of five or six thousand books, the staff selected the subset most relevant to the current session's topic. Each participant was then sent one particular book to read before the start of the event.

The books were assigned to specific readers with the goal of providing each individual with the knowledge that might be the most personally useful. It was not by chance that one of the Carl's Jr. restaurant participants, with a strong finance background, was assigned the 1960 anthropology classics of Edward T. Hall on the cultural impact of space. Anthropology and architecture are not part of the standard reading for finance and business students, so this is the opportunity to provide valuable information to someone whose daily business now involves building and operating "stores."

Weak Signal Research
http://www.mgtaylor.com/
mgtaylor/mgtaylor/wsremerg.htm

If the DesignShop team has learned that your reading habits are usually limited to the major media such as Time, Newsweek, and the Wall Street Journal, they'll give you more off-beat materials. They call this Weak Signal Research—instead of wallowing in the same mainstream data that the mass media dish up for the general public, you get to direct your antenna to the newest, faintest hints of change. Or if the team suspects that your company may be preoccupied with the latest fads, you may be assigned a classic book, directing your attention to the unchanging verities of, for instance, what makes us human.

Here at the DesignShop event, each participant is asked to present the views in the book, *speaking as the author.* Matt explains that each author is to present a summary of the book. "Then we will ask our authors to give us feedback on our work so far in this DesignShop experience. They will comment on the works' viability. Is it going in the right direction? What can be done to make it more viable?"

What at first looks like a cute gimmick—having the participants pretend to be the author—actually forces them to build a mental model of the author's point of view. One value of this is discussed by Jon Foley in his story of how the Authors exercise was used at his company, Agency Group:

> We sent out the books ahead of time. For the Authors exercise, the participants would take off their name tags, and behind those tags would be tags with the names of the authors of the books. Then we would say, "As you put on this new name tag, assume the character. From the author's perspective, tell us why you wrote the book, what could be learned from it, and what our company could learn from it."

This changed the dynamics of the report. Rather than saying they liked or did not like the book, they had to speak from the author's perspective. If they did not like the book, this would help them realize the value of it. Other participants would ask them to elaborate, perhaps on points with which they disagreed, forcing them to think it through again. It was very normal and natural at the end for people to be trading books.

At least half the time, people would realize that most of the books were about the same thing. You might have books like *Unbounding the Future*, *Paradigm Shift*, *The Fifth Discipline*, and *The Art of War*. Participants would recognize that they were all talking about learning, systems, and change.

Critiquing the work done so far in the DesignShop session by analyzing it from the author's perspective is yet another reality test in the iterative cycle of design, test, and design. What would Tom Peters say about your proposed problem design? Peter Drucker? Lao Tzu? Marvin Minsky? You already know what the experts in your field have to say, so if you want a new perspective, doesn't that mean that you should look at new areas of knowledge?

At the Wharton DesignShop event, there wasn't enough time to have the "authors" critique each groups' work thoroughly. But two authors of a featured book, *Unbounding the Future*, happened to be present—us, Gayle and Chris. We were invited into one of the groups to explain our book's topic—nanotechnology—and work with them on their picture of the future. In the course of our Authors' conversation, we saw how profoundly a book could serve to help test and evolve ideas in solving a business problem.

The group that called us in was made up of members from many different organizations—these were people attending Wharton as their company's sole representative. Discussing the state of technology and the nature of the 21st century organization had served to bring out the group's conflicting opinions more clearly. This was a positive development.

They fired off questions about nanotechnology, issues of technical development, timetables, shifts or accelerations in national and international trends, questions about which objects will increase or decrease in value, become more or less cumbersome. Their design of a future organization was based on their perception of what that future would be like. They used their discussion with us as a test session

> *All through history, human knowledge has been like fluid in a set of communicating vessels: an advance in one of them will result in a higher level in other areas. To understand the dynamics of technology, one always starts out with areas of knowledge other than one's own.*
>
> —Peter Drucker,
> *Managing in Turbulent Times*

to critique their design. They used questions and the answers to design and redesign as the conversation went along.

You'd think that after two twelve-hour days, everyone would be exhausted. Not so. The intensity and the novelty of the whole series of modules and learning exercises, now followed by the complexity of trying to absorb dozens of authors' viewpoints, is more stimulating than draining. Despite the group's high average intellectual level, hardly any of the individuals have the time to devote to books that they would like. One of the benefits of the Authors module is that it provides a crash course on the most important new ideas of the last decade and review of classic ideas from across disciplines.

The Authors exercise concluded the second day of the event. By now, everyone had tested their problem statements from many angles, including from the viewpoints of many smart people who aren't even here. Tomorrow marks the move from Focus to Act, and formulating specific plans of action to take back to the individual enterprises.

Challenge

1. Record your impressions and questions as you've been practicing in previous chapters.

2. You have a choice here between two challenges:

   a. Head back to the library or bookstore and find a book you have not read yet in a subject that you may not be very familiar with. It can be philosophy (Karl Popper, Michael Polanyi, The Machinery of Freedom by David Friedman), a new angle on science (try The Counterrevolution of Science by Friedrich Hayek, Society of Mind by Marvin Minsky, Infinite in All Directions by Freeman Dyson, The Selfish Gene by Richard Dawkins), architecture (Frank Lloyd Wright, Christopher Alexander, Jane Jacobs), history (Daniel Boorstin, Barbara Tuchman), or any of a number of other categories. Look for a book whose author has something of consequence to say beyond the merely technical: something philosophical, cultural, political, strategic, and tactical. Read the book and then look at your work so far through the eyes of the author; let the author critique and add to your design. Be prepared to be surprised at what you learn from this critique: Bryan Coffman once facilitated a session where the sponsors insisted that their business strategy be so clear that a fourteen-year-old could understand it. Bryan surprised them by obliging their wishes on the third day of the DesignShop: the fourteen-year-old's critique added some things that the business people had neglected.

   b. Head to the closet of some young person in your family and ask to borrow a set of Legos, clay, Tinkertoys, or some other form of modeling material. Or head to the toy store, craft store, hardware store, or your garage and collect a diverse set of building materials. Make sure you have some means of assembling the items. Then use your kit to assemble a model of your organization, life, or whatever your focus has been in these assignments. Show how things are connected, how they influence each other. Make things spin, roll, move up and down in response to other parts of the model. Label, describe, and document (photograph) your work. Explain your model to your kids, or someone else's kids.

Magic Behind the Scenes

Late last night, long after the participants have left for their rooms, the whole facilitation team is still working hard at transcribing, organizing, and illustrating material to update the journals to be printed and ready tomorrow morning.

It's a surprise to see almost two dozen people appear. During the days, the entire crew has been almost invisible, even to other crew members.

When the team puts their work aside and circles up a ring of chairs, it's to start an intense conversation about how the DesignShop session is going, compare their expectations for today with what actually happened, see how far along the participants are, check what still needs to be done, and decide on the plans for how tomorrow's session will begin. Not only are these people suddenly visible, they're noisy. They are talking a mile a minute, unleashing pointed observations about today's session —none of them has missed a thing—making razor-sharp insights about various organizations' problems, and jumping up to the work walls to sketch out ideas on what to do tomorrow.

This theme of the invisible becoming visible, of the hidden pattern of work emerging, helps explain how the DesignShop process works, and why the entire support team does what it does.

Let's take a look at the most visible parts of the invisible.

Matt Taylor begins: "The basic elements of the facilitation process are easily learnable. They are very systematic, uniform practices of how you do support work. With a straightforward understanding of the DesignShop process, as we've described it in our DesignShop facilitation manual, you can facilitate at a 50% or 60% level, in almost any situation you run into.

> Responsibilities of Krew Leads in DesignShops
> http://www.mgtaylor.com/mgtaylor/jotm/winter96/krewlead.htm

> *The sponsors and the knowledge workers are the engineers who carry out the DesignShop.*
>
> —John Poparad

"Beyond that level, to get the remaining 40% requires a level of mastery, art, understanding of psychology, understanding how the creative process works, business issues, content issues that come from study and experience."

Even looking at the most straightforward parts of the facilitation process resembles peeking behind the scenes at a play, or visiting a special effects workshop for a movie set to see just how they work the magic. It is a science, but it is also an art. In a brief glimpse, we can come to understand at least some of the basic parameters.

A Different Kind Of Facilitation: Knowledge Work Facilitation

Transitioning from Process Facilitator to Event Facilitator
http://www.mgtaylor.com/mgtaylor/jotm/winter96/pftoeftr.htm

The support work done in a DesignShop event is based on:
- a shared vision and goal of an end-state: what people could be at their maximum—creative, cooperative people capable of solving their problem,
- a model of how people learn and become creative and productive, based on an understanding of the human creative process,
- an understanding of the physical environment, tools, and processes needed to support people in creative work, and
- a process designed for each specific event to produce a specific work product of value to the sponsor's business.

Even looking at the most straightforward parts of the facilitation process resembles peeking behind the scenes at a play, or visiting a special effects workshop for a movie set to see just how they work the magic.

Those processes include a new range of support services that haven't been available before. Support team members:
- act as models of creative, cooperative people;
- exemplify that kind of behavior, thereby encouraging it in others;
- challenge assumptions;
- provide information that deliberately "moves you out of the same old box," and
- involve themselves in the actual content of the work.

The Most Visible Parts of the Process

Because of the close coupling between environment, tools, and processes, "facilitating" can mean making use of any and all of these aspects. Let's take a concrete example: What can a facilitator do when it's time to get the group to change their pace? You could stand in front of the room in the traditional manner and make an announcement. You could type up and hand out messages. You could change the light levels in the room. You could even put a particular piece of music on the sound system to effect the change. Let's say the group is blocked and distracted: you could use body language, tone of voice, present a model, or get them "pumped up" as immediate ways of managing the group's energy—again, it's all facilitating.

What Makes a Great Facilitator

"To do a truly excellent job at providing this kind of intellectual support," says John Poparad, "you would be a combination of a very fine professional valet, a Socrates-like mentor, who understood when to enter the process and when not to, and a little bit of Van Gogh would not hurt—a little craziness and an understanding of when to let craziness go—when not to. Find somebody who has life experience, intellectual ability, and a high energy level."

Chip Saltsman talks about recruiting Ernst & Young people to become facilitators:

> It depends on their frame of mind. Half of the people say, "you couldn't pay me enough to do this work." The other half say, "this is the coolest thing I've ever seen; I'd pay you to let me do this."

> You either love or hate the idea of a job that is part improvisational actor, part psychologist, part business consultant, scribe, artist, stage hand, researcher, writer...all in one package. For those who love variety, it is the job they have been dreaming about all their lives but "knew better" than to think that anything this eclectic, challenging, fun, and productive was realistic.

DesignShop staff members "cross-train" so that they can scribe, run the video cameras, do research, structure scenarios, speak to the entire group of participants, modify the environment, build the knowledge wall, create and produce take-home work products, understand the creative process, analyze complex business issues—handle all aspects of the process. This calls for people who are generalists, but who can also go to specialist depth in multiple areas.

In any DesignShop event, people "step up" to particular tasks—ones which they find they have passion for—often in their areas of specialization. But even as they focus most on one particular aspect, they are still trying to monitor how the whole event is going. Rather than limiting themselves, their capabilities, and their responsibilities to specific niches, they are always ready to swing over and help in another role—running a camera, moving walls, writing exercises, scribing for a breakout group. Within particular task areas, one person may be in the responsible lead position, and count on all other team members to assist, but the lead in one area also "flies as a member of the flock" to support work in other areas.

When the team cooperation is really clicking, you will see the support team change tasks and direction seemingly without a word being spoken. It's like watching a flock of birds move suddenly east, then sharply south. You can also see leadership change from hand to hand in the team, almost like a flock of migrating birds, where one leader merges back and a new leader simultaneously flies forward to lead the V formation.

The transitions are smooth because team members all stay in contact with the event and with each other. The Process Facilitator coordinates with the actions of the Key Facilitator—the person doing the stand-up work in front of the room. Everyone stays in touch with everyone else. Even the front-of-the room facilitators are in continual touch with the rest of the facilitation team—getting their perceptions, opinions, and ideas—iterating and reformulating the design as they go along. Many times, in the middle of the Wharton DesignShop, we saw Matt or Gail Taylor go around to all the other team members to ask what they see or think is going on. "I do not just go on my own perception," Matt says.

Many times the communication between the facilitation team is non-verbal. Patsy Kahoe, Process Facilitator for the Wharton session, explains:

> When I am using music facilitation to call the participants back from their breakout team work, I change the type of music, the tempo, and gradually increase the volume. Everyone starts gathering, usually talking loudly. Meanwhile I am watching the main facilitator—say, Matt—at the front of the room. He is reading the participants, judging the timing of when the group is ready to focus on the next piece of work. It might be as soon as thirty seconds or as long as five minutes after a critical mass of participants is in the room. When that point is reached, I will get a very brief eye contact and an almost imperceptible nod from Matt that means bring the volume down slowly, which creates an empty audio space that he then moves into by speaking to the group and capturing their attention.

Rules for Flocking Behavior in the Web
http://www.mgtaylor.com/mgtaylor/jotm/spring97/flock.htm

Navigation Centers: Applying Rules of Engagement
http://www.mgtaylor.com/mgtaylor/jotm/spring97/rules of eng.htm

The communication can also be non-direct. For example, let's say Gail is up front and mentions a recent article particularly relevent to the current dialogue. Depending on how she says it—the emphasis she uses—a knowledge worker might retrieve the referenced magazine from our library, then stand in the back of the room holding it up so Gail can see it. This gives her the option of taking the magazine and reading an exact quote to the group. A lot of our work is "just in time"—getting information to participants or facilitators as they need it. It's all about being attuned to the environment and the people you are supporting—both participants and fellow facilitators.

Working on a DesignShop team also calls for people who are sensitive to mood and focus, as well as alert to barriers to full performance. The support team does nothing disruptive or destructive to mood and focus, whether it's loudly crunching potato chips, arguing with a fellow support staffer, drifting off into a distracting conversation with a participant, or running within sight or earshot of participants and distracting them from the work.

They need to remain sensitive and responsive to the participants' moods, but always remain clear that the task is to guide the participants safely to being creative, cooperative, and able to achieve the event's goals. A large part of this requires sensitivity on when to be visible or invisible, and how to be visible in the times when visibility is called for.

Jon Foley tells about one DesignShop for a group of distracted, unfocused people, and how facilitation actions, rather than words, can make a huge difference in mood and focus. Jon was Process Facilitator, and responsible for the entire process running smoothly. As Jon watched the Key Facilitator standing in front of the participants, he noticed a problem. As he looked around the space to see how the rest of the support team was doing, he noticed the same problem again and again. "The participants," he figured out, "are infecting us" with their distraction. Part of the job of every member of the DesignShop team is to act as a model of creative, cooperative people, to exemplify that kind of behavior, and encourage that behavior in others. Here, just the opposite was happening.

He called the entire DesignShop team together and told them what he had observed. "We need to take back the energy," he said. "We need to surround the participants with our energy and our focus." The entire team took up positions standing behind the chairs of the participants and just listened. But they listened intently, bringing lots of interest to the task. As the participants began to unconsciously synchronize with the team, they also started to move out of their distracted state and into focused activity. Setting an example, "exemplifying a behavior," is one of the basic ways that people learn. Here, by doing nothing more than standing and listening in a way that encouraged that behavior in others, was a silent piece of facilitation.

Does something like this really work? "It works," says Chip Saltsman of Ernst & Young. "I am as left-brain as they come, and what gets me in a DesignShop is the power I have seen, heard and felt resulting from this process."

Some DesignShop Roles

The positions that go with a DesignShop event are unique. The names don't fit any job titles you've ever heard before. We just looked at "Process Facilitator," but the rest are equally strange. What is a "Wall Capture Team"? What is a "Knowledge Lead"? Out of the 12–15 people who might be working a DesignShop session, we are highlighting these spots to show the range of facilitation that can bring home a result for the participants.

Project Manager-Food For Thought

Well, we all know what a project manager is, right? This well-understood role can serve as the start of our understanding of the role of the logistics coordinator for the DesignShop event. This person coordinates and directs the efforts of the support team, deals with the site of the conference regarding things like food and air-conditioning—logistics...that's straightforward enough. Right? Well...maybe that's not all.

The staff brought a large part of the environment with them: the furniture, wall systems, lighting, computers, libraries, art, toys, tools, recording equipment. But the event is taking place in someone else's building. The MG Taylor team begins with an audit of the hotel's environment to identify areas of neglect. They look for adequate natural light and full-spectrum lighting, flexible illumination levels and glare control, fresh air, flexibility in the control of temperature, humidity, and environmental pollution, and high quality acoustics conditions. How many hotels provide great environments? Not many.

Roles and Duties of the Process Facilitator
http://www.mgtaylor.com/mgtaylor/jotm/winter96/profac1.htm

If it's missing, they add it. If it's broken, they get it fixed. If it's wrong, they have it removed. With every DesignShop event, the hotel's maintenance staff has to be added to the support team, and must be trained on how to work a DesignShop session. So does the hotel catering staff.

"Our purpose is to create high performance that services the client. This includes the caterers," says Patsy Kahoe.

She explains that due to the importance of the environment, the logistics behind the event can make the difference between success and failure. The critical nature of the role they play is such that the hotel staff is drawn into becoming a motivated and contributing part of the DesignShop staff. No one has ever pointed out to the caterers before that the row of barren tables, not due to be set up with the lunch chafing dishes for another two hours, constitutes a small island of ugliness and boredom that won't help participants focus. Think about going to the movies or a play—you disappear into the story, into the emotion and the experience, until some flaw breaks your concentration, jarring you out of the experience. (If you want a guaranteed example of how little it takes to disrupt your attention, try attending a play by an elementary school class where the little performers don't yet have stage discipline. You can't help noticing the motions as their eyes shift over the audience, looking for friends and family instead of focusing on the performer.)

At Wharton, the hotel staff brought their all to the event. They worked absolutely silently—you couldn't hear a sound that would tip you off to the fact that a bunch of people were setting up or clearing away a buffet lunch for 100. They worked with the DesignShop team to make sure the buffet tables were never an eyesore or even a visually dead spot. In between meals, they instantly dressed the tables in fresh linen, arranged plants, magazines, and tools attractively on top. The first time, a DesignShop knowledge worker showed them how. After that, they had grasped the notion and were doing their own creative, stimulating decor. The catering team working breakfast educated the team working lunch, and they in turn taught the dinner team. Beverages were always available; meals were absolutely punctual; presentations were impeccable; service was superb.

Art is the imposing of a pattern on experience, and our esthetic enjoyment in recognition of the pattern.

—Alfred North Whitehead

Patsy Kahoe explains how this happens:

My dialogue with the hotel caterers generally starts four to six weeks in advance of the actual event, and focuses on both menus and service. Since everyone will be working long hours, the menus must be planned carefully to sustain energy yet be healthy. I also begin outlining to the catering manager what we are going to be doing, and that we want to incorporate his staff into our team to facilitate the success of the event. Intrigued, they assign us their best people.

The manager and I meet a day ahead of the event with as many of the catering team as possible, from the chef to the busboys. I describe in detail our needs and our reasoning behind those needs, and answer their questions. By this point, everyone is excited to be involved in something out of the ordinary, and they are motivated to be flexible and even more service oriented than usual. By the end of the first prep day they are starting to become part of the team, by halfway through the session they normally have become one with our team. In some instances people from the catering crew have become so involved in the process that they help with tasks that have nothing to do with catering—at one session I found the chef on the floor with our knowledge workers stuffing FedEx packages in a mad rush to beat the FedEx pickup time!

At some DesignShops, the photos of the hotel staff end up on the wall and in journals as acknowledgment. Patsy describes Mary, one of the caterers at a DesignShop that was long ago and far way, who became a part of the team that contributed to the success: "They take great pride: 'this is our work.' The client feels it. Quite literally, the exemplars of what people could be at their maximum and the DesignShop environment encourage the hotel staff to be unusually cooperative and creative. The catering team is inspired, and the participants benefit."

So, rather than being disturbing in its ever-changing nature, the evolution of the environment to support the work at hand happens almost magically via the DesignShop facilitators—invisibly, soundlessly.

When the support team is working well, the food, the pens, the hypertiles appear before they are needed. The participant's reaction might be, "How did it show up? How did that happen? That table was not here. There was no silverware, and now there is."

If the magic is really working, then the participant is completely unaware of the graceful facilitation that made their modeling equipment appear or their empty dishes disappear, or made the breakout room bigger and added a table. Instead, the participants are rapt and focused on their work, just as a theater audience is caught up in the drama and unaware of the stage technician back in the wings running the fog machine. It seems a right and proper part of nature that the lighting should have changed just then, that a fascinating article should appear up on the Knowledge Wall just when you needed that exact information; that you put out your hand and there are the tools that are most useful.

The closest images that we have are of the butler, who soundlessly appears at your elbow with the cold drink just the moment before you realize your thirst, and the valet laying out precisely the right clothes for the day, so you get dressed without hemming, hawing, and discovering that the shirt has a button missing. Now imagine the same level of service provided for your mind.

More Mind Support-Artists, Modelers, Scribes

The goal of all these forms of graphic facilitation is capturing the essence of the participants' thoughts in words and pictures. This work organizes and documents information. It translates discussion and words into vivid, memorable content, images, sequences of images, and relationships.

At the simplest level, the artist is illustrating or reflecting what someone is saying. However, it's more than just an assist to group memory. It is making information useful to others: making lists, charts, spreadsheets, maps.

It is also extracting information. Says Michael Kaufman, "If you see somebody who has an idea but can't get it out, just draw it for them. Don't force them to do it themselves." If the graphic documentor leads the group in developing diagrams, flow charts, maps and visual models, the process may be helping them think through and communicate key concepts and ideas.

A graphic representation can chart the group's evolving ideas. As a session progresses, and as the artist draws pictures of what the participants have to say, concepts begin to appear on the work walls. Then circles and arrows begin to lasso concepts, connecting them to each other, linking them to facts and data lists. As the images accumulate, the group can often see new patterns within its own information.

The participants are rapt and focused on their work, just as a theater audience is caught up in the drama and unaware of the stage technician back in the wings running the fog machine. It seems a right and proper part of nature that the lighting should have changed just then, that a fascinating article should appear up on the Knowledge Wall just when you needed that exact information; that you put out your hand and there are the tools that are most useful.

John Poparad notes: "There is some artistry, but it really requires skill in listening. To do that well, you must understand the essence of the dialogue as well as be able to do the translation into graphics. The deeper the 'artist's' training in logic, communication skills, business concepts, science, and the specifics of the business being discussed, the more value can be added and extracted by the graphics."

Over the course of a DesignShop session with a good crew of scribes and artists, you can see a visual language develop: icons and images to represent key and recurring ideas. Think of a Chinese character—a pictograph—that captures entire paragraphs of information in one or two characters. Write the same information out in English text, and you have pages of information before you arrive at the concept level. With an icon, you have one character, one image, telling a story of central importance to you.

An alert artist can facilitate and crystallize a management change: Chip recalls how, at an E&Y DesignShop event, an artist heard the group seize on the recurrent theme of "escape from Los Colinas," a business unit several participants were trying to leave in order to join a new enterprise.

Escape from Los Colinas: it sounded like *film noire*, a B movie, Now Playing At A Theater Near You, something right out of the 1940s or 1950s. In minutes, the artist had completed the movie poster that captured the story, the drama, and presented it to the participants.

This quick graphic turnaround is part of the magic that makes DesignShop sessions successful. It is powerfully rewarding to have your ideas become "real" very quickly. The graphic shows that they have transmitted their idea successfully. Now, with art in hand, they have the ability to do it with other ideas. The feedback that they can get fast graphical implementation of their ideas is tremendously motivational.

The value of having an artist, scribe, and modeler on hand, quickly becomes evident to participants. In just a little while, they start grabbing the artists to capture their work. By the end of the DesignShop event, when tactical plans are being developed, the demand for artists soars. Says Chip, "They'll need to convince others about their ideas, or just to transmit ideas like a meme—an idea that goes into another mind and replicates. Very often artwork does the job."

It's not uncommon for the experience to be so valuable that an executive decides that a specialist in knowledge work is what is needed as a personal assistant back home. At one point in Bryan Coffman's career, he worked for man whom he describes as "a one-man DesignShop, a visionary who knows where the financial ends meet. He would come up with an idea, and I would sketch it out for him to give him visual feedback."

Michael Kaufman adds, "What Bryan is doing is creating feedback loops, and iterating the information at different levels—lower or higher." So the graphics can take the ideas, and feed them back more abstractly, and then as more detailed representations. The originator of the idea gets to look at the drawing and say, "Is that what I mean? Is there a piece missing? This makes sense at the abstract level, but what about when we drop to detail? Do I have something else in mind that needs to be captured as well?"

Here the artist was helping the executive iterate his own thinking and develop his own ideas. Just as most of us have a dominant hand, we also have dominant talent sets. This kind of knowledge facilitation helps us at our sticking places. Someone who has been trained in creative process issues will pay attention to how you manufacture an idea, and learn what parts of the process you need help working through.

Michael talks about another person filling a similar role in a different company. But here, the graphics are leveraging the executive's ability to communicate:

> There his role is translating the executive's thinking into useful material for other people. He'll do slide shows, desk top publishing, charts, whatever. It scared him a little at first to find himself at high-level or even board-level meetings.

The artist deals with what cannot be said in words.

—Ursula K. LeGuin

The key was getting things out very fast—making the ideas accessible and available so other people could use them. Without him, the executive probably wouldn't be as effective at getting his ideas implemented.

If you're ever short of ideas of what you want as a bonus or perk, just think about how someone might facilitate for you.

Further Into the Invisibility

Matt Taylor says: "As the knowledge workers get better at writing the exercises, at doing the graphics, at selecting the music...there is less work to be done by the standup facilitator."

The obviously visible position of Facilitator—whether the Key Facilitator who stands in front of the room, or the Facilitators in breakout groups who may metamorphose instantly from Scribe to Facilitator to Modeler—begins to take us a further step into the invisible patterns of the process.

Rob Evans of Ernst & Young gives his perspective: "What the person in the front of the room does is more about design than facilitation. I would call the person a 'designer.' The term 'facilitation' is misleading. It suggests that people who consider themselves facilitators already have the skills, and they can step into this environment using their old processes and get DesignShop process quality results."

The Key Facilitators have worked in-depth with the sponsor to come up with a design which will become the journey for this DesignShop event. Over the weeks prior to the session, the design of this journey has been further discussed, explored, rethought, and reconfigured by the entire support team until it has matured. The entire team has come to have a common vision of the goal of the journey and a sense of the shape that journey will take. The Key Facilitator's knowledge should be the most in-depth imaginable.

The nature of the design and the vision of the journey rest on several foundations:
- an understanding of the goal the sponsor wants to reach,
- a deep understanding of the sponsor's organization and their business,
- an evaluation of what the participants need to learn in order to be able to reach the goal,

- an understanding of the way people learn and create,
- a large, evolved repertoire of ideas and strategies to give people that learning, and
- a "written in pencil" plan for how to give the participants that learning in this situation.

Double Vision

As the Key Facilitator stands in front of the room, as the Process Facilitator watches and "takes the pulse" of the participants, as scribes scribe and writers write, they all keep two images in mind simultaneously. One is the vision of where the participants have to be to achieve the goal; the other is a no-nonsense evaluation of where the participants are right now. Are they learning? Are they stuck? Are they where they need to be?

As long as learning is going on, and the participants are moving toward the goal, the design for the DesignShop activities is considered valid. The Key Facilitator is there to keep implementing the design: to keep the learning going, to exemplify desirable behavior, to prevent dysfunctional behavior, to keep the group working the problem until they have extracted maximum value, to urge them on if they have come to closure too soon.

"Facilitating" in a DesignShop Event Is Not Your Normal Facilitation

DesignShop facilitation calls for a different type of interaction than what is customarily done by people called "facilitators" or "management consultants." The Key Facilitator role, in particular, is a wonderful lens to use in focusing on just how different this style of work is from the way things are normally done in a non-DesignShop environment.

The facilitator is not the star. The ideal facilitator would be invisible to the participants; the environment would be so compelling and the exercises so engaging that the work of the facilitator would never actually be noticed.

The facilitator is not the star. The ideal facilitator would be invisible to the participants; the environment would be so compelling and the exercises so engaging that the work of the facilitator would never actually be noticed.

No Hiding Out for the Facilitator

Most traditional rules of facilitation are designed to protect the facilitator. For example, traditional facilitators are not supposed to be engaged, and they aren't supposed to be knowledgeable about content issues. They are just watching the process. This, in effect, is to protect the facilitator from the participants.

In a DesignShop session, the facilitator needs to be a model, an exemplar of being cooperative, communicative, and creative. Hiding out behind a wall of rules, not engaging in discussion, not contributing ideas, not disclosing feelings and thoughts isn't going to cut it.

In a DesignShop session, the facilitator needs to be a model, an exemplar of being cooperative, communicative, and creative. Hiding out behind a wall of rules, not engaging in discussion, not contributing ideas, not disclosing feelings and thoughts isn't going to cut it. Rather than being buffered by and sheltered by these facilitation rules, the facilitator is called on to place himself or herself on the line and in the path of direct conflict, if that is what it takes for the objectives to be met, for the company to succeed.

"In certain threatening circumstances," says Matt Taylor, "I will deliberately show complete openness, expose my vulnerabilities to the whole group, at a very early point. It tells them it is OK. I have to exemplify the behavior I want them to display."

Traditional Methods Unacceptable

An obvious implication is that facilitators experienced in traditional techniques need to dump their standard intervention strategies for controlling behavior. A traditional facilitation technique classifies people according to "types" and justifies mistreating them in ways that lets the facilitator control their behavior—say, by moving up in front and turning his back on a "dominator type." Other forms of encounter groups "legitimize" facilitator safety while brutalizing participants. Not acceptable here.

Chip offers this comment: "This is not an encounter session. It is not an intervention. It is not a 'group-grope' and it isn't brainstorming." None of these traditional methods exemplifies the behavior of people being creative, cooperative, and performing at their maximum.

People are not "types" to be controlled—they are individuals who all have the potential to be creative, cooperative and full of good ideas. Chip exemplifies this attitude when he talks about facilitating "difficult types": "I love it when a breakout team complains that one of their members is being cynical and shooting down ideas. Because once someone cynical latches onto an idea, he or she can really take that idea and run with it. And a cynic adds value through not letting the team get carried away on a positive tide of groupthink."

No Pretense of "Objectivity," "Remoteness," or Being Outside the Game

Traditionally, facilitators learn to split between process and content. They are also taught to believe that they can be "objective"—detached and indifferent to the content, focused purely and cleanly on process. But consciously or subconsciously, any facilitator is going to make process decisions based on content. So unless facilitators understand that they are unavoidably in the content already, they are doing a disservice to the client.

Here, everyone is in the game with participants; no one stands on the outside. DesignShop facilitators contribute their own content ideas if they have them, but they don't pretend they are content-neutral. And as we've seen, DesignShop facilitators offer outstanding business insights.

What Is Important Here Is Not Style

Facilitating a DesignShop event doesn't require any single style of facilitation. Facilitators can and do work in a variety of different styles. Different styles are often much better at various points during the process development. You pick your strengths, and from that set you develop your style of facilitation. Any style is appropriate as long as the facilitator is willing to invest in the design process, to take risks, to be very open, to be a co-designer, to collaborate in the work, and to stay focused on the outcome.

It's Not Just the Furniture Or Any One Thing. It's the Whole Thing.

People who have done facilitation work before tend to miss the integration of environment, tools, and processes that make the DesignShop experience work. Sometimes they identify a particular feature, understand its importance, but then

Seven Domains Model
http://www.mgtaylor.com/
mgtaylor/glasbead/sevndoms.htm

Figuring out what experiences, what exercises, what adventures need to be created to help the participants solve their problems tomorrow is a primary function of the facilitation team.

assume that this will give them all the magic. They'll say, "Hey, those big work walls are great. I'll get those and then I'll have the whole thing." Although big work walls are a tremendously useful tool, there's a lot more to the DesignShop process than just this.

Other folks will notice some aspect of the process and think that this is the magic ingredient. "Ah," they'll say, "I'll take my standard exercise and add this detail to it." Or they will think, "Oh, the big deal is that it is interactive, so I'll make my exercise interactive." Or, "Hey, the exercises are written, so I'll make them written." Or, "I get it—stay in Scan a long time." True, very true, but that's not all.

No Preset Program...But There Is a Design

Traditional facilitators walk in with a preset program which they are going to run participants through. That is not what is going to happen here: the journey changes to accommodate the needs of the participants.

Or, "traditionalists" will try to turn it into a rote formula. This is like saying, "The Wharton DesignShop facilitators used these exercises in this sequence, so I'll just tweak this a little and use it for solving our unique business problem." This is a guaranteed waste of time, and possibly even harmful.

The problem in all these examples is that people are seeing the pieces without seeing how a DesignShop event comes together as a whole.

The Designers at Work

Back within the circle of the facilitation team, there is no question that they see the design as a whole. They understand the creative process issues that have been woven into it, and how to evaluate where the participants stand and where they need to go. The analysis is roaring along and appearing on the workwalls—multiple conversations all focused on these issues. Consider these diagnostic comments the facilitator team made: "They are having a problem with their identity; they aren't sure who they are now that the situation has changed...they need to spend more time with their vision...this group is confusing the bottom line with their motivation for being in business." The team put their fingers right on the areas of weakness for each group. Figuring out what experiences, what exercises, what adventures need to be created to help the participants solve their problems tomorrow is a primary function of the facilitation team.

Navigation Centers: Designing Sessions in the Nav Center
http://www.mgtaylor.com/mgtaylor/jotm/spring97/session_design.htm

Magic Behind the Scenes

What is going on here is happening at very high speed. But if you filmed it, and then slowed it down, playing it frame by frame, you could see that for this work they are using the same design and process principles on themselves that are being used in the DesignShop event at large. It is happening so fast that the stages all seem to blur together... What are we here for...the parts of scan...focus...act...test...back to scan...vision...identity...building...testing...revisiting the cycle again.

Tomorrow, all external signs of this design process will disappear. Instead, there will be exercises and work groups, but not a mention of theory. But the theory and its implentation had better be right. If any of the participant groups are going to walk out of here with a tactical plan in hand, it's got to happen tomorrow.

Scan Focus Act Model
http://www.mgtaylor.com/mgtaylor/glasbead/SFA.htm

Seven Stages of the Creative Process Model
http://www.mgtaylor.com/mgtaylor/glasbead/7stagcrp.htm

Challenge

1. Record any ideas that stood out to you while reading the chapter. Write down key words that describe seamless facilitation experiences you have enjoyed—workshops, hotel, obtaining information by phone, returning merchandise, going out to dinner. Have there been times when the facilitation was blatant or incompetent? Describe these experiences.

2. What can you do to "create high performance in everybody you touch in the service of the client"? What does it mean to facilitate and provide knowledge work support to your colleagues at work, or to your family and friends? What skills do you bring to this area of knowledge work, and what skills would you like to learn? What people and skills do you need to have around you to best support your own knowledge work? How do you find them?

Tactical Planning at Warp Speed

It's Friday morning, the last day of the Wharton DesignShop. Outside the hotel in mid-Philadelphia, there's sweltering heat, high humidity, and occasional thunderstorms—which do nothing to break the heat. Combine the weather with the high-crime environment outside the hotel, and it means that many of us haven't been outside in several days. To participants from more human-friendly external environments, it seems that the DesignShop event is an oasis constructed in hell. The two long days behind them and the nine-hour marathon ahead don't seem to have tired anyone out. The participants come in gladly, picking up breakfast as they head toward the large group meeting area.

As people ingest their doses of caffeine, Matt and Gail sketch out the tasks ahead. Today it all comes together. Each organization will leave with a detailed and critiqued action plan. For two days you can see some people have been resisting the urge to say, "Yes, that's all very well, but what exactly are we going to do?" and "That goal is too ambitious—how could we possibly accomplish it?" Implementation issues have been deliberately ignored in order to get the right goals set and the participants speaking a common language. Now it's time to figure out how to get there from here.

Or rather, how to "bring there to here." The key is to envision the preferred future state, and then see how to "bring that preferred future back to here every day, in every action you take." Who would guess that this simple reformulation of the implementation challenge could make a difference?

MG Taylor Axioms
http://www.mgtaylor.com/
mgtaylor/glasbead/axioms.htm

Leaping the Abyss: Putting Group Genius to Work

Gail Taylor points out that, "Today will be 80% of the work." What does she mean by that? The whole group has been working their tails off the entire time. Sure, it's been a non-standard kind of work—different from what they do back at the home office—but it's been intense. So what could "80% of the work getting done today" mean? Maybe it means that all of the "real" work will get done today, because today is when the action plan—the most concrete product—gets written.

We asked Chip Saltsman of Ernst & Young what he thought Gail meant by this. Chip's numbers are a little different, but the idea is the same:

> If on the first day we get X amount done, then on the second day we'll get 2X, and on the third day we'll get 4X done. On the third day, if we say, "We're half way through," people say "huh?" But, we'll get more done on that last day than we did during the prior two days. Once the group is aligned on what their answer is, they are capable of incredible output, working in parallel.

As everyone prepares to separate into organization-based teams, Matt has a final challenge:

> When I was a builder-architect and said we could build a building 10% faster, people would say "So what?" But if you said that we had nine months, but would do it in six weeks, bam! A big change is easier to get alignment on than a little change. Don't exhaust yourself in the little changes. We have to make deep changes, or be victims of change.

Matt's advice as they launch themselves into work helps add to the creative tension. Chip adds,

> You want to be building up creative tension. If you are shooting an arrow, and only draw back the bowstring halfway, the shaft barely travels. If you pull the bow back to your ear, the arrow really flies. Creativity comes out of the conundrum of the need to be organized and flexible at the same time. People who say, "I need to work under pressure, I need to be worried"—that's creative tension. Many of these insights are well described by Mihaly Csikszentmihalyi in his book *Creativity*. He points out that, in creativity, a state of tension exists between being:

> REBELLIOUS — CONSERVATIVE
> PASSIONATE — OBJECTIVE
> HUMBLE — PROUD
> IMAGINATIVE — ROOTED IN REALITY
> PLAYFUL — DISCIPLINED

Tactical Planning at Warp Speed

For the next three hours, the various organizations work intensely and creatively on their plans.

Transitioning from Focus to Act

In what ways does the strategic and tactical work about to be done in the DesignShop session differ from the same type of work done by the same people back home? Chip offers,

> At a DesignShop event, everything is happening faster. The work is much more collaborative. This may be a group of executives who have never come together before to work on these issues, but the communication is outstanding, because you've begun speaking the same language. They may be deluded that they all speak the same language in their work life but, in fact, they speak 'dialects' depending on location and function.

How do you tell when you are ready to move from Focus into Act? And what is that moment like when all are focused solely on one company and its issues, in contrast to the wide range of groups gathered here at Wharton? Chip explains:

> In a large group, the transition to Act usually comes around some kind of an emotional synthesis conversation. They have to talk it out in a long, emotional discussion—an intense conversation. In order to reach their destination, they have to walk away from something. It's obvious that the group has reached a decision, and it is now time to act on it. Sometimes you feel the "we gotta do that" feeling.

> This is a culmination of a pattern that started back on Day 1 during Scan. You've spent two days getting them loaded up to do the work on Day 3. The linear types want to do Day 3 when they walk in the door—they want to solve it first. However, the creative process doesn't work that way.

> During Scan and Focus, you are also working through the questions of identity and vision. When you are dealing with identity, you are asking, "Who are we? What kind of problems and conditions are we are dealing with?" You look at it from many different vantage points and develop lots of different ways to see the problem.

> When you are developing vision, you ask, "How do you see it going into the future? What does "there" look like? What's the difference? What is it about the new "there" that allows different operating conditions?" You get your hands dirty sometimes when you're busting some cherished beliefs. "Who said anything about bicycles? Why do we have to be a bicycle company? Why

Scan Focus Act Model
http://www.mgtaylor.com/
mgtaylor/glasbead/SFA.htm

not a transportation company? Why not a toy company? A racing company? Who said we have to do it that old way? [It's like Carl's Jr.—are we a lunch concept? a sandwich concept? what are we?] Expect that there will be moments of "What the heck am I doing?"

In working with intent, you have to see if you have the resolution to go through with it. When the group has that conviction, you hear, "By golly, we are going to solve the problem." You can ask yourself the test questions—Are you excited yet? Do you have the juice to make it happen?

You have got to have a problem to solve. And the group has to feel that this is a problem worth solving. Often it is up to the leader to articulate this, to stand up and say, "We aren't going back to the old way. I'm burning the boats behind you." Very often, you need to achieve Intent before you get the Insight on how to do it.

Insight is the ah-ha! the Eureka! The moment when everything slips into place. In the rest of our lives, we use words like "breakthrough," "epiphany," "getting religion." It's the moment you imagine a design and allow for a new thing that will make the future happen.

How reliably does the insight, the ah-ha, the answer, show up for people? Do people know when they have the answer? Here is Chip's perception:

Most commonly, they have the answer, but they don't know they have it.
Next most common, is that they have the answer and know it.
Third, is that they don't have it, and they know they don't.
Last is that they don't have it, and they think they do.

When a great innovation appears, it will almost certainly be in a muddle, incomplete and confusing form to the discoverer himself it will be only half understood; to everyone else it will be a mystery. For any speculation which does not at first glance look crazy, there is no hope.

—Freeman Dyson

The most mystifying is the common state of "they have the answer and they don't know they have it." What on earth does that mean?

It sounds unlikely, but it echoes as a common pattern through the various DesignShop experience stories. It means that someone in the room has spoken the golden solution, or scribed a golden solution up on the board. But so far, everyone is still hunting around rough pebbles and fool's gold, passing by the nugget again and again. Remember back at AEDC, Matt was saying, "What if it wasn't the law? What if it wasn't the law?" like a broken record, but no one could hear him. This was completely obvious to all that were outsiders to the situation, but when you're right in the middle of it, those habitual barriers and mental strings that we don't even recognize any more can block our view of a beautiful, effective solution.

The habits, mental strings, and old concepts have to be left behind.

The facilitator's job is to keep participants in the struggle, keep them engaged, moving forward, working the problem. The facilitation team is thinking, "What are the barriers that we need to remove to get them to insight?"

What the facilitator is *not* thinking is, "How do we force them into this particular answer?" As a facilitator or as a sponsor "voice of authority," you may just be itching to jump up and yell: "Look! Here's the solution to the whole problem! Just drop all this other nonsense and get with it." Resist this urge, because people don't learn from being told, they learn from the experience; they need to experience it.

The facilitation team continues vigilantly providing direction toward the goal, easing the way, but allowing the result to emerge on its own. It's analogous to how a butterfly hatches. If you think that the chrysalis is a barrier that needs to be removed and decide to help the butterfly out by slitting the chrysalis open, the butterfly will crawl out the doorway you have made. But you'll find that it will never be able to unfurl its wings, never be able to fly, never be a butterfly. Struggling to free itself from the chrysalis is an important part of the process of becoming a butterfly. Biochemical changes go on in the butterfly as it struggles, rests, and then struggles again to forge its way out of the container of its old form and into the shape and mobility of its new life. Without the biochemical learning of the struggle, you don't get the desired result.

When the group emerges from its chrysalis after the struggle, it's got wings, the energy to fly, and the deep learning that will continue to help guide each individual as he or she performs tasks during the upcoming Act segment, and also months from now and miles away.

People have to work on the problem enough to make it their own. Not until you've wrestled with it, do you own the problem and own the solution.

How Does the Facilitation Team Prepare for the Moment of Insight

The facilitation team has been concerned with how to get the participants to the moment of insight. They have also prepared the next set of steps for moving into Act, once insight has been reached.

It is often simply from want of the creative spirit that we do not go to the full extent.... And the most terrible reality brings us, with our suffering, the joy of a great discovery, because it merely gives a new and clear form to what we have long been ruminating without suspecting it.

—Marcel Proust
Remembrance of Things Past

How do you prepare for a decision that hasn't been made yet? You can do it because, most commonly, the participants have already created the solution to the problem, even though they may not recognize it yet. The pattern of the solution is more apparent to the facilitators, or to anyone who is not wrestling to rid themselves of a conceptual barrier.

In a DesignShop session being held for a single company, the fifty to eighty participants will break into teams during Act. So using that pattern as a guide, Chip describes the continuing process:

> The night before, we'll have chunked the work into six-plus-or-minus-two bits of work. We'll select the ones we think we're going to work on.

At the moment of insight, we have created topics around which to form teams. Once the teams have crystallized around a "there," or made their decisions, we use those topics—usually on hypertiles—to validate that those are the topics that need work. Sometimes we eliminate some or add others on the spot. The participants "vote with their feet," join the topic that most interests them, and then they get to work.

In one DesignShop session for an E&Y client, the chunks related to a series of product lines. But for another one done for E&Y internally, some of the topics for the groups were:
- communicating to outside world
- what they were going to sell
- how they were going to sell it
- Internet consulting

Often, a synthesis team will be coordinating the work of all other teams. After all, there can be as many as eighty people in a DesignShop event.

The facilitation team will ask themselves, "How do we put closure on this, so that people can resist the day-to-day pressure?" Therefore, you will often have a team working on a covenant or contract.

Sometimes during Act, a new team will materialize. At an E&Y event, for example, we realized that we had to assign account execs to 300 clients. So a team came together, made the list, and then went back to their original teams.

On the last day, the morning of Day 3, the facilitator's job is to stay out of the way. By now there is usually violent agreement about what needs to be worked on. Very often participants aren't assigned to groups. They sign up for topics for which they have a passion.

> Now we are in the second half of the creative cycle: building and testing. The work is engineering: you design, you put the skeleton together, and flesh it out. You need to go through a couple of cycles of design, build, and test—multiple cuts at the same problem coming from multiple directions. You need to bring it in front of others to test it: "Well, have you considered this?" "Well, no." So they go back to their group and continue to flesh out the problem.

Reaping the Benefits from Focus

Wait a minute—doesn't this all sound just too rosy? Too easy? Unrealistic?

The reason the work goes so very quickly and yet maintains excellent quality is because you paid your dues yesterday in Focus. During Focus, every group looked at the whole solution—not at parts, the way you are now working in Act. During Focus, you did repeated stress tests of the whole situation and of entire proposed solutions.

You can stress-test an idea along many dimensions. Having two or three groups working separately on the same thing is a great way to test their solutions.

The stress tests were to look for fatal flaws and essential elements. The search for fatal flaws either went on implicitly, as in building a 3-D model, or called out explicitly, as in these examples from Chip:

> Try solving the problem, but without a key thing that they think they need. So, for E&Y it was "design a consulting practice that has one third of the people you think you need." Solving the problem without a key element brings up, "What's gotta go in the lifeboat?" You get down to the real essence.

> "You are bought by a corporate raider. You have six months to hit aggressive targets or you're history. What do you do? Can you take away the things you think you ought to have, but don't need?

This forces them to think about it not working. Since they are going to be thinking about that anyway, you may as well have it addressed explicitly and use it to test and improve the solution.

After that, every group works on different pieces of the problem. Often you get a lot of insight by having two or three groups working on the same thing. There is a constant reshuffling of teams and, with that, a constant amount of idea sharing. Either implicitly or explicitly, because they have reported-out, the ideas are exchanged throughout the group. Repeatedly, there is time to take what they are developing and stress test it. We will test the structures that the groups are proposing. We suggest: "We can divide up the work this way."

Back to Act

"Usually we have one full group check-in session." Chip explains, "The facilitators do very little talking. We facilitate the conversation so it's not dysfunctional. We test to make sure the participants don't have more to say on a particular subject. To test, we'll say, "Let's move on." Well, sometimes they have a lot more to say! When they weren't getting any more out of it, then we would move on to the next group."

The first big payoff of the ruthless stress-testing, design, and redesign in Focus is that the plan evolves like lightning. There isn't any of the standard stuff such as appointing a committee to research and plan for six to twelve months.

The next payoff is that every responsible party has already kicked the tires. If you have pulled representatives of all the stakeholders together, then the entire value web is already educated and signed up to work on the plan. Because you put the time into developing a common set of experiences and a common language, everybody is finally talking about the same thing. The standard business of months of education, selling the plan, watching it get misunderstood and distorted isn't there. In three days, start to finish, you're ready to fly with a new course of action.

E & Y Clients Do a DesignShop

Chip told us about a DesignShop event for an E&Y client, a major consumer products company. They had done an excellent job during Scan, so good that at the end of their Scan on Day 2, they had covered the work walls with 30 or 40 product ideas that were worth $100 million or more apiece.

Tactical Planning at Warp Speed

Their Focus and Act segments illustrate how testing can locate weaknesses which can then be fixed in the midst of building the Tactical Plan. It also provides an example of another issue that concerns facilitators: how to achieve closure so that people can resist the day-to-day pressure of the old environment.

As this company moves from Scan to Focus, they are looking at the work walls covered with a plethora of $100 million product ideas. Chip, standing up in front of the walls, would point to an idea and ask, "How many people here think that this one idea is easily achievable?" And then hands would go up. Eighty percent was Chip's cutoff point. Anything that got less than 80% of the participants' hands up in the air wasn't a candidate. For some ideas it was 100%—a sure thing.

At one point he stopped pointing out ideas. He turned to the participants and said: "On the board behind me is a billion dollars of easily achievable business, right now."

The room became completely silent.

Potential victories covered the walls in front of them.

Then the participants broke into groups for the next exercise: to start testing for areas of weakness in this pie-in-the-sky dream. Each team was handed an abundant supply of Post-It Notes and given the same mission: Explain "Why We Can't Do It." They had to write as many Post-its as they could, listing barriers that would prevent them from moving forward.

While the participants were off at work in their groups, the facilitation team implemented an architectural change that was going to create a major mood alteration. Using kids' building blocks, the team built a big brick wall that stood as a barrier between where the participants would be sitting and their $1 billion of sure-fire new products on the work walls.

When everyone came back for the last exercise of Day 2, there was a brick wall between them and their goal. Then, things got even worse. The next exercise was the report out dealing with "Why We Can't Do It."

The Surprising and the Straightforward give rise to each other As they rotate and cycle without end. Who can exhaust them?

—Sun Tzu
The Art of Strategy

Group after group showed up with their pile of yellow stickies and read through all the reasons why the company was never going to reach the goal of a new $1 billion in products. They were all cultural, organizational reasons: "We won't work together." Each yellow sticky in turn went up on the brick wall, until the surface was covered with them. It was a visual representation that the cultural issues were what stood between the people and the achievement of their goal.

With all these problems staring at them, blocking them, the participants were told that they were finished for the day. Time to go home.

The president took the barriers like a real blow. The participants went home a sobered bunch.

But, they were asked not to think about the problem that night. Instead, they were asked to sleep on it, and write down their first idea upon waking the next morning.

Day 3: Moving from Focus into Act

When they showed up in the morning, the brick wall and the yellow stickies were gone, but the tension of what it all meant hadn't dissipated. This was deliberate. The designers wanted the tension created by the brick wall to be the springboard for moving from Focus to Act. It was.

According to Chip, "After about two-and-a-half hours of discussion and they were ready to go Act. Teams formed around eight promising product lines, one on option prioritization, synthesis, barriers and vision. After a one o'clock check in, the president huddled with his executive team to polish the vision while the rest of the teams plowed on."

The final report-out of the day was staged so that the product lines went in order of increasing drama.

The second to the last report was done by the Barriers team. The Barriers team built another brick wall, smaller than the original monster, but replete with the emotion and symbolism of the first. With the wall lurking there, they presented a vision of how they would like the company to be, a plan for getting there, and a personal committment to follow.

Tactical Planning at Warp Speed

Now it was time for the last group to report. What could this group possibly say or do that would overcome the crushing weight, the impossible barrier of all those reasons for failure?

Suddenly, bricks and yellow stickies went flying as the president smashed his way through the brick wall. The whole group was on its feet, cheering, applauding. "Here's our vision!" he said, the work that he and his team had been doing to guarantee success. The president worked his way through the new operating imperatives that had been created that day, swept the barriers aside, and presented the new vision.

People came out of the DesignShop event pumped up. The group left on a huge high.

> "Later, we got a call from the president. He said, 'The corporate jet doesn't need fuel to get back home.'"

The wide-ranging work of Scan and the stress-testing of Focus left them stronger. The stress-testing of cultural issues was clearly uncomfortable. But the way out of the problem is *through* the problem—and, in this case, "through the wall" as well. This group left the session with a dynamite plan, and the path smoothed of obstacles in order to help that plan succeed.

The unmistakable statement of the physical presence of the wall and the unmistakable statement in the president's smashing the barrier did more convincing than hours of discussion or debate could. It put an intellectual, behavioral, and emotional seal on the work that has been done.

Symbolic acts have a strong, powerful emotional impact. At another DesignShop event facilitated by Ernst & Young, they performed a symbolic act to indicate that the past was gone. On a red card each participant was to write the thing that they were leaving behind. On a green card, each wrote the idea that they were bringing home. Leave this old attitude behind—take this new idea home.

"Hmmm," said Chip as he thought about it. "We should have burned the bad thing, maybe used flash paper, do something to blow it up. That would have been even more effective."

On the day of victory no one is tired.

—Arab proverb

The Eagle in Action

Back here at Wharton, the progress in the groups is strong. People are working intensely. Ideas and iterations happen quickly. There are no pauses in work process, no lulls. It really is fast-paced action.

The F-15 group with Col. Bill is having a great time. They work like those old DesignShop pros over at the AEDC breakout.

The DesignShop process spread into the military the same way it has spread among commercial organizations—through word of mouth by people who have seen it work. In this case, the motivating force was the migration of Col. Bill Rutley from heading up AEDC to leading the System Program Office (SPO) for the Air Force's F-15 fighter aircraft.

He had been the force behind getting DesignShop environments, tools, and processes established at AEDC, and he brought this enthusiasm with him to the SPO. In April 1994, shortly after taking his new post, he sponsored the first F-15 DesignShop event.

Col. Bill had good reason to want the best tools available. The F-15 is in a difficult position. This plane has been flying for twenty years, and it's getting old. And yet, its successor, the F-22, has been delayed so many times that now it looks as though the F-15 may have to fly until the year 2020.

How can you keep an aircraft that old flying well enough to fight wars? Especially since there appears to be some kind of rule saying that a class of aircraft can't be upgraded when it will be replaced within five years by a new aircraft. With the F-22 being delayed by small increments, this means that the F-15 design could be forced to stop evolving when needed.

Moreover, the funding cycles for the aircraft are messed up, leading to instabilities in the flow of dollars. Somehow, the Air Force has got to keep winning wars until 2020 with an old aircraft and unreliable funding. Quite a challenge for Col. Bill and his team attending the Wharton event, despite their intensive training in DesignShop processes.

Tactical Planning at Warp Speed

Col. Bill had great success introducing DesignShop techniques at AEDC, but since that command changes hands every couple of years, he'd had to move on. We were curious about his next command—are the techniques being as well-received at F-15? Col. Bill:

> Here we have worldwide responsibility for over 700 airplanes and a prime contractor, plus subcontractors and international contractors. We are on the road all of the time. I am on the road 250,000 miles a year.
>
> Compared to AEDC, the DesignShop work with the F-15 program has had a tougher road because there are much more complex organizational needs—but it is having a serious, positive effect.
>
> The F-15 challenge is more difficult because it has a beginning and an end. AEDC has no definable end whatsoever. But by the year 2025 or so, most F-15s will be out of service. There is a complete life/death cycle and no return after death. Also the F-15, like AEDC, had not thought about where it was going to be in the future. It will now have twice the life anyone anticipated. But due to the short lifetime expectation for the aircraft, no one thought beyond one to five years out. SPOs [System Program Offices] have a very short reach.
>
> Here's how life is at F-15: You get a phone call from Washington, and someone is mad and wants something today, and so that item is shipped. You get a call from England, and they have a jet down, and you work that now and drop everything else. There is a higher level of fire-fighting and near-term focus than at AEDC.
>
> AEDC has a sense of history. I was able to capitalize on that by using the DesignShop experience to remind them of it. Now at F-15, there are also some things to capitalize on. There is a real loyalty to the airplane. It is like the World War II Spitfires—very emotional. There is a sense of the history of the airplane and what it means to the war fighter.
>
> I constantly point out that, of the people who will be flying the airplane, some have not been born yet. We have a tremendous responsibility to make the right decisions in the next few years. Because of the way our budget cycle works, if we screw it up today, the recovery will not occur until close to the end of the life of the jet. The critical investments are being made from now to the year 2000, and we have to make the right decisions.
>
> A budget downturn is necessary, and what we have to do is to reengineer, reconfigure, reinvent the box it will fit in, and redo this thing with our contractor teammate so that the war fighter never knows the difference. The fact

that things are changing back here is irrelevant to them. All they want is a plane that does the job every day, every place.

With the F-15, we have already had breakthroughs. We call one the Eagle Enterprise, which addresses the problem of how to neutralize geography, time, and cultural differences. We recognize that we are scattered all over the place, and we have to have technology and ways of thinking about each other and working with each other that neutralize time and culture differences. Deacon is the head of that. He is a bright young guy making a lot of headway. That is evolving.

The broader effort with Matt and Gail has been two-fold: One, to effect the cultural evolution of the F-15 program and to aid that. This combined command is only three years old, although the airplane is 20. Previously, there were two separate commands in separate locations. Although the F-15 SPO still has two locations, Wright-Patterson Air Force Base and Robins Air Force Base, they both work for the F-15 SPO Director. Now they are all one organization working with the same mission.

There is still a lot of that left-over culture from the two organizations. They are not completely one organization. It's a merger situation in which our predecessors kind of stapled the organizations together. You can still see the cultures of the old organizations, with really large differences. It used to be that the group at Wright Patterson did not even speak to the people at Warner Robins. Now, due in large part to the DesignShop series, Wright Patterson is beginning to understand what Warner Robins is doing, and Warner Robins is beginning to understand what Wright Patterson is doing—it is starting to be more and more one team.

We found a facilitator at the Wharton event who had also been at the key F-15 "merger" DesignShop session. While not as colorful as burying a hatchet, Gunner Kaersvang recounts, it was indeed a dramatic change which emerged as a natural part of the process of working in this environment and having a common experience:

> I was at the particular F-15 DesignShop session when they were integrating the north and south sections. There was a lot of animosity between the two groups. All of a sudden, it clicked. They had a fuss they called a "furball." Then the two groups were milling together in the middle of the room, and they were so excited that they were talking so loud that I could hardly get them to hear me. It was incredible.

Tactical Planning at Warp Speed

Col. Bill is now having some success with using the DesignShop processes to work with those outside his direct command:

> We are also bringing in more and more people who work on the F-15 who do not work for me. I do not "own" about 8000 people out there who do things for us. Engines, for example, are technically out of my control. In fact, they work very well with us and work to our requirements. They are coming in through the DesignShop approach as well.

> Here's part of the reason—If you sit down and are separated by tables, like in a routine staff meeting, everyone is already in a fixed position when they come through the door. There might be utility in doing that for routine things. There is no utility in doing it for serious thinking—serious D&D [dialogue and debate]. Everyone has to get his passions, questions, and feelings on the table without being called an idiot. It worked that way at AEDC, and it is working that way here.

And, in fact, here at Wharton we can see that it is working just fine. It would be understandable if everyone associated with the F-15 was burned out and frustrated—they have been working for so long to keep an old system working, with resources that alternate between sufficient and insufficient, seemingly at random, based on politics in Washington rather than on the needs of the war fighter whose life is on the line. This is more than enough reason for morale problems, one would think.

Instead, we see a highly-motivated, upbeat team which accepts their situation cheerfully and focuses on coming up with creative ways to deal with it. One task for this DesignShop session is figuring out how to better communicate the effects of randomly fluctuating funding to Congress. It is a complex system in which erratic funding cuts can lead to serious waste, not just of money but potentially of human lives as well. Often it is not the exact size of the budget that causes the problems, but instead the sudden changes. It must be like trying to run an industry at the whim of a bunch of emotional Norse gods without memories. Col. Bill words it succinctly for us: "Washington is going down a slippery slope and they cannot see the abyss. This is due to their feedback loops. You have a one-year budget system with two-to-four-year feedback."

The problem should not be so hard for Washington to understand.

Now, up on the F-15 wallboard is a diagram of the F-15 funding, decision making, and work process. The discontinuities, the break points where problems arise, stand out bright and clear. This summary diagram can now be the basis of a new tactical plan for communications with Washington.

This is just the beginning of a more ambitious project that would enable Washington to get a much better feel for the effects of their funding decisions. Matt explains:

> The long-range goal, about 4-5 years out, is to take something like SimCity software and actually put the F-15 "game" on it, and then hand it to Congress. Then they can experiment: "If I do this with appropriations, and this with readiness, and this with that over there, here's what happens to casualties and the country's ability to win a conflict."

Bill concludes his story with an explicit discussion of the issue of morale and commitment:

> Our entire group should get together every ninety days. I am convinced that to manage a group you should do that. But for us to get together every six months is about all we can do.
>
> Outside the DesignShop process, normally you will have one meeting addressing one topic—but not within any context, unless you are lucky. You sit around a rigid table and get a briefing and send it back to the drawing board. For a lot of things that are routine, day-to-day activities, that works, and you would not want to do a DesignShop approach for them.
>
> But with all of that taking place as individual actions, without DesignShop events you have no idea where you are taking the entire program. It ends up somewhere by accident, and you do not know where the strategic vector is going. People just do not know. They say, "I don't know where I am going, and Rutley is supposed to figure it out."
>
> But when you have people from every corner of the organization together, and bring all that to bear, it forces people who don't want to be accountable to find out that accountability is neat, and they begin to engage. It is fun to watch. There are some who do not want to engage. They do their job every day, but it is hard to get them to engage beyond that. There is a place for that, and it is OK. But using the DesignShop methods, you get more and more people to engage, and it spreads like wildfire. It was like that at AEDC and is getting there at F-15.

Tactical Planning at Warp Speed

Rapid Iteration:
Design, Build, Test. Redesign, Build, Test.

Not only is the Wharton F-15 group going like a house on fire. So is the E&Y team, and the AEDC team…all the groups.

After three hours of impassioned and detailed planning, with each team assisted by facilitators, the groups emerge ready to present their results for peer review and more stress-testing. The comments this time are more content-oriented, less focused on making sure that the presenting team has used a process that digs deeply enough. The comments and questions include:

- AEDC is asked whether they can consider offering services overseas; it's clear they've addressed the issue.

- Ernst & Young is queried about whether they will be able to get the internal support for their plan; yes, it looks good.

- F-15 is challenged: are more resources absolutely needed, or is there another way? After discussion, it appears that, yes, the team is right: given the mandate that the F-15 is ordered to fulfill, there is no other option. It emerges that faulty government accounting systems are at the heart of the problem, and the team is addressing that.

- Carl's Jr. is questioned on how they deal with having 400 COOs—the general managers. Their plan is seen to address the issue by giving them more responsibility. This critical issue of balance between the corporate business and local entrepreneurs is addressed further. So is the question of feedback on experiments—that looks good: the results of a given promotion are already available overnight.

- Orlando Regional Health System is queried on alliances and outsourcing. The response is reassuring; these are being addressed.

Overall, the teams are feeling confident about their plans, and the peer review has given them some items to recheck. It's time to iterate—the big group splits into organizational units again and takes another shot at their plans over lunch and through early afternoon.

What if someone wasn't confident about the plans? What if the stress-testing by the group had revealed a fatal flaw? What if the questioning had produced an additional flash of insight that would suggest a totally new solution?

Design, test, redesign, test again. This is what has been going on in the small groups all day long. This rapid iteration—quickly cycling through the process again and again, rapidly building a prototype solution, testing, then building a second, third, fourth, fifth prototype—has led to results that are strong, balanced, and able to withstand environmental stress. And if they break under stress—plow them under, and design again.

Wrapping It Up

At Wharton, each team has had its own facilitator with them throughout the day. Their roles have shown a whole different set of variations today: lots of testing, lots of suggesting of content ideas. One key focus of the facilitator is to make sure the participants are putting together action plans, "to do" lists, schedules that avoid what Chip calls "the empty imperative." If you hear a "somebody needs to take care of this," it has to be changed into not just "Who's going to do this?" but "Who is taking care of it and by when?" You want to really get it specified: "Bill Smith will handle X by August 2." or "All phone calls will be returned within 24 hours."

The tactical plans that are being built have detailed schedules, written specifications—things that usually take weeks or months to create.

By 3:30, it's all come together. There's another brief report out session to give each group a chance to put their results in presentation form—always a clarifying experience. Many have done graphics to illustrate their plans; these are extremely helpful.

Tactical Planning at Warp Speed

There is a sense of satisfaction, of completion, and for the first time during the DesignShop, some serious fatigue on the part of the participants. We're coming down off a high. We're thinking about catching a plane out of this hot, humid city and going home to our families.

A few participants, new to the process, are concerned about being able to take home all of their work. They are assured that not only will they get copies of what was written on the wallboards, they will also be getting a list of all the books brought as part of the library, a transcript of all of the large-group discussions, the models underlying the process itself, a synthesis work product that captures the key issues and extends the thinking done here, and even the music log. And all of it will be sent to them, Fedex, on Monday at the latest.

Jim Nicholson, a newcomer to both AEDC and to the DesignShop process, is focused on the specific results attained by his organization: "As a new member of the AEDC team, this was a new experience for me. It let the team members include me quickly. We are not leaving with just the start of a new product—we have a very demanding schedule."

John Poparad, also with the AEDC group but very familiar with the process we've just been through, sums it up: "Part of the joy of DesignShops is the ability to create a world and live in it for a while in a fully creative, non-critical manner, and then withdraw."

A senior executive, with experience as both a participant and sponsor of earlier DesignShop events, summarizes the interactions between the extremely different organizations that have made up the Wharton participants: "At a strategic level, there was a lot in common on the issues. We are all going in the same direction. For everyone, it is the transition that is the difficulty." It's a double transition that everyone is facing—the transition back to the home environment, and the work to implement the transition to the vision of the future that everyone has just detailed out.

The final farewell from Matt may bring closure to the event, but it opens the door to all the work to be done once everyone is back home. With a joke from Col. Bill Rutley and a burst of laughter, participants race to grab suitcases and dash to the airport. Carrying the plans and visions that they have created over the last three days, they are about to bring the future back to the present.

Tactical Planning at Warp Speed

Challenge

1. Record ideas and questions from this chapter to add to your growing library of observations.

2. It's time to pull together and iterate your vision, and then delineate how you will bring the vision the preferred future back to here every day, in every action you take. It's also time to test again to make sure the vision is large enough to embrace your whole potential and the potential of your enterprise. "Don't exhaust yourself in the little changes. We have to make deep changes, or be victims of change."

3. Go back to all of your work from previous chapters:
    models of collaboration
    models of environment
    models of overcoming limiting practices
    models of the problem-solving toolbox
    models of education
    models of your enterprise as an integrated ecosystem
    a physical model of the enterprise or a critique from a respected deep thinker of facilitation.

    Now pull it all into a single synthesis: a whole picture. You can mindmap it, or create a longer document. You may even wish to use a business planning template, but don't attenuate the value of your work by unnecessarily forcing it into some arbitrary form. This synthesis may be difficult and could take a while. That's OK: persevere. Work through it until you get the "ah-ha," and the patterns of the whole system clearly emerge.

4. Test the synthesis for viability and depth of change.

5. Describe and diagram how you will bring this vision back to "here" every day.

Designing the Ride

Keith Cushman of AEDC: "This process is designed. Most meetings have an agenda. That means you know *what* you are going to talk about, but not *how* you are going to talk about it. In a DesignShop experience, you know in pretty precise terms both *what* you are going to talk about *and how* you are going to talk about it."

Keys to a Successful Sponsor Meeting
http://www.mgtaylor.com/mgtaylor/jotm/fall96/chipsalt.htm

Designing the What and the How begins a month before the actual event. In a Discovery Day session, the sponsor or sponsor team, the Key Facilitator, the Process Facilitator, and other potential facilitation team members gather to develop clear objectives for the DesignShop event:

- Define the sponsors' goal, the nature of the specific task on which we will focus. A broader definition opens up a larger idea space to explore, enabling solutions to be selected from a more fabulous set of possibilities—which may end up pleasing you far more than an answer to your original problem. Is the work going to take the project through one, several, or all steps of the process of design and implementation?
- Get a general idea of what sorts of products should be generated during and after the DesignShop session.
- Assemble the right participant list.
- Decide on general logistics arrangements.
- Take a first cut at the design of the actual DesignShop event.

*Science is the art of
phrasing questions and identifying
their attendant assumptions.
The obstacles to furthering
knowledge lie in formulating
the right questions
and in circumventing
ambiguous answers,
never an easy task.
The best practitioners
know that incisive questions and
skillful analysis
will ultimately yield their reward.
New questions
may require fresh insight,
unencumbered by the baggage
of past experience,
and a probing mind
to test old concepts.*

—Robert W. McFarlane

**Designing Value Chain
Support Systems**
http://www.mgtaylor.com/
mgtaylor/jotm/fall96/valchnds.htm

To create an event for a specific company and a specific problem, the facilitation team will use a DesignShop-type environment and subset of the processes—a "Discovery Session"—for the purpose of designing the main event. Not only is each Discovery Session custom-crafted for each sponsor, but every time the sponsor brings in a new problem to be the focus of its own full-scale event, a new Discovery Session is crafted to accommodate the new problem.

You do your work in a DesignShop-style space set up to accommodate your group size and the kind of work you'll be doing. There is the same kind of facilitation that you would have in a DesignShop.

The session might be designed to start immediately with an in depth Take-a-Panel/Share-a-Panel exercise to get all the viewpoints out on the table. This is the same wide-ranging learning that goes on in a good Scan. Almost immediately, the exercise produces an extremely good set of ideas, lots of information about the company, insight into the problems, and understanding about the participant's points of view.

Using the big work walls to map out the information, the facilitation team will collect information on your culture, intentions, and contradictions about your industry and the problems you face.

The sponsor team brings technical depth: intimate, intricate knowledge about their business, the industry, the issues, and the nature of the problem. The DesignShop team has to soak up this unique knowledge from the sponsor and meld it with their knowledge of the process of bringing people through to a creative solution.

In addition to learning the content which the sponsor can provide, the facilitation team also has to determine the boundaries of that content. The sponsor and his company are already experts at solving problems in the context within which they normally operate. The "unsolvable" problems are those that require them to operate beyond that context.

The key to discovering what needs to be learned about culture, intentions, contradictions, and what constitutes going beyond normal context lies in the art of asking the right questions. Many questions will have the goal of finding the hidden boundaries and assumptions around a perceived problem—questions that bump up against the profile of your work rules, assumptions, and processes for how you do things. Imagine placing that profile on a map of all knowledge. What parts of the map are well covered? Which areas are Terra Incognita? These are the places of the most promise in which to go exploring. Which tools or processes are present in your tool kit? Which are missing? According to Chip, Matt will often "introduce really way-out ideas to a conversation to see how the sponsor teams react to them, to know what they will or will not accept, and what their blind spots are."

In addition to understanding the company's culture and the problem, the facilitators want to build excitement about the challenge. This excitement creates focus, increases energy, and helps drive the creativity required to get to a good design of the DesignShop activity.

The dialogue continues all morning.

Over lunch, you might do a version of the Authors exercise. Every participant would select a book from the big pile on the table. Some of the books may be related closely to the topics that will appear in the DesignShop session, but most of the books have a more vague relationship. The only common theme is that the books all deal with complex systems in a range of different fields. The bibliography at the end of this book has some titles you might find on the table.

You skim your book while you eat lunch, and then the group reconvenes. Each participant then plays the role of his author and tells the group what he has to say concerning the problem to be solved by the group. This can be an effective tool.

Rob Evans gives a colorful description: "You can think of this as crop rotation for the mind—for people who have been chewing on a problem and not getting anywhere."

This exercise further helps the facilitators understand the client's situation from many vantage points, and it provides the ability to see the problem in a systems context.

Together, the sponsors and the DesignShop team are going to design the event. As Chip says, "It's not something that the design team 'does to' the sponsor." It's also not something that the sponsor does to the design team. Neither the answer nor the process is canned and off the shelf. The design must provide a challenge to the client, yet also accept and work with the client's thinking style.

By the end of the day, you'll have crafted a first iteration for the design of the three-day DesignShop event. Crafting a DesignShop session is not necessarily an easy or comfortable process for the sponsors. The process is non-linear, so crafting an agenda is unlike a typical conference or meeting planning. You can tell how well the sponsor meeting went by how effective the DesignShop event is that you were able to create...

Designing *How*

The art and craft of constructing the exercises and determining the actual sequence of events is an education in itself. Rob Evans says, "It really requires working side by side with someone in the process and learning from experience."

Design of the Value Chain DesignShop
http://www.mgtaylor.com/mgtaylor/jotm/fall96/valchn01.htm

Rob, who is now developing a group of facilitators for E&Y's center, has been training with MGTaylor, taking facilitation workshop classes, working on support teams, co-facilitating Ernst & Young events, as well as cofacilitating with MG Taylor in MG Taylor WorkShops that teach E&Y and MG Taylor knowledge workers this system. Rob is describing something that is very like a Guild, the same way that doctors continue to learn medicine—with lots of hands-on experience, lots of exposure to how a senior practitioner does it. It is a passing of the craft.

There is a logical structure that underlies the creative and design process, but there are important elements which are strictly judgment-based. You might almost call them aesthetic criteria. Like any complex process, there is a large body of knowledge on how to successfully work with intricate sequences and processes. Reading theory is an excellent foundation, but learning by doing—trial and error, modeling off a successful pattern—is essential.

A DesignShop event is usually built on the pattern of an intellectual model.

Scan Focus Act Model
http://www.mgtaylor.com/mgtaylor/glasbead/SFA.htm

The Wharton DesignShop event was built on the model of Scan/Focus/Act, the most commonly used model for these events. Scan/Focus/Act is also the easiest model to use. Many large DesignShop sessions are three or four-day events, so for the Wharton three-day event, day one was designed as a Scan, day two as the Focus, and day three as the Act.

Each day of the DesignShop session will repeat the pattern model as well: so Day 1 will have its own Scan, Focus, and Act components, and so will Day 2 and Day 3. Chip includes: "By using this matrix as a rough template, a facilitator can construct a robust design to help a group achieve high levels of performance and surprising creativity."

To get additional richness, the design plays several additional models together against the company's situation. So, while participants are involved in Scan, they will also start working with some additional model. The model we are going to look at playing against Scan/Focus/Act is the Creative Process model.

Creative Process Model

The Creative Process model is one of the three or four pieces of knowledge which almost every facilitator would choose to have with them on a desert island. It is the easiest model to dismiss as a waste of time, creative sentimentality, self-indulgence, too touchy-feely, fluffy, and modeling overkill. The only thing you can say in its behalf is that it keeps showing up again and again in successful DesignShop events, and seems to be the key to devising a way to get companies to solve their problems. So, if it weren't for the fact that it works—you could feel free to ignore it.

This model of the creative process has two halves. The second half, Designing, Building/Engineering and Testing/Using, is where we are usually the most comfortable, because that is where we already know what our mission is, and all we have to do is build it. Action-oriented folks, or people who can't tolerate the anxiety that goes with the first half of the cycle, want to head for the building stage right away.

The first half of the cycle holds the uncomfortable stuff: Identity (Who are we as an organization?), Vision (What are the opportunities? What can we accomplish?), and Intent (What do we want to do?). Often by reframing these issues into the

Seven Stages of the Creative Process Model
http://www.mgtaylor.com/mgtaylor/glasbead/7stagcrp.htm

larger context provided by Scan, solutions that were not apparent before become clear. As a result, it produces a phase called Insight.

Just to show how the intangible, fluffy issues of Identity, Vision, and Intent get in the way of a logical, can-do attitude, look at this example of a recent DesignShop event:

Gail Taylor and Chip Saltsman were key facilitators for a major conglomerate, a company that brought together things as disparate as imaginable under one roof. In the DesignShop session the participants struggled miserably, as they clearly did every single working day, with the issues of what did these different things have in common, where are the synergies, how do they fit or not fit together? The words that they used to describe their problem were, "We can't make decisions; we just have trouble making decisions."

Value Chain DesignShop Analysis
http://www.mgtaylor.com/mgtaylor/jotm/fall96/valchn04.htm

Had they analyzed the problem correctly? Was there something wrong with their ability to make decisions?

The company was good at talking and generating ideas, and even good at selecting action. But they were miserable at actually doing something. Part of the problem was that the firm was a hierarchy, but not everyone knew who owned who and where responsibility lay. They tended to go through a lot of motions, but no action resulted.

As Chip listened to the participants talk, he said, "I heard no passion in the report-outs." The only passion was arguing over parking spaces!"

Gail observed the same thing. She fed her perceptions back to the participants: "Here, I see a company whose vision is to make money, and you want to do it with some integrity."

It brought the participants up short. "That's not what we want," they objected. Shortly afterward, they started talking to each other and communicating more freely about issues of passion and compassion. The team was hungry for more meaning in their life and in their work.

On the second day, writers came up with a scenario that helped them crystallize their search for meaning.

It was called: "Do or Die."

A variant of the Backcasting Exercise, Do or Die time traveled the participants two years into the future. Here is what they were faced with: "The worst of all possible things has happened, and your entire company has tanked. You are standing in line at the unemployment office, and the guy next to you asks what happened. Tell us the sad story. Tell us about what went wrong. Tell us how this became all screwed up."

Like Backcasting a positive outcome, Backcasting a negative outcome has a profoundly powerful effect. In this case, it is to bring your worst fears to the surface and release you from the emotional constraints that never let you talk about them before. After all, the worst has already happened: the whole company went down in flames, you are all out on the street, and the reasons for it aren't taboo any more—they are being written up as business gossip in the newspaper. It's time to come clean: "We were all so busy protecting our own turf, that we never saw what was coming at us. We can't stand listening to ideas that weren't invented here."

There was nothing wrong with these peoples' decision-making skills and abilities—they were fine decision makers. They were bright, talented, and competent. But they were treating "inability to make decisions" as the problem, when in fact it was merely a symptom of the real issues of Identity and Vision.

The Creative Cycle Never Stops

At first glance, we might assume a company runs the Creative Cycle only once: when the first decisions are made about "who we are as a company, what our mission is, whether we have the will and motivation to do it." From there, the company moves on to building product, testing it in the market, and never looks back.

But is that really it? Even if you brought the product to market with wild success, are you now finished forever? No...you're back to "what do we do next?" Over time, as your product evolves and the environment changes, the old identity and the new reality no longer sync up. AEDC's identity went out of sync as soon as the environment, via Congress, wouldn't let them be the same people they had considered themselves before. Carl's Jr's "we are a sandwich concept" identity meant they couldn't be a dinner business unless they changed their identity or convinced America to eat sandwiches for dinner. That's the pesky thing about life— the challenges and the questions just go on and on.

Matt:

There are still many organizations out there, looking for the one-time change. They can get suckered into the idea that this one technique, this one right answer is what will get them out of their current jam. Instead, they need a way of learning how to stay out of jams permanently. The new task of learning is to catalyze changes, renewal, problem reformulation, and innovation.

To grow, you need to be continually learning, and in the process redefining yourself in a spiral that moves ever upward. In movies, theater, novels, even fairy stories, we get to see the whole Creative Cycle play and replay. In any story about an individual hero, or the basketball team, or army platoon, or math class, the dynamic is one of repeat challenges. The hero needs to show growth and transformation, because the alternative is decline and death. Each challenge is a new step up the ladder, the problem set is tougher, and it demands new resolve— new Identity—from the hero.

How Do Scan and the Creative Cycle Interplay?

OK, it looks like the Creative Process Cycle is going to be around for the long haul. So how do you get two models to "play against each other"?

On the first day of the Wharton DesignShop event, the participants launched into Scan with the initial Backcasting exercise. They were assigned to groups and asked what were the important discoveries and innovations, themes, basic assumptions, and paradigms by which they had lived their lives over the last century. This produced lively group debate, disagreement, and, in the process, learning.

When the entire group reassembled and reportouts were requested, note that the answers the groups had prepared were *not* requested. This learning was instead folded back in to provide the basis of what came next. The participants were asked to stand as individuals and select the one event in the last century which had the most personal significance to them. This kind of question touches directly on the issues of the Creative Cycle: Identity, Vision, Intent, and Insight. Who am I? What do I care about passionately?

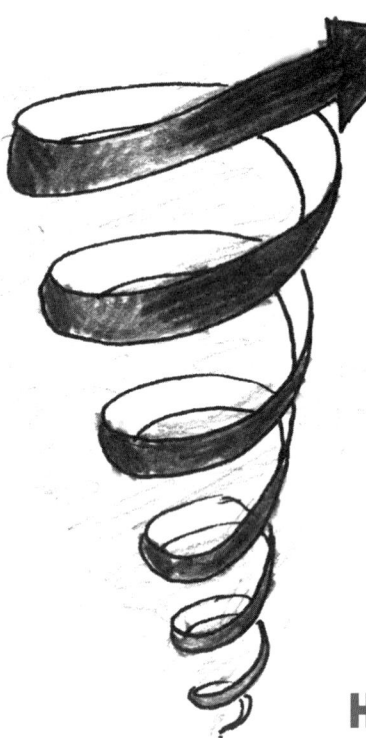

There was unexpected richness produced by this—people learning about themselves, people getting insights into other points of view, theoretical things like "paradigms" suddenly became full of personalized meaning.

Going through the process as a participant didn't feel dizzying. But when you start to think about designing an event with cycles running inside other cycles the room starts spinning. Why all this cycling?

Nonlinear Process : Growing an Idea

In a knowledge economy, people should be able to design a process that produces an idea as a result, even when the system they are dealing with is inherently too complex for one human to understand. This process needs to be nonlinear, especially when working with the first half of the creative cycle.

During the last century, the Western world became skilled at working with linear processes. There is a real urge to fit everything into a linear mode. Rob, who already comes from a background rich in facilitation, teaching, and exposure to many of these issues, sees how skilled and comfortable we are with linear work. "People are used to putting together linear meetings where they can show how each piece of the meeting contributes a bit of the final solution. And we're pretty good at meeting skills: make an agenda, push the agenda, manage the discussion."

But the problems that stymie us are those with overwhelming complexity. These are precisely the places where the linear solutions fail us. People let linear methods undermine them when they say, "My problem is so complex that I can only consider one or two options."

"You can see the whole DesignShop process working best," says Chip, "when what you have is a big, complex problem, with lots of people geographically dispersed." Chip goes on delineating complexity after complexity, gleefully describing a business nightmare.

Rob points out how difficult it is to describe nonlinear processes to all of us who are so accustomed to the straight and narrow:

> The nonlinear design processes are the hardest to translate. They are a lot more like growing a garden than putting together a clock. It's a little like

Complexity Theory Applied to the Enterprise
http://www.mgtaylor.com/mgtaylor/jotm/summer97/complexity.htm

The significant problems we face cannot be solved at the same level of thinking we used when we created them.

— Albert Einstein

understanding the role of scaffolding or concrete forms in creating a building. You could say, "Why are you wasting your time putting up scaffolding or building forms, things that don't match the final shape of the building, things that you build and then just tear down?" But the forms are what we use to pour the concrete for the real thing. To get the real building in the right shape, we do a lot of things that don't match the final shape, but they contribute to the end product.

But this is a whole different process. This is more about designing an outcome, an exercise in assembling complexity. In Kevin Kelly's book *Out of Control*, he talks about the difficulty of trying to reclaim farm land outside Chicago and returning it to prairie. "It is difficult because..."

Chip picks up: "In the natural world, you can't assemble complexity into what it's going to look like in its final state. You don't build a prairie by putting in this plant species and that bird species. Prairies emerge from processes. For example, they need fires periodically to clear out competing species. The seeds of some prairie species will only germinate from the heat of fire."

In complex environmental situations, the linear approach of "go in and directly construct the desired endstate" doesn't work. For the complex, multidimensional problems that we increasingly face in the business environment, nonlinear processes are the only way to deal with the complexity.

So, like restoring a prairie, the process of creating an idea is to go through the cycles of winter, spring, summer, fall; flood, fire, rain, drought. Yes, we may need to reimport water if the spring that fed the area was diverted, but much of the task is providing a rich enough matrix and allowing the process to cycle through to reestablish balance.

Maybe the best way to describe this is as "the process of growing an idea."

Growth During a Nonlinear Event

The DesignShop equivalent to winter/spring/summer/fall is recursion and iteration: repetition. Running through a process again. And then again. Each time from a different perspective.

Designing the Ride

"Recursion" or "iteration" or "repetition" does not mean Goldilocks-and-the-Three-Bears testing, where the first bowl of porridge was too hot; the second bowl too cold; and the third bowl of porridge was just right. Goldilocks is testing only; she isn't redesigning and learning to make Perfect Porridge.

The notion here is to build, test, tear down. Redesign, build, and test again. That is why the sessions are not brainstorming. In brainstorming, you generate ideas, and then you go off to implement them. Here, you bring the ideas all the way to test, then fold them back in and design again.

"It's like plowing the crop back in." Like a farmer raising alfalfa with the deliberate intention of plowing it back in to enrich the soil with nitrogen for the next season's crop.

Like the process of learning to create using clay on a potter's wheel:

> You use the mass of your whole body, transmitted through your hands, to guide the clay to what you believe is the center of the large, horizontal potter's wheel. You start the wheel spinning rapidly and your hands shape the clay into a cone. At high RPM, you do a visual test. Do you see a perfectly symmetrical cone? Or, do you see a wobble, a distortion in the shape? If you do, you are off center. Maybe you test again—holding a fine pencil tip steady, does it trace an even line around the perimeter of the sphere? It looks okay, you think.
>
> You start to build, using your hands and the wheel's centrifugal force to open the interior and raise the walls of the pot. The pot climbs up to fulfill its mature height and shape. In that instant, your hands feel a slight wobble—barely detectable—a centering flaw. The distortion becomes wilder and wilder. The flaw amplifies, yawing wildly out of control and into collapse.
>
> Growth tested the stability and structure, and they were found wanting. The pot is gone, but not thrown away. You fold the structure back into the pliable clay. The learning that produced that pot—its short-lived beauty and its flaws—has been experientially folded into you, the potter.
>
> You reshape the clay and put it back on the wheel to center it again. Next time, you will do better. Your new knowledge will transmit through your body, into your hands, into the clay, until at last the vessel you envisioned in your mind stands before you.

Designing the *What*

Let's shift from looking at the How of the DesignShop process, to looking at the What. "What" is the technical content that we want to offer to people to help them solve their problems.

*Information
is the difference
that makes a difference.*

—Gregory Bateson

Rob offers this explanation: "In Scan, you are trying to get insight into pieces of given solution and patterns of the whole that will lead to a solution. We need to understand what do they need to Scan and take on board to come up with a robust enough solution. You have to understand different vantage points, the patterns of the ultimate solutions, along with specific information that they can't forget. What do they need to learn to make progress?"

Scan Focus Act Model
http://www.mgtaylor.com/mgtaylor/glasbead/SFA.htm

What do people need to take up during Scan? What do they need to learn? They will need information, data, and theory in order to create a context for action. What new information and new concepts will spark participation in their process of design?

We generally start with the things that the client needs to think about, and then we come up with metaphors to help them think. What issues are they going to have to grapple with?

This part of the issue is more familiar turf: straight analytic stuff such as, "What larger system is our company or problem a part of? How does that system behave?"

In selecting metaphors through which to understand the problem, the team is searching for an "unrelated" system to the situation at hand. The two-fold purpose: to actually learn how other alien or obscure systems manage similar processes, and to see your own situation from a radically different vantage point, since we know that is a powerful technique for generating creativity.

When the facilitation team was designing for Wharton, they thought about the problems facing organizations in the future. One problem is that the future looks chaotic, turbulent, swept by strong forces. But somewhere, there have to be patterns. Somewhere, there must be adaptive processes that let entities survive or thrive despite the turbulence. A great metaphor to study—the ocean.

Many businesses attending the Wharton DesignShop event are tied into other interconnected systems, the way Orlando Hospital is tied in to Medicare, technology, changes in the legal climate, and demographics. All those conditions are changing, and your business is being dragged along. How do you survive it? Or how do you change course? A great metaphor to study: rivers.

Metaphors that derive from complex systems are rich sources of knowledge. The Wharton participants found many of the key issues intended for discovery by the writers of the Metaphor exercise. The participants discovered other valuable information beyond that intended by the writers. In different settings for different problems, these same phenomenon could be thought about and used in very different metaphoric ways.

Look at the notion of the rainforest. In the Wharton event, the facilitation team selected the rainforest as the metaphoric system against which to study the problem of how a business copes with the interdependence of constantly renewing systems. And in that situation, how do some species gain competitive advantage through strategies of designing for state change?

In another DesignShop session the key customer question regarded bundling and unbundling. There they also worked with the rainforest as a metaphor, asking the question, "How many things can you take out of the rainforest before it doesn't work any more?"

The complex systems in nature are not the only fruitful source of metaphors. The more colors you have on your palette of metaphors, the better choices you'll be able to make.

Chip, who generates marvelous historical metaphors, shares a few: "If the issue to be understood is leverage, don't read about the ant. Instead, ask yourself: 'Who else has achieved amazing leverage?' Rob came up with the notion of Cortez, and I just ran with it: How did Cortez conquer the Aztec Empire with just 400 guys?" We had great results working with that metaphor.

In another DesignShop activity, speed to market was identified as a central issue. Very early on we introduced the notion of the Mongol Horde. It was very inspiring."

In the simplest of terms, you could say that when you overlay what content and skills need to be learned, with how the participants need to travel through cycles of growth offered by the underlying models, you have the pattern for your DesignShop event. Now, you create or select exercises which best serve as structure for each moment of the DesignShop session—as the many stories throughout this book have shown.

Robust and Reliable

How much of this complexity does a sponsor need to scoop up before doing a DesignShop event is possible? If the DesignShop session is to succeed, the sponsor must bring to the party an in-depth knowledge of the complexities of the situation. Sponsors handle the complete complexity of the What, and generate much of the valuable content there.

In the simplest of terms, you could say that when you overlay what content and skills need to be learned, with how the participants need to travel through cycles of growth offered by the underlying models, you have the pattern for your DesignShop event.

The How—the process of building creativity—is another matter. It's nice, it's useful, but it's not necessary for the sponsor to understand it in order to use it to solve business problems. Historically, lots of sponsors have fabulous DesignShop session results while never really coming to terms with the nature of the DesignShop process.

Rob Evans explains:

> Facilitators need to understand the logic behind the environment. Facilitators need to understand the theories. Understanding theory leads to good practice. But a tremendous amount of the process can only be learned through on the job training in which you "shadow," work alongside, a skilled facilitator.
>
> Learning to design a nonlinear event, you have to watch how it works, and try it out yourself—design the sequence of activities, test to see how it works—a level of mastery that can only be gained by experience.

Rob insists on the need for experience in order to understand nonlinear processes, because even very bright people with only intellectual exposure keep trying to find a way to make the process into a single action point or a linear process.

Designing the Ride

"But *what*," asked a friend, a VP of Technology Development who was hearing about the DesignShop process for the first time, "did the facilitator *say* that made them have the breakthrough?"

Our friend is still looking at it in a linear fashion, still looking at the first moment of insight as being the critical instant and at the facilitator as being the critical component. Somewhere in this question is the thought that this is the moment when the magic happens, and if you could just repeat those identical words then magic would happen for you, too.

No—incorrect analysis.

At the moment of the aha!, the Eureka!, the insight, the facilitator may have said nothing. (All rather like Sherlock Holmes and the Hound of the Baskervilles— "the wonder, Watson, is that the dog did not bark in the night.")

Or then there was the CEO who asked, "What percentage of productivity improvement or degradation is produced by making changes in your process, versus your tools, versus your environment?" To a certain extent it is artificial to draw a distinction between environment and tools, or environment and process. Information is embodied in material objects, and that information affects people. It is just a matter of scale. The environment is just the tool that is all around you. The process is the psychological environment. It is seamless and it changes. But so many of us are bound and determined to try to make the distinction.

So, that question might be answered by another question: "Does your car go faster depending on whether the front right tire or left front tire is flat?" The car needs four functioning tires, because it's an interdependent system, just as your business is a system with interdependent environment, tools, and processes. Should you put more investment into your environment? tools? process? Well, which tire of your car is flattest?

The good news and the bad news is that there isn't one secret, magic incantation that works the spell. The way the magic works is this: the participants have spent an adequate amount of time in a properly structured environment.

> *The environment is just the tool that is all around you. The process is the psychological environment. It is seamless and it changes. But so many of us are bound and determined to try to make the distinction.*

> *A discovery is said to be an accident meeting a prepared mind.*
>
> —Albert Szent-Gyorgi

They have had great environmental conditions and all the right tools to get the job done.

Barriers that impede their creative work process have been continually swept out of the way.

The knowledge, education, and training they need to solve their problem have been made available. They have been soaking up that new knowledge as fast as the fire hose can pour it out, and immediately applying it to problems.

They have worked iteratively with all their knowledge and their designs: learning, designing, testing, and then doing it again.

Project Management techniques have been used properly to schedule the work, to allow participant feedback to change the schedule, to give participants continual, non-punitive feedback on their work.

They have been swapping information and listening to each other.

They have been allowed to explore the full creative cycle again and again.

Their levels of creativity and cooperation have risen to the levels needed to manufacture a breakthrough idea.

The facilitation team:
- Designed the event to allow creativity to emerge.
- Helped write the questions that sparked the debate that led to the Aha!
- Shielded the participants from the outside world so they could focus in a collaborative space.

Over the course of this process, the probabilities of certain events have shifted. The odds of creative insights occurring go up, minute by minute. As information is shared, the odds of pieces of knowledge converging to create a vital conclusion go up, minute by minute. The odds of someone figuring out how to solve a problem go up and up as new tools, new metaphors, new models are learned. Suddenly, it all clicks to produce a solution. And you can say pretty reliably how long the total process will take, and roughly when the group will have done enough work that the insights will start occurring.

What is surprising—at first—is not that this process can happen, but that it is reliable and robust. Create this kind of environment, get the right people together, pour in the right knowledge, use the hidden patterns called out in processes like the Creative Cycle, and you have very high odds that you will emerge from it with the kind of productive results you need. The first enunciation of the "breakthrough words" may have been spoken by anybody in the room—the president, a secretary, a customer, a competitor, a stock analyst. The amazing thing is that after 48 hours of the process, everyone was capable of hearing them.

The Seven Domains Model
http://www.mgtaylor.com/
mgtaylor/glasbead/sevndoms.htm

Look at an example of the reverse. Many dollars and years of research show that if you crowd rats into a boring and hostile environment, you get a lot of stressed-out, ulcer-ridden, dysfunctional rats who fight a lot. It doesn't take skill in forecasting to predict that, on any given day, there will be many rat fights. This means you have built a robust environment capable of producing abundant trauma, even if any individual rat decides he is hanging up his guns and fighting no more.

Structured environments can have as powerful an effect on humans. Chip speaks with a certain conviction of the Marine Corps boot camp and their drill sergeants as the ultimate statement in unforgettable structured environments. As with any powerful tool, they can be used for good or for harm. The religious cults and "self-improvement" movements of the 1970s and '80s would use structured environments with long days to induce fatigue, protein deprivation to dull thinking and judgment, and ritual activities and other forms of control to convert new recruits. In the previous chapter, you no doubt noted the insistence on all those ethical and behavioral rules by which facilitators must abide, all the picky attention to details of food and environmental conditions. These aren't just niceties, they are absolutely critical elements—ethical necessities which must be present to provide a beneficial environment.

OK. So what would you logically expect if you put people into an environment structured to increase their intelligence, heighten their judgment, increase their creativity, speed up their rate of learning, and augment their knowledge?

Chip: It isn't about lighting a match in the powder magazine. It's about stacking lots of the cards in your favor. Oh, yes, you have to say stuff, but the aha! has to come from the participants.

Gail describes it as creating a "saturated solution." It's like making rock candy: you keep adding sugar...and more sugar....and more....and you leave the string in there until suddenly the rock candy crystals start to form. You keep augmenting the environment, and augmenting, and augmenting until a solution to the problem starts to form, and seems to emerge all by itself.

The Day Before

As the month before a DesignShop event goes on, the sponsors and the facilitation team are pulling together the event: getting participants committed, the read-aheads created and distributed, pulling the full facilitation team together, getting the space. During this month, and then later during the event, they fundamentally rethink the event topic and re-analyze what is needed for the client to make progress.

DesignSession and WalkThru
http://www.mgtaylor.com/mgtaylor/jotm/spring97/sam_journal2.htm

The day before the DesignShop session starts, the sponsor team and the DesignShop crew do a walkthrough session. The DesignShop environment is set up, the space configured—books in the library, art on display, toys available for modeling and playing. Among the team doing this setup are people from the client company, who are going to be working on the DesignShop event as part of the facilitation crew. They have already had training sessions to introduce them to the space, the concepts, and to help them discover what the role of a knowledge worker is all about.

Now, the proposed events of the DesignShop session are recreated from scratch, and then the early sections are designed in detail. This is the same kind of iterative work that happens for participants: fold the old design back into the creative clay and let the next design emerge. The team is asking themselves—is Scan/Focus/Act the right model? Is this the best metaphor, is this the right problem, is this the best solution, could we do it from a different vantage point, should we change the sequence? Day 1 is rigorously designed. Modules, assignment, and team configurations are chosen. Day 2 is a little less fully planned, and Day 3 may be rather sketchy.

A set of action plans map out the expected sequence for Day 1—how the breakout rooms will be resized and arranged; what exercises need to be written when; what toys or props need to be on hand. There are lights, "scenery," music, camera, writers, actors if need be—the facilitation crew is like a professional theatre company that will bring a paper structure into three dimensions, adding depth, emotion, color.

One knowledge worker likened the DesignShop experience to her past experience in theater: "There is a structure similar to improvisational theater. You have a beginning, and you know how you want to end. In between you have a lot of options, and you work with what the audience hands you."

Staying Responsive: Lots of Improvisation

To guarantee relevance and effectiveness, the exercises will be polished or finalized minutes before they are to be used. At its simplest, this means that an exercise might feature articles from that morning's newspaper, or might be built around an idea or wording from a participant in the previous exercise.

But the change can be much more profound than that. Participants can cause the nature of the sequence or the exercise to change completely at any time. Exercises and sequence might have to be reinvented from the ground up.

How can the participants change the schedule, when they don't even know what it is? Remember back when the participants found they didn't have an agenda or schedule—what! no agenda! Well, neither does the facilitation team. Oh, sure, they planned out Day 1, and sketched the sequence out on a work wall. But then the facilitation team pays attention to every step, every minute of the DesignShop process, and asks if what the participants are getting out of an exercise is matching the expected goal for that exercise.

The facilitation team will not actually interfere and ask the participants how they feel, but the facilitators will watch and listen for whether or not the group is learning, communicating, grappling with key issues, making progress.

Facilitators are always asking themselves, "What do the participants need?" If what they need is not being given to them now or planned for the upcoming exercises, then it's time to course-correct and find a direction that will move them

There is a structure similar to improvisational theater. You have a beginning, and you know how you want to end. In between you have a lot of options, and you work with what the audience hands you.

through their dilemmas, or take them exploring in a place where they can find solutions. The original plan is always subject to modification if the design goals are better met another way.

Throughout the journey, the facilitation team members are continually asking themselves what is working, what is missing, or what needs to be done to bring that future goal to the present.

As a facilitator and process manager, Chip looks to see "if they are engaged, focused in on the project, seriously working on it, hooked and captivated by the problem."

Gail asks, "What can block the information from flowing? What kinds of memes block the information? I'm always thinking, 'I've got to find new ways to making this thing healthy.'"

Bryan Coffman: "I ask, what vantage points are we focusing on? Where are they in the creative process? Have they gone all the way through the complete creative process cycle? To draw from a rich set of possibilities, I'll use the models as an aid to formulate questions."

Michael Kaufman: "I'll walk around with another facilitator, and we'll ask each other if learning is going on. Dr. Deming said continuous improvement was continuous learning. The more learning, the better."

Jon Foley: "I think about the African Queen story, and ask myself: On Day 3, where do they need to be to be at their maximum? What do they need? Do they need intent and insight? Do they need goal?"

Chip: "I ask myself, 'Have the participants done enough work on this phase? Are they ready to move on?' And then I'll test to see if they are ready to move on."

Timing the length of an exercise—steering participants away from premature closure of an idea and bringing them to closure when it's complete—is determined by gleaning feedback from the participants. Have they extracted all the value to be had from this exercise yet? Often the people squawking the loudest about not having a schedule back in the beginning turn out to create the actual schedule by insisting that "there is more to talk about here; we're not ready to move on."

But what keeps the process oriented? With so much flexibility, could the process careen off to some disastrously unproductive end?

Staying Oriented: Lots of Rigor

Underneath all this flexibility and improvisation, the facilitation team is keeping their eyes rigorously focused on the goal. No matter how turbulent the process, the goal remains as the target for the journey.

If events develop in a way that obviates the planned design, the event is redesigned. If the planned design is working, they stick rigorously to it. Matt:

> Often, during the process, you'll hear things like "These people aren't happy," or "This doesn't seem to be going anywhere." Maybe the sponsor says he's unhappy or uncomfortable. He's the boss, right? But does he understand the creative process? No, he doesn't. He's the boss, but he is not a sensor of our system.
>
> A sensor measures and feeds back the difference between performance and expectations. The "expectation" is where the boss wants to go. He said the goal is a strategic plan that will get his company to survive the next decades. We have designed an event whose end product is expected to be the kind of strategic plan he defined. Right now, he would settle for a book; but he wants a strategic plan. That is the standard of the sensor of the system.
>
> If something is innovative and new, it changes something or challenges an assumption. Change or challenge to a commonly-held model should generate some uncomfortable feedback—discomfort is a natural part of the design process.
>
> Now, the question is how we choose to respond to this discomfort. If you get upset about being upset, that is bad: a positive feedback loop. Or, we can treat it as a signal informing us of where we stand in the design process. So instead, steer him to the outcome, and not to his opinion of the process or how he feels. It's not a reason to change the design of the process. We designed it, and we know where it is going.
>
> We are going to get a true strategic plan, which means it's going to be uncomfortable. The agreed-upon goal is not to have happiness, but to rethink your

If something is innovative and new, it changes something or challenges an assumption. Change or challenge to a commonly-held model should generate some uncomfortable feedback – discomfort is a natural part of the design process.

processes and develop a significantly different strategic plan. During the journey, we will be hearing about all the ambiguities, uncertainties, and other things that could be "weak signal" threats to our organization. So, I cannot use those anxieties as a feedback. Keeping that in mind, I will make things as comfortable as I can.

Together, we are going to get significantly down the trail to accomplishing this significant task. The world will be different if you have accomplished that. We are going to disturb the universe.

Challenge

1. Jot down the ideas that captured your imagination while reading the chapter. Add whatever questions were raised as well.

2. Keep a copy of the Creative Process model and Scan/Focus/Act with you, and for a week or so, see if you can find correlations between the model and the way things work in the world. Gather examples not only from your work or home, but from nature and history as well.

3. You don't have to be planning a DesignShop to apply the principles discussed in this chapter. Choose a project from the work you have already specified in previous challenges. Diagram your approach to design and implementation of this project over time using the Scan/Focus/Act model and the model of the Seven Stages of the Creative Process as templates to help your thinking.

4. What questions should you ask in the Scan phase to break out of the box? How will you test the ideas uncovered during the Scan? In the Focus phase, what tools will you use to support implementation in the Act phase?

Giving Up the Illusion of Control: Fear, Frustration, and Other Forms of Loathing

When you as a new DesignShop participant also happen to be the leader of an organization or group back home, you eventually start to think, "We should have one of these…I should sponsor one of these." You begin to play out the scenario, and about ten seconds later a powerful feeling hits you in the gut. We know, because we felt it—sponsor fear.

Perhaps the role most important to the success of a DesignShop event is the sponsor. The sponsor represents the organization undertaking the task. He or she makes the decision to embark on the process, sets the challenge(s) to be addressed, and must work in advance with the facilitators and knowledge workers to specify needs, problems, and objectives so that the process is tailored to support the defined goal.

Leaders like to think they have control over what is going on in their organizations. Of course, this isn't true at all. Organizations are seething masses of conflicting goals and plans pursued by dozens or hundreds or thousands of uncontrollable individuals, most of whose primary agendas have nothing to do with the health of the organization itself. As the saying goes, what is amazing is not how well the bear dances—what's amazing is that the bear dances at all.

Life shrinks or expands in proportion to one's courage.

—Anais Nin

Introduction to Complexity
http://www.mgtaylor.com/mgtaylor/jotm/summer97/complexity.htm

So the appearance of control is always an illusion. But the DesignShop process rubs your nose in this fact. Because you are tapping into the unknown or underappreciated skills of your teammates, and because time is compressed, completely unexpected things can happen fast. Of course, that is why these events are held in the first place—if you knew in advance what the outcome would be, you wouldn't need to go through the process to find out.

Despite the ever-present forces of chaos in their organizations, leaders are good at maintaining some level of control, or at least some appearance of control. That is how they became leaders. The DesignShop process requires that they relinquish that—a skill which has been key to their success. How do they feel about that? Nervous. Stressed-out. Scared.

To explore the effects of these emotions, we went to the staff, who see it all the time. Jon Foley: "As you're doing a DesignShop session, the outcome evolves. If you start the event saying, 'this is what the outcome should be,' you have lost the benefit, lost what you could get out of it."

Bryan Coffman: "There is a philosophical threat in that there is no rank here: the structure is loose and the agenda evolves, as opposed to when you all sit around a table and the biggest blowhard gets to talk all of the time. It's also different from having a facilitator who goes around the table getting a 'chip' from everybody, like you are in kindergarten. There is a big philosophical threat inherent in the design of a DesignShop event—inherent in the philosophy."

Frances Gillard: "If you as a sponsor send your staff to a DesignShop session, you had better be there. You either have to be there or, when they get back, you'll find they have moved on to thinking that you may not understand."

Some leaders find the thought of not being in direct control of the process so threatening that they choose not to have their organization take part in it at all.

Bryan: "Even if you are at the DesignShop session, you can still lose control. You can really hate it, and that is one reason some leaders never do it again. Often, the ones who cannot handle the thought of losing control do not even make it to the first day. They wind up canceling the DesignShop event before it starts."

Giving Up the Illusion of Control

Perhaps the word "fear" sounds a little melodramatic. But when you have seen the energy and speed of action at one of these events, and picture your organization undergoing that, it is scary. Remember that entire departments and divisions can be created and wiped out at these events. Corporate plans and goals can entirely change. The word *fear* sounds accurate to us, and also to Jon Foley when he remembers his first time as the sponsor of a DesignShop event:

> I was the sponsor of an important DesignShop session which was supposed to start on a Tuesday. The most difficult time for me was on Sunday afternoon:
>
> I'm sitting in front of the computer. Everyone else working on the event has gone out on a break—it's time to get some lunch. But I'm on a roll and I don't want to lose the energy, so I'm working on one of the exercises, and all of the sudden I froze up in fear. I wanted to call my boss and say, "I don't want to do this. We will not be ready by Tuesday morning, I want to call it off on Monday morning. I just want you to know that I'm going to do that—I have the authority to do that, I'm going to do it."
>
> But before I made the call I realized something. I had been on a high ropes course in which I had to face a situation that brought out physical fear. When it hit, I literally had to do one thing at a time. Move this hand three inches that way. Move this foot three inches that way. Turn my head. Move this hip. It was how I got through my fear up there until I could get fluid and start doing things.
>
> And I recognized that this feeling that hit me was the same fear-based adrenaline surge that I remembered from the high ropes course. So I did the same thing: ask myself what's the next word I'm going to type, and I would type that word. It took about ten minutes, then I was through it. I blasted through it and was on track again. But I had to face it totally alone. It was the only lonely thing I had to do.

Matt explains, "That fear is natural and not wrong. It should not be avoided. As a facilitator, I feel it all of the time."

Like entering the military or going skydiving, there are two traditional ways in which someone becomes a sponsor: by volunteering, or by being drafted.

Bryan: "Usually a personal friend of the company's president says, 'Look, this is the weirdest thing. It is very strange. It is not always fun, but you should try it.' So they do."

We cannot escape fear. We can only transform it into a companion that accompanies us on all our exciting adventures.

—Susan Jeffers

Sponsoring a Session
http://www.mgtaylor.com/
mgtaylor/jotm/spring97/
event_sponsor.htm

However, the real white-knuckle road to being a sponsor is when your boss drafts you for the role.

Todd Johnston: "When your boss has ordered you to sponsor a DesignShop event, you feel enormous pressure—like it is all on your back. First, you are stepping into an environment that is unfamiliar. Second, there is real or perceived pressure from the boss, who tells you to deliver certain output. Meanwhile, the boss isn't going to come to the DesignShop event. They just want to see the results."

Long before the participants show up at a DesignShop session, the sponsor is on site for the "sponsor meeting," in which goals are set, and then the walk-through, at which the staff lays out the sequence of exercises and experiences custom-tailored for this event.

Frances gives an example of how this process typically goes:

> We had a sponsor from the Air Force, Colonel Tom, a bright guy with his own set of very definite ideas. He came in with an agenda for the sponsor meeting, and said, "We are going to do such-and-such at the DesignShop session."
>
> The sponsor meeting and the walk-through were done in the DesignShop environment, not done in a standard office. In a DesignShop environment, we can give the sponsor a sample of the different kind of process that we are proposing. In a standard office environment, we wouldn't be able to show them any examples. How would a sponsor be able to understand and agree to something he had never experienced? Col. Tom was convinced to give it a shot.

As a frequent facilitator, Bryan has had to hold the hands of many nervous sponsors:

> During the walk-through, first-time sponsors will try to steer the agenda so they reach a certain comfort level. What they do not realize at first is that by trying to manipulate or steer that agenda, they are in fact ensuring that they will not get the results they need. They learn that quickly. Working with a first-time sponsor is often one of the really challenging aspects of the facilitator and staff roles—to give them a comfort level without interfering with the process. There are not many sponsors who are not nervous the day before their first DesignShop event.

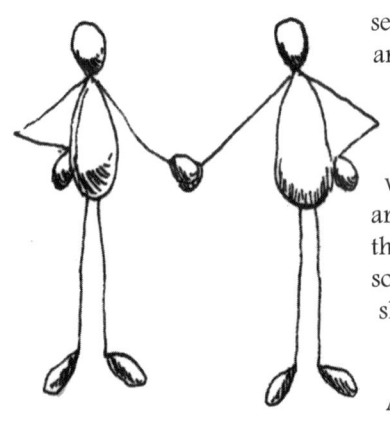

Giving Up the Illusion of Control

During the DesignShop session, the sponsor is there at all times—excited, nervous, surprised, anxious, trying to remember to breathe. These are all the same emotions that an expectant father has once Lamaze training has ended and now he's in the delivery room doing The Real Thing. If you're not extremely nervous, so it is said, you don't understand the process.

Because they are leaders, sponsors tend to be highly action-oriented, with a strong drive to make decisions and develop specific plans. Therefore, they tend to have trouble during the early Scan phases of the process—it seems too unfocused, too unrelated.

Chip elaborates: "First-time sponsors may feel that they have put their career on the line for something they have not yet learned to trust. Their angst level is usually highest at the end of the Scan day, when it will appear that no useful work has been accomplished.

Think about meetings where the group floundered around for a long time, finally came up with some options, and then had a very productive last half hour. This is Scan/Focus/Act. Or have you ever had to write an article, and you studied, made a few outlines, and then you're in the shower and suddenly the answer was in front of you and you just had to write it down? The 'writing it down' is the Act. The key point is—we all go through this, we just don't usually have a way of thinking about it. You can't shortcut straight to Act."

Gunner sees common reactions following a similar timetable:

> By the end of the second day, they are going around whispering, "This is a waste of time and I am never doing one of these again." Then about halfway through the third day, when the plan starts coming together, they are saying, "This is the most wonderful thing that has ever happened—can we have another one when we develop the plan to a certain point?"

Potential sponsors need to ponder this: You will be creating a bunch of change agents in your organization. They will make things different. If you don't want people doing this, then don't implement the process. Without it, your organization will not do as well as it could—it may even die. But if you give your people this exposure to enhanced creativity and productivity, and then thwart it, they will be frustrated and the best ones may leave.

There is the risk you cannot afford to take, [and] there is the risk you cannot afford NOT to take.

—Peter Drucker

Scan Focus Act Model
http://www.mgtaylor.com/mgtaylor/glasbead/SFA.htm

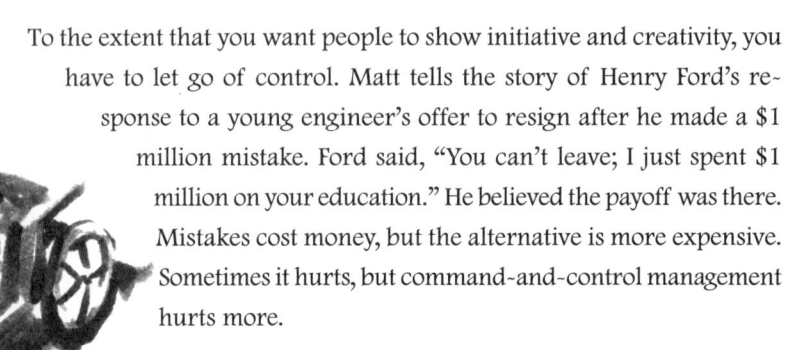

To the extent that you want people to show initiative and creativity, you have to let go of control. Matt tells the story of Henry Ford's response to a young engineer's offer to resign after he made a $1 million mistake. Ford said, "You can't leave; I just spent $1 million on your education." He believed the payoff was there. Mistakes cost money, but the alternative is more expensive. Sometimes it hurts, but command-and-control management hurts more.

Pulling all this together, we can come up with a few "Operating Rules for Sponsors":

- Be there at all times or be left behind. When events happen, they happen quickly.
- Expect the group to expand the challenge.
- Let hierarchical relationships be ignored for now. This is not a time to "pull rank."
- Relax and be open: there's no need to bring predetermined answers for the group to "get" and "sign on to."
- Avoid prejudging the process—wait until the end.

Transition Manager's Creed
http://www.mgtaylor.com/mgtaylor/jotm/fall96/trnmgcr.htm

It's kind of fun to do the impossible.

—Walt Disney

Beyond Sponsor Fear: Sponsor Confidence and Participant Discomfort

The most experienced sponsor at the Wharton event was Col. Bill. He has long ago left sponsor fear behind and moved to the next phase—confidence that the process works, combined with a bit of amusement at how it affects some participants:

> There are the people who do not believe in what they call "touchy-feely." They want to blow all of this away and have the standard situation where they have an agenda, they will listen for 15 minutes, and then the colonel will make a decision. At the start, they thought that was how the F-15 program was going to work. And occasionally I do make decisions that only I can make. But for the most part, they have found out they really are empowered to make decisions.

Giving Up the Illusion of Control

The touchy-feely stuff takes the classic "Type A" personalities and blows them apart. I love watching them react. Look at the videos and watch their faces get red. You can tell what is going on. There ought to be a medical warning on DesignShops, especially for Type A's. I tell them, "We might as well draw the chalk outline on the floor now, because I'm telling you that you will work for 12 hours and decide you accomplished nothing. You are going to feel bored beyond belief and bang your head against the wall in your room, thinking you have wasted 12 hours and could have been filling out reports or watching your contract or whatever. Instead you have been in here playing with toys and talking about the universe in the year 2025, when you cannot figure out Saturday."

Type A engineers especially have trouble initially getting used to DesignShops. The only thing worse than a Type A engineer is a lawyer. The worst thing in the world is a Type A lawyer with an engineering degree. That is a horrendous combination. We had a couple of people close to this specification.

Another one of our people once described the participants' reactions to me this way: "We are frustrated because we are constantly circling. Then they throw something unexpected in there. There is no schedule. We do something, and we thought we were going to report-out about it, but we didn't. Then we come back the next morning to something different. They are constantly producing a level of chaos and trial." I said, "Sounds like the real world, doesn't it? Why would you expect this to be any different?"

Overall, I'd say that 90% of the people adjust to it over time.

Process Need Not Be Enjoyable

As you enter a DesignShop environment for the first time, you see the unusual setup, hear the music, and are surprised by the presence of toys. Your first thought is that the process must have, as a primary goal, getting the participants to have a good time. Matt explains that having a good time is not a prerequisite:

> How they feel does not matter. Naturally we want them to be relaxed, content, happy, cruising along with a smile on their faces, as much as possible. That is a natural human desire on our part. But if they absolutely hate it, that means nothing to the process. The process doesn't care. The process does not require that they like it. The process requires only that they do the work. Then later they can decide whether they like it or not, based on the results.

Believe me, we have had people who hated DesignShop sessions at first and love them today. That is not our concern. You cannot manage that. There is too much concern for that kind of thing in organizations today—people in the hierarchy are constantly trying to appease their bosses, make their bosses happy. That is a positive feedback loop that is unstable. That is not our goal. We want to make them effective. We want to bring out their genius individually and as a group to break through on an issue that is important.

That is our mission, and our feedback loop is based on what they do productively, not what they say to us. We can take that into account, but we will not modify our process based on it. We modify based on what we see them actually do.

Resistance to the Procedure

The facilitation team has seen participants who have trouble with the process, especially in the first half, before the results start to emerge:

Bryan: "People want to have the standard things: a keynote speaker, a focus group, have people say 'here, do these things,' and walk out with a solution. In this context, the first two days seem like a waste of time."

Frances: "There can be a personality clash where some people don't want to do the Scan phase at all. They just want to get in there and act. A lot of them don't really see the value in the first day or day and a half, because they are not into their comfort zone."

Matt: "So what if it feels funny? You change your habits and what is your body/mind going to tell you? It tells you to change your habits again, and go back to what you are used to."

Pat: "Discomfort is necessary."

Gunner: "You never get any place without it."

Pat: "It is the discomfort you feel from any kind of stress. Any kind of threat will do the same thing to you."

Stress and fear are no strangers to most participants—they have plenty of it back on the job. At Wharton, the Ernst & Young team told us that they "don't have retirement parties from E&Y, they just have lunch for the widows and orphans." Another comment from a participant was that at his company, "Fear permeates. It's fear that won't allow our people to share knowledge in a knowledge base, because knowledge shows that I'm an expert. If I have to ask for information, I am showing weakness."

When Fear Gets Extreme

Elsa Porter tells of a friend whom she convinced to attend a DesignShop event on the topic of energy. He had a strong negative reaction, the strongest one we've heard:

> He thought that it was cultish. He thought that it was dangerous. He thought that this was similar to EST in terms of deprivation. You had to work twelve hours, and they got you so tired. He went on and on. What he did physically was to cut himself off—sat on the outside, walked around during discussions. He was very disruptive in terms of his own behavior.
>
> He and I both belong to the same online discussion network, and he was criticizing it for several weeks afterward, and I was defending it. It was the first time that had occurred to me—how threatening it can be.

An emotional reaction this strong is rare, but facilitators and sponsors should be aware that it can happen. We talked earlier about structured environments ranging from the military to the 1970's proliferation of religious and EST-like groups. If someone has been through a structured environment like that, they will be identifying similarities of structured environments, but not this structure. Any "structured" environment is not this structure, just like any "facilitated" meeting is not providing DesignShop-style facilitation.

A DesignShop session requires a large investment of time and money, and the facilitators need to be prepared to take action to preserve that investment if the process is being disrupted. Upset participants can be taken aside for calming discussion, or in extreme cases can be excused from the process. In the many years that DesignShop events have been held, pulling a participant out of the process has rarely been necessary.

New Behaviors:
Example of the Venture Capitalist

Far more common than strong negative reactions are strong positive ones, particularly getting positive participation from unexpected sources. Matt remembers betting on such participation, and winning:

> Years and years ago, it must have been 1981 or 1982, people came to us and talked about a new company—a spin-out of AT&T. They have this new switching technology and are bringing in all these venture capitalists. There were about 20, because it was too big for any one firm to do. The venture capitalists agreed to hear the proposal together to develop some sort of consortium to fund the company. They asked us to design a process in our first management center in Boulder to facilitate all of this.
>
> They were thinking that this is just a location where they would have a regular facilitated meeting. But we said we would have a process, there would be a brief introduction, and that it would not be a day of present-and-shoot. At that point, when we were sitting around planning the day, one of the young support people was telling me about venture capitalists—that they would not do this. "They do not engage," etc. I responded that, "Scientists, engineers, community developers, teachers, and so on don't do this either, except for the fact that they do this in DesignShop sessions." He said, "I'm telling you that so-and-so (who was sort of the big bull moose of all venture capitalists) will not write on your wall." We made a gentleman's bet. How long do you think it will take? He said, "In the whole twelve hours, you will be lucky if you get him to write on the wall at all."
>
> So we got them together, and I said this was what we were going to do, this was the process, and so on. "Considering investing in this company is a very complex issue. You have all seen the business plan, now we need to get your concerns. Take a marker and write out on the wall what you think is the most important thing you need."
>
> And he takes the pen and walks up to the wall and writes and says, "If you are going to be good, this is what we have to have: etc. etc." I looked in the back of the room and his aide was shaking his head. At the end of the day, the aide came up to me and said, "How did you do that?" "I handed him the pen and told him to go to the wall and write." "Yes. But how did you do that?" I handed him the pen and told him to go up to the wall and write.

The reason that it worked is that we asked him a question in which he was really interested. We gave him the opportunity to do what most of us really like to do, which is to stand up and share what we require. As it turned out, no one had ever asked him that question before—"What is it that you require; what is it you want? Before we start, shouldn't we know?" He wasn't running the meeting. If we had said, "In order to proceed, sir, could you explain..." then he would have run the meeting. Because it was a DesignShop session, we didn't let him run the meeting. We let him set what he could control, which were his criteria.

As for the other venture capitalists, some of them loved it. Some of them were neutral. Some of them were so focused on the deal that they did not really notice the process. They knew something was different. They knew that it worked. We pretty much all agreed that it worked.

Sometimes, it's those who are most opposed at first who are most enthusiastic at the end, as the staffers can testify. Christopher Fuller gives an example: "In Orlando, there was a gentleman who liked to exert control and who liked to stand up and direct the process. The last day, he was the one who shook everyone's hand and said we did the right thing. After being there three days, you learn to work together."

Frances continues: "Usually, the people who come in most vehemently opposed, because they are so bright and have been through so much and know that it is just another seminar, are the ones who come out totally knocked out by the process. They have never experienced anything like it."

A savvy sponsor can prepare his or her people for the process, minimizing resistance and maximizing acceptance up front. Col. Bill tells what he did at AEDC to introduce his people to the idea:

> I had to sell the whole process. I had town meetings. I had sessions every six months for an hour-and-a-half.
>
> We asked people to tell co-workers what they saw and felt. They were to be evangelists—talk about the good, the bad, and the ugly. Plus, I got video clips that were really good. I asked for clips of the regular work-level folks telling what they had seen. I had two or three really powerful ones.

Whatever you can do, or dream you can, begin it. Boldness has genius, power, and magic in it.

—W.N. Murray, 1951
The Scottish Himalayan Expedition

One was a guy who had been at AEDC for 25 years. He said, "At first I thought, here is another one of these things that I have to go to, and get another pin to put in the lapel, and sign another thing pledging my life. All the big muckety-mucks in their suits and ties and uniforms will stand up and exhort us to do good work. Then we will go back to the work, and they will go back to their offices and the golf course, and nothing will change. That was not how it worked. Not only were they working with us, they were not wearing suits and ties and uniforms. They were just Joe and John instead of Mister or Colonel They stayed with us and worked the whole time. This is real."

This is a guy who has real credibility with his co-workers saying, "this is real." I used that videotape a lot. For every town meeting I used it.

The lesson from all this is that DesignShop sessions can release a whole gamut of emotions, from fear to exhilaration, just as any other organizational work can. But because they focus on big issues, and do so very quickly, the usual emotions are intensified. Careful preparation by sponsors and facilitators can minimize the negative emotions, enabling more participants to feel the happy excitement of a successful DesignShop process.

Challenge

1. Continue the practice of recording ideas from this chapter without looking back at it. Record questions that are raised in you as well. After doing this, go back to the chapter and flesh out your notes.

2. What guidelines can you devise to help you sponsor your own dreams and plans? How do you make sure that you can ask the tough questions, search out the bizarre ideas, get the work done, and endure the ambiguity and discomfort that naturally comes with some parts of the creative process? Identify people who can help—how can you engage them to do so? (Look for your own win-win solutions.) Think of ways to give yourself the space and time required to continue the practice of actively scanning as a part of your creative process?

Bringing the Future Back Home

Like leaves scattering to the winds, these teams who have achieved so much together now separate onto planes that will carry them to California, Florida, Illinois, Texas. Even members of the same companies are often returning to distant branch offices, and may not see each other again.

Surprisingly, there is none of that bittersweet nostalgia that usually comes with marvelous experiences that end and will never be recaptured. Instead, there is the feeling that the experience, the DesignShop event itself, hasn't ended. Why?

Back here in Philadelphia, one obvious point is that the whole support team keeps right on working, even after the last participant is gone...although participants can stay and keep working alongside, if they want to.

Preparation of the various work products from this event continues seamlessly as participants leave the DesignShop session on Friday. The knowledge worker team produces the entire three-day event as a database—a knowledge base—so that all the information, the entire experience, is captured, indexed, searchable, and findable. They'll build a web site for the DesignShop event. There is the video, the transcripts, the read-aheads, the online searches, the evolving Knowledge Wall, everything becomes available to help a participant recreate the experience months from now.

Now, from the perspective of the last three days, they will produce a new work product that synthesizes, explains, heightens, and extends the work done in the DesignShop session. This work is in addition to and beyond the journal which

Ten Step Knowledge Management Model
http://www.mgtaylor.com/mgtaylor/glasbead/tenstep.htm

captures the chronology of the DesignShop event. This new piece of work is intended to take the thinking further.

But the participants, though heading out of the door for home, are also still in DesignShop mode. When they walk into their offices on Monday morning, they have a list of specific action items generated at the session to start implementing. And, within days of their return, the materials that the support team is working on right now will be there on their desks. The adventure continues.

Participants now have to make their future visions real. Taking it back home is one of the toughest challenges faced by the DesignShop participants. Back home, you're facing the ongoing structure of physical environment, tools, techniques, policies, people's beliefs, knowledge, or lack thereof. It's not uncommon to return from a DesignShop event and experience a tremendous sense of culture shock. Worse, you're facing an established structure. Usually, this means that the structure is going to win; you're playing a game with the deck stacked against you.

Chip offers this note: "This is the toughest thing—how to internalize the gains from this event. We keep in touch with the senior people. They need to make things tangibly different, move into a different space, get rid of meetings that are not called to take some action, bring the future to the present."

"Structure wins," says Matt. Think about the millions of New Year's resolutions made each January 1: I'm going to exercise more, smoke less, drop my weight, give up this Bad Habit and adopt that Good Habit. The evidence is overwhelming that despite willpower and intellectual understanding that more fruits and vegetables and exercise and stress reduction are essential, the odds are that the new goal will not succeed. The reason is not Personal Weakness and Huge Moral Flaws. The reason is structure: a structure in place supporting the status quo. The structure makes the old way convenient. What does the structure of other people's actions do to support or hinder? Unless you can restructure enough of the environment—getting rid of the barriers to the Good Habit, getting rid of structures that support the Bad, adding structures that support the new habit—the old structure wins.

A typical pattern in business is coming back from lectures full of enthusiasm for team building, or TQM, or whatever, and trying to educate the people back home.

After fighting an uphill battle with people who don't get the idea, you forget all about it and go back to life as usual. What has happened is simply that you returned to the same old environment, the same old structures, and with people who have the same old knowledge. Unlike you, they have not just gone timetraveling to see the future and returned with knowledge, revelations, and powerful secrets.

Somehow, you have to communicate the power of this shared experience to people who weren't present. You have to share your new knowledge with them: that dark taboos have dissipated under the light of day, that the old "problem" has disappeared and been replaced by a new vision of how you are going to do business. That in three days you have managed to come up with a complete strategic and tactical plan with practical, implementable steps on an issue that you hadn't been able to crack successfully in three years. That you have learned some things about increasing your own creativity and productivity—things that you yourself might have thought were kind of weird or pointless five days ago—but now you would like others to make this a standard way of working for yourself and others. Wouldn't it be fantastic, you're thinking, if my whole team back home could be this creative and cooperative on a daily basis! We would be unstoppable!

The response you can expect? "This can't really be my manager saying this…maybe it's sunstroke. Or too much stress. Overwork. Or bad airline food on the flight home."

Good luck. Transferring your insight, your vision of the future, and instituting the changes you will need to make to have it succeed is one of the toughest leadership and educational tasks around.

You Might Think of This Problem as Being "Merlin's Challenge"

Much of the success and the failure of the glory that was Camelot—King Arthur, Queen Guinevere, Merlin, Lancelot and the other Knights of the Round Table, Morgan le Fey, Mordred, objects of power from the sword Excaliber to the Holy Grail—turns on exactly this point.

Merlin, born in the future and living backward in time, knew what the future held, because he had already been there. No one doubted his wisdom or his powers, which had been proven repeatedly over the years. And yet, with this most critical vision of the future, with his knowledge of which path led to tragedy and which to triumph, he could not find a way to communicate, educate, enlighten, and transform the actions of the people of Camelot. Noble king, queen, and brave knights, a whole world doomed because they would not—could not—listen. Merlin, for all his magic, could not create a way to get his message across, to transfer his experience of the future into something that could transform Arthur's thinking.

*For of all sad words
of tongue or pen,
The saddest are these:
"It might have been!"*

—John Greenleaf Whittier

Camelot has many of the dynamics of a business: the corporate Knights gathered at the Round Table, the reliance on the wonderful technology of the sword Excalibur, a variety of personnel problems and office intrigues, the need for leadership to face painful truths. And, as with any body of people endeavoring to move forward, so much wonderful that could have been achieved. If only…

Solving Merlin's Dilemma

You've got a couple of things going for you that Merlin didn't:

First: You have a very detailed vision of your desired end state. You are not just aware of the tragedies you have to avoid, you have worked out how to avoid them, dissolved the problems that have stymied you, and have a subset of your company sharing a vision of a truly desirable goal and a plan to get there.

Second: Because you have worked on a real business problem, your tactical plan has action items and assignments for specific people that begin making a change on your office environment the minute you get back.

Third: As part of your plan, you have probably selected certain visible, physical changes that you are going to make immediately upon your return. These physical changes literally import something from There—the DesignShop and the Future Vision—into the Here and Now. With each change you make, the Here and Now becomes a bit more like the future you envisioned.

The changes you make will probably be of two types. The first are changes relating directly to your new business plan. The second are changes you decide to make to bring various aspects of the DesignShop environment, tools, and pro-

Bringing the Future Back Home

cesses home with you. If over the last three days you found things that helped you be creative and productive, don't wait until you do another DesignShop event to experience them again. Don't forget about them. Grab some paper or a wall and sketch out the things that you want to add to your work environment. Then do it.

By the third day of a DesignShop session, many participants will have recognized that the improvements in creativity, intelligence, cooperation, and the resulting superior work performance have come about because of the supportive environment. By changing their environment, intelligence-suppressing factors and creativity-suppressing factors have been removed. People have been given an enhanced set of knowledge tools and processes that let them be more effective—they are using power saws and drills instead of rocks. People are operating closer to their maximum capacities.

There can be real culture shock arriving back home to the old unchanged office environment, with its traps of marginal functionality, barriers to creativity, and lower levels of productivity.

When this happens, and it will, remember that it's not that the people back home aren't willing to change—the problem is that the organization is held in place by structure.

To create a DesignShop environment, MG Taylor has done an audit and removed from the environment every known obstacle they can—physical, psychological, social. They have created an environment you can play in. They have facilitated the environment by setting the moods which are designed to encourage creativity and cooperation. Then, people behave

The natural energy for changing reality comes from holding a picture of what might be that is more important to people than what is.

—Peter Senge

Seven Domains Model
http://www.mgtaylor.com/
mgtaylor/glasbead/sevndoms.htm

very differently. One of the real goals of the DesignShop process is to teach you how to recreate this improved environment yourself and create your own high performance organizations. What can you do to recreate as much as possible of that environment back home?

Most people don't have the freedom that Col. Bill had to build a Management Center based on DesignShop principles, send employees to train as facilitators, and get intensity by running a two-year, ongoing program of DesignShop events and smaller DesignSession activities. Even Col. Bill's personal office is heavily DesignShop-influenced: "My normal environment is not too far off of a DesignShop environment now. My executive officer is a knowledge worker who learned with MG Taylor. That makes him a much more effective executive assistant. He operates much better than if he did not have that training, knowledge, and understanding. I love it. I wish I could operate that way all of the time.

"The benefits are tremendous," says Col. Bill of using knowledge workers to provide intellectual support. "It puts the value where I can put value—using my brain. I get to think about the enterprise and what we are doing and how I can help create the vision for it and how we can work on that."

But even if you can't have your own personal knowledge facilitator, there are dozens of ways that anyone can begin changing their structure at home. Ralph Graham uses his office as a mini-"Management Center," employing the same kind of physical, collaborative exercises used in AEDC's Gossick Leadership Center. Managers and individual contributors in different companies have changed the way meetings are run in their groups. Many people have come home with an appreciation of how useful toys, modeling equipment, and art materials are, and have stocked their offices with them. Col. Bill:

> The important part of being a kid is the ability to explore and extend. I have toys in my office. Some people have puzzles, basketballs, stuffed animals, etc. They will fool with it—it works. I don't do it as often as I ought to do it. One of the books I read recently says you don't have to come home from the office exhausted. It talks about the ability to play. If you have something to play with in your office—stop for five minutes and fool with it. If you have a ball around, it is hard to resist. Look how much fun participants had with building the models.

Introduction to NavCenters
http://www.mgtaylor.com/mgtaylor/jotm/spring97/navctr_intro.htm

Bringing the Future Back Home

By starting to change the structure in these obvious, visible ways, other people in your company just can't help noticing it. Change begins to spread.

One highly effective thing that almost everyone does is display information or images that really crystallized something essential about your company or the vision. Maybe it's something you developed during a breakout session, or maybe something from the final work product. Charts, posters, and graphics are all candidates.

A DesignShop participant for a leading American technology firm—a client of Ernst & Young's—had a flash of insight during a DesignShop event: "We're just like the Lion King!"—referring to the Disney movie of childhood, exile, and triumphant return to kingship of young Simba the lion. Hearing that insight, an artist went to work and created a poster showing the company as the Lion King surrounded by the parallels between the complex world of savanna and jungle, and the participant's realm of business and technology. The poster was included as part of the final work product that arrived on all participants' desks on Monday morning.

Almost immediately, copy after copy of that poster was up on the participants' walls. And just as quickly, people started asking—"What is that?" From there, more and more people heard the story of the DesignShop session, the experience, the Aha!, the vision. The picture, plus the story, communicated the learning and the vision that had been achieved. For once, no one had to give up and say, "Well, I guess you just had to be there to understand." Instead, they heard fellow employees saying, "How can I get one of those posters?" Within weeks, over five hundred posters supporting the vision of the company as the Lion King were displayed on office walls.

The goals of the DesignShop event don't stop when you walk out the door. That is why the final work product acts as a lever for future growth: indicating what you need to keep working on, points you need to have reinforced—good stuff that came up during the three days that there wasn't time to address, but was captured and now can be worked with at home. Facilitators stay in touch with sponsors to keep working on how to get the results implemented. Participants get the contact information for all other participants, so even though they may be widely geographically dispersed, they stay in contact to keep working the solutions. Addi-

*People started asking—
"What is that?"'
From there, more and more people
heard the story
of the DesignShop session,
the experience, the Aha!, the vision.
The picture, plus the story,
communicated the learning
and the vision
that had been achieved.
For once, no one had to give up
and say, "Well, I guess you
just had to be there
to understand."*

Introduction to the Work Product
http://www.mgtaylor.com/
mgtaylor/jotm/fall96/
workprod.htm

tional workshops can help spread what has been discovered throughout more of the company.

So how well did the Wharton DesignShop participants do? How much value did they really get out of their three days in Philadelphia? How well did they do at implementation?

The Ernst & Young Story

We have visited with some of the Ernst & Young people during this story, but we haven't taken a focused look at the company itself.

Ernst & Young LLP is a management consulting giant—the second largest in the world. They have well over $6 billion in global revenues, and a roster of glamorous clients including Kellogg's, TRW, Digital Equipment, and Northern Telecom. E&Y had sent five participants to the Wharton DesignShop event.

At Wharton, we met Lee Sage, he of the fiercely set shoulders and the umpire's face. Because titles aren't emphasized at DesignShop events, we didn't find out until later that he is a partner at E&Y—a major player responsible for their global re-engineering practice, about $750 million in annual revenue.

Lee and four other E&Y partners were sent on the expedition to Wharton with a mission: find out whether there is something important going on with DesignShops, something E&Y needs. Sending five partners to a three-day event was a significant investment of time for E&Y—whatever it was, it had better be awfully good.

Lee looks back at his initial reactions and recalls a metamorphosis:

My partners and I went through that first day, thinking all the while that, "We can do this, there's nothing here, we know how to do this. This is sizzle in packaging, but no substance."

And then about late afternoon or evening of the second day at Wharton the little voices started to say, "Be careful, there is something here. Don't conclude too quickly: there is something here. Look below the surface as to what is really happening."

By the time we got through the third day, we saw the amount of collaborative thinking, the convergence, and the amount of work that we were able to do as a group. This convinced us to come back and say, "We need to carry this forward and do a couple of internal DesignShop sessions on some business problems."

Lee brought his excitement back to E&Y:

We assembled forty Ernst & Young professionals—not all partners, there were some managers as well as partners from various offices and practice areas. We had two three-day DesignShop sessions, and by this point we were beginning to see that the work environment, the collaborative style, the new thinking that the DesignShop process and environment caused to occur was beginning to grow on us. We were starting to grasp what was happening to us in the power of the process. We did not understand all the reasons why Matt and Gail do certain things when they do them, but we were finding a positive experience in going through the process.

As E&Y held more DesignShop events internally, one of the first lessons to hit home was the connection between the special environment used and the quality of the learning achieved:

We at E&Y spend millions and millions of dollars training our own people. Now, with the DesignShop process, our professional organizational development bunch is close to being convinced that our people learn through experience and observation, not through lecture and viewing overheads, and that this new environment is helping. This may sound obvious—people learn better experientially than by sitting and listening—but before we had the DesignShop environment and process, we had no way to make it happen.

The whole environment of the DesignShop session—what you do, what sharing goes on, what experiential learning occurs by having fifty people working on a common business issue—has been breathtaking for us. It has been staggering for us to find out what our people capture and retain in business without one overhead being used. It's phenomenal.

This should change the business environment. Today, if you look at a typical Ernst & Young office throughout the world, you'll find 80 to 90% of our space devoted to individual space, and the balance is group space. The association with Matt and Gail Taylor and the DesignShop process has convinced

Five Es of Education Model
http://www.mgtaylor.com/
mgtaylor/glasbead/5Esofed.htm

In the first half of 1996, we have had somewhere in the neighborhood of twelve of our clients go through three-day DesignShop events.

In every instance, we are getting done in three days what we would have historically accomplished in somewhere between six weeks and three months.

— Lee Sage

us that it should be exactly the opposite. We need 80-90% group space and 10-20% individual space.

Based on this, back in October 1995, our consulting executive committee, which makes the decisions on major investments, committed to going forward with this whole approach and building our own DesignShop-style environment.

MG Taylor helped E&Y build their own Design Center: the 12,000 square foot Accelerated Solutions Environment. In the same way, the Gossick Leadership Center was custom-tailored to AEDC's needs, the accelerated Solutions Environment is designed to handle E&Y's multiple design activities. E&Y uses the center for ongoing work with their clients, and uses it internally among E&Y employees for work that they do on behalf of their clients. The DesignShop vision has become the path on which E&Y is taking their own corporate development. It has become the method by which they work, and by which they work with their clients.

In explaining why E&Y is adopting the DesignShop process so enthusiastically, Lee returns again and again to the issue of speed:

> The business we're in—management consulting—can be frustrating, because you are obviously dependent upon other people to actually pull the switch and get things done. So, we are always very interested in new approaches and ideas that can get us through the design process and get into implementation faster, and that was the major draw that brought us to the DesignShop process.
>
> Because of competitive pressures and customer issues and shareholder activism and so forth, executives today at the major companies around the world need to get benefits faster than ever before. So the design of the solution—as well as getting the alignment of objectives and the executive group sponsorship and so forth, all at once and quickly—is a major reason why we are so excited about and have become so heavily involved with it.
>
> The key is being able to drive through the design activities and get the buy-in built much faster than we have been able to do in any other way. In the first half of 1996, we have had somewhere in the neighborhood of twelve of our clients go through three-day DesignShop events. These are companies like Digital Equipment, TRW, British Petroleum, First Chicago Bank, Monsanto, Hewlett Packard, and Xerox.

In every instance, we are getting done in three days what we would have historically accomplished in somewhere between six weeks and three months.

That is an increase of a factor of ten to thirty: a solid order-of-magnitude improvement in speed. It's accomplished through a deliberate effort to stretch the participants:

There's more parallel processing in the MG Taylor approach than what you would have found typically in our previous methods. Gail Taylor tells a story in which elementary school teachers, as they see their students not learning, try to solve the problem by "dumbing down" the material. As Gail says, that is exactly the wrong thing to do. You should be stretching them, pushing them, and pulling them into other scenarios and new angles to consider. We have grown to the point where we believe that. It's not yet totally incorporated into our approach and methods, but parallel processing, team activities, getting much more done faster—these are key elements for us.

Given that the process is producing excellent plans so quickly, how can that speed be maintained during implementation? Here E&Y got a pleasant surprise:

That is another huge plus in using the DesignShop process. Previously, if we were in a six-month consulting assignment, the amount of time, visibility, and internalization we got with the decision-makers and key executives at the client company might have been six hours over a six-month period. Now, with the DesignShop process, you get them for 35-40 hours in a three-day period. Their ownership of the designs, the decision-making, the commitment to go forward, the allocation of the resources and so on, all get done in three days, because you are able to get a much higher level of individual participation. And this is participation by individuals with much greater influence and—pardon the use of the word—power inside their organization.

In a typical consulting engagement, you wouldn't get that amount of time, and you wouldn't have it as concentrated. Therefore, the buy-in, implementation, and effective execution of the design is diluted and degraded, whereas in the three-day deal they come out of there ready to shoot the rockets and go.

We've already seen some dramatic examples. Typically it used to take a month to set up a meeting and get a decision made. But now there have been four situations—at places such as Digital Equipment, and the merger between First Chicago and National Bank of Detroit—where people were coming out of

DesignShop sessions on a Wednesday night, and on Friday morning they are presenting to the Chairman.

E&Y is now beginning to combine the DesignShop process with its huge existing base of solutions for business—a skills-and-knowledge base already bringing in a billion dollars of revenue per year. Lee tells of an early example showing what kind of results are possible:

> This is a case we just had recently: two companies have merged, and these two companies are both very large and successful in their own right. They come together, and one company has the tradition and history of building their own systems, their own applications; they were all internally developed and managed, maintained, and so on. The other company was a package-oriented company. They would go buy whatever they could find and develop very little, and let the outside firm take care of the management and the upgrades and so forth.
>
> Well, you bring those two organizations together and obviously there are some philosophical differences. How they are going to manage data, what is the architecture of their technology, what kind of applications are going to be used, what is the competitive advantage, what is the core competency that they need to manage and maintain internally versus what can be acquired outside that doesn't really possess any real differentiation? There is a huge amount of work to be done on these things.
>
> This group came for a three-day DesignShop session and, in the clients' words, they got 90% of the work done—decided upon, with an action plan agreed upon—in the three-day deal that they didn't believe they were going to get done in six months.
>
> They agreed to the strategy, the technology, architecture, what applications were unique and provided differentiation, and, therefore, would be internally maintained and developed, what would be packaged solutions, what would be transformed or carried over into the other organization, which ones would go across the bridge in opposite directions and the like. They believed that they built synergy and relationships that they couldn't have done otherwise.
>
> They believed that they got things done, as I said, in three days that they couldn't get done in six months. And it's worth a lot of money to them, because it allows them to get busy on implementation and begin to save money that in normal circumstances they wouldn't have begun to realize for another year.

Bringing the Future Back Home

Six months' work done in three days. Synergies that couldn't have been achieved in any other way.

Lee summed it up: "It's very quick, powerful, very decisive. It's faster and it's better."

That was in 1996.

Since then, clients have come back for second and third DesignShop events—and some for eight and nine— in rapid succession. When Chip told us about the president of a major consumer products company smashing through a brick wall, he was describing a group holding their second DesignShop event. Their first DesignShop session had focused on cost reduction. At the end of the event, during which they'd discovered how to make a savings cut of $250-300 million out of their supply chain, the president told the facilitation team that he wanted to come back for another DesignShop session in one month. This one he wanted to focus on growth—and that is where he picked up the $1 billion in new product opportunities.

MG Taylor is introducing DesignShop processes to more and more E&Y branches with successful work for major medical industry and tax and audit clients. Teaming with MG Taylor, they have held a series of DesignShop events for high tech, aerospace, consumer product, telecommunication, and medical industry clients from their Fortune 500 roster.

The theories and practices tell you what to manage and change instead of managing people. Now, the client and E&Y have had a taste of a different, better way to work. Potentially, this can revolutionize the way they do business.

In 1997, with a year and a half of DesignShop experience under their belts, E&Y is doing very well. Revenues, which had been on a cheery growth curve anyway, were up over 100% in one year.

More Follow-up

The other stories are just as interesting, whether they are the corporate stories or tales of the individuals involved.

- For CKE—the hamburger folks—the positive impact of their first DesignShop event has been dramatic.
  Before: After four years of declining same-store sales, CKE's stock was down to 6 7/8, with only one stock analyst even willing to follow their progress—everyone else had listed CKE as a "sell."
  After: As soon as the analysts saw the first prototype store based on the DesignShop work, there was a tremendous response—they could immediately tell the difference, as did the customers. Sales went up immediately at that store, and went up consistently at each store as it was re-done.

  Eighteen months after the DesignShop session, Bill Espinosa tells us that CKE has announced the new image a success and is rolling transformed Carl's Jr. locations out at the rate of four stores per week. Sales are up 40%, a consistent upward trend that shows the redesign is working in the long-term. The stock price has risen from 6 7/8 to 32—enabling a 3:2 stock split raising $71 million in equity in one year—directly due to the DesignShop event results. Twenty months after the Wharton event, CKE took its next step and began its spread to the East Coast by acquiring Hardee's, the fourth largest burger chain behind McDonald's, Burger King, and Wendy's.

- Frances Gillard—the shy secretary who went with trepidation to her first AEDC DesignShop session and ended up convincing her husband to handcraft a coffin in which to bury the hatchet—convinced herself that this strange facilitation DesignShop stuff was actually a wonderful new career. Her gut instinct to get in on the ground floor of something this dynamic has paid off. She has since left her job as Center Master at the Gossick Leadership Center to become an entrepreneur. She and her husband have opened a successful joint business in Tullahoma where he offers custom woodworking services and she offers facilitation and knowledge support to businesses and individuals. She has since become heavily involved with opening new management centers and educating new Knowledge Workers to the DesignShop process.

---

*Make the organization smarter all around you.
Improve the quality of the dialogue between your group and others.
Let your passions and values show.
Connect the people you influence with others who can broaden their understanding of the larger system.*

—Gifford & Elizabeth Pinchot
The End of Bureaucracy & the Rise of the Intelligent Organization

An Enterprise of One
http://www.mgtaylor.com/mgtaylor/jotm/fall96/entofone.htm

- Wharton was the first and only DesignShop Event for Orlando Health System, although a few individuals, like George Fortier, a consultant with the OHS team, attended several prior DesignShop activities. Because the Wharton event was a gathering of many different organizations, Orlando was not going to get the intensive focus on their issue that they would get if the event was custom-built to serve their needs. And, unlike the AEDC team who knew the ropes and could dive right in, the Orlando team were virtually all first-timers. Given this, was Orlando able to reap any benefit at all from its participation? It wouldn't be surprising if the take-home value was minimal. We checked in with Gary Strack a year and a half later to see what his perspective was.

  Gary: "It stimulated thinking in our organization about the future and forced us to revisit our strategic plans. It hasn't fundamentally changed the way we work. It's hard to quantify the impact of the DesignShop process, because it's not measurable. But it has influenced our thinking and therefore influenced our organization in many ways."

- For AEDC, the Wharton event was one in an ongoing series of DesignShop sessions which continue today. One of the items on AEDC's agenda at Wharton was to phase in a new contractor with the aid of a departing contractor. This raises the whole question of labor/management relations, which had once been so rocky. What has happened?

  Eighteen months after Wharton, relationships between contractors, labor unions, and managment are excellent, and continue to work successfully. The hand-off from old contractors to new ones flows smoothly as new members are merged into Team AEDC through the DesignShop process. As the word on AEDC has spread, General Basilio of the Air Force Materials Command now uses AEDC as a model of how to have better partnerships.

  The most impressive part of the AEDC story is the network of partnerships and alliances—the web of value—that now links commerical industry, military customers, and educational work to do good together and contribute more fully to all aspects of American aerospace.

Today AEDC has increased its full service to the country to become a joint operation with all service branches. In addition to an Air Force Commander, they now have a Navy Vice Commander, and the Army also now does testing there. In the future, it is expected that the Army will bring people there full-time.

AEDC based the network on a covenant: a statement of principles committing everyone to do good together. "If you are doing anything complex, first sign a covenant of principles before you sign a contract," says Colonel Bill. Far from being an empty gesture, the covenants have in fact led to contracts, and tens of millions of dollars of commercial testing work continues to grow for AEDC.

- The task for the F15 Eagle team at Wharton was to develop a vision of how to get F15 jet to go into 21st century in an effective, efficient way. The Wharton DesignShop event provided the roots of what became the "Intelligent Partnership" strategy for linking the war fighter, the contractor team, and the taxpayer. Arising from the DesignShop work, the notion of the covenant has also become the basis for how the F15 has successfully structured itself to move into the future. This covenant has been signed by thousands of people, and continues to gain participants.

The Intelligent Partnership covenant lays out the principles under which anyone associated with the F15 will operate as a team.

The Partnership has to decide what is better and more efficient for the contractor to do, and what is better for government to do, so that what happens is best for both the taxpayer and warfighter. In many ways, it is not simple—the government entities are giving up activities that they've been doing for fifty years. Col. Bill stressed the importance of doing it properly: "You don't want to damage the war fighter. You don't want to damage the taxpayer. You don't want to damage individual people, whether they are in industry or government. Jobs will change, and work can change from one side of the equation to the other without hurting anyone. The F15 group learned that through the DesignShop process."

In order to have their strategic vision become real, the F15 team focused on "what do we have to do, starting today, to make this happen." This bringing the future to the present, bringing the There to Here, is something that F15 learned straight out of DesignShop activities.

First they came out with the Intelligent Partnership strategy, then a strategic plan, and a detailed tactical plan for operating. They came up with a dynamic process for evaluting the needs of the airplane. They developed an effective decision-making process to decide how to spend limited dollars on the airplane. The war fighter could now set priorties to ask for budgeting money. Everybody has agreed on what the key decisions are, on what money should be spent for, what is the most valuable. The whole decision process is now focused on what is most valuable; both the process and the quality of the decisions have improved. Squeaky wheels go away. They may squeak, but just squeaking loudly no longer generates funding, because in the new process everybody agrees on what is most important.

The F15 team is now working on organizing their next DesignShop event.

- And Col. Bill?

Back in 1994 and 1995, Jim Champy, author of *Reengineering the Corporation*, had intensively studied a handful of leaders from across the country who had successfully transformed their organizations. Of these people, only one was not from industry and finance: Col. Bill, who was transforming AEDC using the DesignShop process. Champy's management consulting firm rounded-up Col. Bill and a half dozen other executives to come and teach Fortune 500 companies and Harvard Business School folks what they had learned.

Col. Bill must have liked the teaching experience. After holding two top jobs for five years, Col. Bill chose to compete with 120 other colonels for a teaching post. He won out and is now teaching leadership, management, and communications to MIT and Harvard students.

AEDC based the network on a covenant: a statement of principles committing everyone to do good together. "If you are doing anything complex, first sign a covenant of principles before you sign a contract," says Colonel Bill. Far from being an empty gesture, the covenants have in fact led to contracts, and tens of millions of dollars of commercial testing work continues to grow for AEDC.

- Back in 1990, it was Jack Yurish and Vince Wasik's leveraged buyout of National Car Rental that brought that company to a DesignShop session. National is now implementing that prescient plan, developed almost a decade ago.

    Jack Yurish and Vince Wasik have moved on to other ventures and adventures. They continue to use DesignShops as a potent tool. Jack attended the Wharton event to keep his thinking sharp on the type of flexible, interactive organization structures companies need to survive the complexity and change of the future.

    Vince, through his investment capital firm, Morningside Capital, runs his new companies through DesignShop activities to jump-start them and give them a competitive edge. One of Vince's main objectives is to help African-Americans realize the rewards of the free enterprise system. In August 1994, he invested in Carson Products, a company run by an executive staff of African-Americans, manufacturing hair care products for African-Americans. In October 1995, Vince took the company to a DesignShop event with the intent of getting everyone on the same sheet of paper, and moving the company forward to the point where it could be taken public. The results were so dramatic and produced such tremendous progress in such a short period of time that Merrill Lynch, the main underwriter, said "No, we don't have to wait three years before an initial public offering. We could do it in thirteen months."

    As we write this, Carson Products has just gone public with a ten times gain in value, after completing many mergers and having recently bought out a division of Johnson Products.

- Michael Kaufman, the facilitator who so impressed the E&Y team in their breakout group, has moved to Palo Alto to work in the West Coast's first KnOwhere store. Coming right out of the world of DesignShop events, these stores give people across the U.S. access to the creative tools and toys, books, the weird and wonderful furniture, office design services, and the DesignShop facilitation teams—the people who custom design the ride to creativity and provide valet service for your mind. People from big businesses and small, cruise into KnOwhere locations to hold one-time

KnOwhere Store
http://www.knowherestore.com

DesignShop activities targeted on a specific business problem. Or they get the facilitation team to help outfit their personal work environments or create their own management centers. Sounds like Michael is heading for serious, high-tech fun, and the Silicon Valley is getting a new form of creative technology that it can profitably use.

For people working in the form of art called "business," the creative process continues forever. But just like a painting is a work of art that stops at an interesting place, this book has to pause somewhere.

In the appendices and bibliography are tools to help you continue on your journey. Start making changes. Travel to the future and bring your vision home.

We would like to leave you with the kind of closure and drive to action that propels people out of the DesignShop event on the last day, and sends them home motivated to do what it takes to change your environment into that envisioned state. Our last set of exercises is designed to help you get yourself back to the future.

Challenge

1. This is the last opportunity we have to work together in the main body of this book: we the authors, and you the reader. We have established a ritual of recording impressions and questions upon completing each chapter of the book without looking back at it for analysis. It has become a comfortable habit by now, and we will ask you to do it one more time.

2. What are parts of the old structure that you want to leave behind? Write these down on a separate piece of paper.

   Now take a match, and burn the things that are part of the past.

3. Structure wins. The best of visions perish if the structure that must be employed to realize them is not simultaneously set in place. What pieces of the environment, tools, policies, processes can you establish now to help facilitate your work and incubate your vision? How can you bind these together so that they reinforce each other and cease to be pieces, but a self-organizing whole?

   Take these with you into the future.

4. It's time for you to formulate the questions. What is your next challenge? How can you keep learning? How can you keep powerful collaboration going without the slipping back into the traditional sense of control? What questions do you need to ask of yourself to take the next leap?

Following Up

For more information on the DesignShop process and related ways of improving your organization's ways of working, contact:

MG Taylor Corporation
2044 Sea Loft
Hilton Head Island, SC 29928 USA
email: info@mgtaylor.com
web: www.mgtaylor.com
phone: 888-knowhere (888-566-9437)

Additional facilities in Cambridge, Massachusetts and Palo Alto, California

Pergamit & Peterson
PO Box 60775
Palo Alto, CA 94306 USA
email: gayle@pergamit.com, chris@pergamit.com
web: www.pergamit.com
phone: 415.233.1116

For Taylor-designed Client and Partner Management Centers, Navigation Centers, and Work Environments, see: http://www.mgtaylor.com/mgtaylor.htm

Axioms

A DesignShop axiom cannot be proven to be true: it simply is. The value of an axiom is found only by discovery -- through applying it to real situations.

- The future is rational only in hindsight.

- You can't get THERE from HERE; but you can get HERE from THERE.

- Discovering you don't know something is the first step to knowing it.

- Everything that someone tells you is true. They are reporting their experience of reality.

- To argue with someone else's experience is a waste of time.

- To add someone's experience to your experience, to create a new experience, is possibly valuable.

- The only valid test of an idea, concept or theory is what it enables you to do.

- You understand the instructions only after you have assembled the red wagon.

- If you can't have fun with the problem, you will never solve it.

- Every individual in this room already possesses an answer.

- The purpose of this intensive interaction is to stimulate one, several or all of us to remember and extract what we already know.

- Creativity is the process of eliminating options.

- In every adverse condition, there are hundreds of good solutions.

- You fail until you succeed.

- Nothing fails like success.

Bibliography

Further Reading

In 1977, the Taylors compiled a list of 500 books that contributed to the basic foundation of their first management center. Books have always been an integral part of the DesignShop environment. Here is a short list to get you started.

Environment

Alexander, Christopher, Sara Ishikawa, Murray Silverstein, Max Jacobson, Ingrid Fiksdahl-King, Shlomo Angel. *A Pattern Language: Towns Buildings, Construction.* New York: Oxford University Press, 1977.
> Years of extensive research has yielded archetypal language—pattern language—for design of environmental elements ranging from communities and open spaces, to buildings, to areas such as window seats; use of this language gives lay people a practical application of architectural principles.

Alexander, Christopher. *A Timeless Way of Building.* New York: Oxford University Press, 1979.
> This new theory of architecture uncovers the patterns which bring a room, neighborhood, town, city, or region to life and give it unique identity.

Boulton, Alexander O. Frank Lloyd Wright, *Architect: An Illustrated Biography.* New York: Rizzoli, 1993.
> Boulton traces the life and work of the twentieth-century American architect who called his innovative ideas "organic architecture."

Brand, Stewart. *How Buildings Learn: What Happens After They're Built.* New York: Viking, 1994.
> Buildings improve with time—if they're allowed. Brand shows how to work with time rather than against it.

Hall, Edward T. *Hidden Dimension.* New York: Anchor Books, 1990.
> Hall introduces the science of proxemics to demonstrate how our use of space can affect personal and business relations, cross-cultural interactions, architecture, city planning, and urban renewal.

Hiss, Tony. *The Experience of Place: A Completely New Way of Looking At and Dealing With Our Radically Changing Cities and Countryside.* New York: Knopf, 1990.
> "Simultaneous perception" allows our surroundings to disturb or soothe us as we engage in our tasks; computer simulations can determine the effect of simultaneous perception and aid in careful urban planning which will allow our environments to enrich the lives of future generations.

Organizational Strategy

Schwartz, Peter. *The Art of the Long View: Paths to Strategic Insight for Yourself and Your Company.* New York: Doubleday, 1996.
> How to use scenario planning for developing strategic vision, navigating the future.

Stack, Jack with Bo Burlingham, ed. *The Great Game of Business: The Only Sensible Way to Run a Company.* New York: Doubleday Currency, 1992.
> Employee teams will focus and perform best if they perform like owners—with full information on the business including all financial matters.

Wing, R. L. *The Art of Strategy: A New Translation of Sun Tzu's Classic, The Art of War.* New York: Doubleday, 1988.
> The fifty-two passages contained in this translation of classic essays can be used as worksheets showing the way to a clean and aesthetic triumph over life's obstacles by observing, calculating, outwitting and outmaneuvering adversaries and avoiding battles.

Bibliography

Complexity and Emergent Systems

Bateson, Gregory. *Mind and Nature: A Necessary Unity.* New York: Dutton, 1979.
> Bateson applies his research on cybernetics and information theory to anthropology in an early venture into bringing the human and technological realms together.

Bateson, Gregory. *Steps to an Ecology of Mind: Collected Essays in Anthropology, Psychiatry, Evolution, and Epistemology.* San Francisco: Chandler Publishing Co., 1972.
> This collection includes a wide range of Bateson's early journal publications and speeches, and including his metalogues (dialogues with his daughter), his theory of schizophrenia, and his research on aquatic mammals and on semantics.

Jantsch, Erich. *The Self-Organizing Universe: Scientific and Human Implications of the Emerging Paradigm of Evolution.* New York: Pergamon Press, 1980.
> For many years the de facto landmark publication on self-organization, this book includes a heavy focus on dissipative structures and autopoietic theory.

Johanssom, Borje, Charlie Karlsson, Lars Westin, eds. *Patterns of a Network Economy.* New York: Springer-Verlag, 1994.
> The advances in spatial and network concepts of economics, and the technological innovations that power them, have wide-ranging implications for international trade and the global economy.

Kauffman, Stuart. *At Home in the Universe: The Search for Laws of Self-Organization and Complexity.* New York: Oxford University Press, 1995.
> Darwinian selection alone cannot explain the complex systems and general laws that define the universe; another force, the emergence of self-organized order from chaos, is a concept we are just beginning to understand and apply to complex social and economic phenomena.

Kelly, Kevin. *Out of Control: The Rise of Neo-Biological Civilization.* New York: Addison Wesley, 1994. (Also available on the Internet.)
>In the new era, robust adaptability and autonomy of living organisms becomes a model for human systems from telecommunications to the global economy to drug design.

Kuhn, Thomas. *The Structure of Scientific Revolutions.* Chicago, IL: University of Chicago Press, 1996.
>In this landmark book—initiating the concept of paradigm shift—the author hypothesizes that scientific progress does not come only by evolution, but by a series of interludes of gradual progress punctuated by intellectually violent revolutions.

Minsky, Marvin. *The Society of Mind.* New York: Simon & Schuster, 1988.
>A seminal book on the role of agents in cognition, language, and a unified theory of the mind.

Resnick, Mitchel. *Turtles, Termites and Traffic Jams: Explorations in Massively Parallel Microworlds.* Cambridge, MA: MIT Press, 1994.
>Exploring the counterintuitive world of decentralized systems and self-organizing phenomena, Resnick examines how people resist decentralized ideas and proposes an innovative computer language that helps develop powerful new ways of thinking.

Toffler, Alvin. *Powershift: Knowledge, Wealth, and Violence at the Edge of the 21st Century.* New York: Bantam Books, 1990. Also available on audio cassette.
>The next century will herald a new system of high-tech wealth creation, and a tremendous upheaval as a new system, with workers owning the "tools of production" in the form of knowledge, become the "prosumers" who define the market.

Toffler, Alvin. *The Third Wave.* New York: Morrow, 1980.
>The second of Toffler's trilogy, Third Wave traces the nature and rate of social change from the Agricultural Era of the hunter-gatherers through the second wave or industrial revolution, to the third wave—the information revolution in which we are now participating—and its implications on human production and society.

Waldrop, Mitchell. *Complexity: The Emerging Science at the Edge of Order and Chaos.* New York: Simon & Schuster, 1992.

> Waldrop traces the development of the emerging science of complexity and its implications to our organizational and economic systems through a multi-disciplinary focus, from biology to mathematics to emergent economic systems.

Learning and Organizations

Axelrod, Robert. *The Evolution of Cooperation.* New York: Basic Books, 1984.

> Axelrod explores the balance between egoism and social interaction and its implication in our changing social structures in areas such as cooperation, mathematical and strategic games, conflict management, and consensus-building.

Nonaka, Ikujiro and Hiro Takeuchi. *The Knowledge Creating Company.* New York: Oxford University Press, 1995.

> The success of Japanese companies is in creating explicit knowledge (manuals, procedures, etc.) from tacit (experiential) knowledge through the work of middle managers who bridge the gap between top management ideas and the chaotic realities of the front line.

Senge, Peter. *Fifth Discipline: The Art and Practice of the Learning Organization.* New York: Doubleday/Currency, 1990.

> Five "component technologies" provide the vital dimensions necessary to build organizations that continually enhance their capacity to realize high goals: personal mastery, shared vision, mental models, team learning, and systems thinking.

Weiner, Norbert. *The Human Use of Human Beings: Cybernetics and Society.* Boston: Houghton Mifflin, 1954.

> "The purpose of this book is to explain the potentialities of the machine in fields which up to now have been taken to be purely human and to warn against the dangers of a purely selfish exploitation of these possibilities in a world in which to human beings, human beings are all-important."

Wilson, Robert Anton. *The New Inquisition: Irrational Rationalism and the Citadel of Science.* Phoenix, AZ; Falcon Press, 1986.
> An off-beat look at skepticism, knowledge, science, philosophy, materialism and 'rational science' in the context of twentieth-century society.

Technology

Asimov, Isaac. *The Foundation Trilogy* (Foundation's Edge,.....) New York: Caedmon, 1982. (Available as a sound recording read by the author.)
> Asimov weaves the futuristic story of galactic history in the time between two empires as thinkers struggle to reduce 10,000 years of chaos to 1,000.

Bailey, James. *After Thought: The Computer Challenge to Human Intelligence.* New York: Basic Books, 1996.
> New, more powerful computers will "think" in terms of pictures and paths, not numbers, challenging the primacy of humans as reasoners.

Brand, Stewart. *The Media Lab: Inventing the Future at MIT.* New York, Viking, 1987.
> A look at the work of one of the most exciting R&D labs in the world, and how it is individualizing tomorrow's media.

Drexler, K. Eric. *Engines of Creation.* New York: Doubleday, 1987.
> A broad look at a future with nanotechnology, space development, machine intelligence, hypertext publishing, Engines calls for improved ways of debating technology policy.

Drexler, K. Eric. *Nanosystems: Molecular Machinery, Manufacturing, and Computation.* New York: Wiley, 1992.
> The first hard-core textbook giving the analysis behind the case for molecular nanotechnology—challenging but helpful, even if all you read are the illustrations.

Bibliography

Drexler, K. Eric and Chris Peterson with Gayle Pergamit. *Unbounding the Future: The Nanotechnology Revolution.* New York: Quill, 1991.
> Manipulation of matter at the molecular level to create new products with atom-by-atom precision will impinge on every part of our lives and revolutionize the whole world.

Fuller, R. Buckminster. *Ideas and Integrities, A Spontaneous Autobiographical Disclosure.* Englewood Cliffs, NJ; Prentice-Hall, 1963.
> The pioneer of designs and concepts such as the geodesic dome, the Dymaxion world map, and countless other structures that have changed the face of the world describes the development of his creative innovations and demonstrates how we may harvest technological advances to benefit all humanity.

Negroponte, Nicholas. *Being Digital.* New York: Knopf, 1995.
> With bits replacing atoms as the basic commodity of human interaction, the revolution in information technology is liberating computers from the confines of keyboards and fundamentally altering how we learn, work, and entertain ourselves.

Rheingold, Howard. *The Virtual Community: Homesteading on the Electronic Frontier.* New York: Harperperennial Library, 1994. (Also online.)
> It is our essential task to transform ourselves from mere social creatures into community creatures if human evolution is to proceed; Rheingold is making those steps with millions of others via the electronic media, an ecosystem of subcultures made possible by rapidly expanding technologies.

Weiner, Norbert. *Invention: The Care and Feeding of Ideas.* Cambridge, MA: MIT Press, 1993.
> The father of cybernetics looks at the history of ideas and inventions, some of the social and economic patterns related to those inventions, and the innovation and change that are required if future technologies are to serve all segments of the world's population.

Weiner, Norbert. *The Human Use of Human Beings: Cybernetics and Society.* Boston: Houghton Mifflin, 1954.
> "The purpose of this book is to explain the potentialities of the machine in fields which up to now have been taken to be purely human and to warn against the dangers of a purely selfish exploitation of these possibilities in a world in which to human beings, human beings are all-important."

Wieners, Brad and David Pescovitz. *Reality Check.* San Francisco: Hardwired, 1996.
> Compilation from Wired magazine of technological projections, listed by date of expected arrival.

Education, Learning, and Creativity

Bolt, Lawrence G. *Zen and the Art of Making a Living: A Practical Guide to Creative Career Design.* New York: Arkana, 1993.
> This innovative, unconventional, and profoundly practical career guide attacks the conventional thinking and describes new approaches to the twentieth century workplace.

Briggs, John. *Fire in the Crucible: The Alchemy of Creative Genius.* New York: St. Martin's Press, 1988.
> The author discusses the roots and development of genius and creative ability.

Leonard, George. *Education and Ecstasy.* New York: Delacorte Press, 1968. (also available from San Francisco: Big Sur Recordings, 1970. Cassette.)
> The highest form of personal fulfillment is education.

Leonard, George. *Mastery: The Keys to Long-Term Success and Fulfillment.* New York: Plume, 1991.
> The five keys to mastery are Instruction, Practice, Surrender (being a student), Intentionality (visualization and exercise), The Edge (pushing the limit); using these keys, people can sustain activity on the plateaus that are necessary until a new level is reached.

Bibliography

Gardner, Howard. *Multiple Intelligences: The Theory in Practice.* New York: Basic Books, 1993.

>The ability to solve problems or fashion products valued in one or more cultures is intelligence, and all people have in varying degrees seven types of intelligence: linguistic, logical, musical, spatial, kinesthetic, intrapersonal, and interpersonal. (In later books, Gardner has added "naturalistic" intelligence, referring to those who can distinguish among and classify features of the environment.)

Halprin, Lawrence and Jim Burns. *Taking Part: A Workshop Approach to Collective Creativity.* Cambridge, MA: MIT Press, 1974.

>Includes suggestions and examples of enhancing creativity in a wide variety of "disciplines" through group relationships.

Heinlein, Robert. *Time Enough for Love.* New York: Ace Books, 1994 (reissue).

>Through fiction, the author approaches the future and the human potentialities within it; the story about a man who discovers that love and mutual respect are the true reasons for wanting to live forever.

Heller, Steven and Steele, Terry Lee. *Monsters and Magical Sticks: There's No Such Thing as Hypnosis?* Phoenix, AZ: Falcon Press, 1987.

>Defining hypnotism as an altered state of mind, the authors take a look at the frequency with which we are all hypnotized, how we accomplish such altered states, and how they can effect our productivity, creativity and overall health, and our personal and organizational orientations to future possibilities.

Expanding Your Learning Power

Adler, Mortimer J. and Charles van Doren. *How to Read a Book.* New York: Simon and Schuster, 1972.

>In this popular revision of the original classic, the authors describe how to achieve higher levels of reading, how to determine quickly the author's point of view; they present the various ways to get the most out of reading different types of material.

Buzan, Tony and Barry Buzan. *The Mind Map Book.* New York, Dutton, 1994.
   Graphics can free your ideas to grow and expand constantly; graphic techniques such as mind mapping can help you mirror and magnify your brain's patterns of perception and significantly increase your ability to learn, think, and create and to join with others to pool thinking productively.

Kistler, Mark. *Draw Squad.* New York: Simon & Schuster, 1988.
   Step-by-step, the author takes us through principles, examples, and exercises that enable the least "visual" of us to draw quickly and confidently.

Koberg, Don and Jim Bagnall. *The Universal Traveler: A Soft-systems Guide to Creativity, Problem-Solving, and the Process of Design.* Los Altos, CA: W. Kaufmann, 1974.
   The authors identify essential types of questions that must be asked if problems are to be solved efficiently—questions concerning the nature, origin, and complexity of the problem to be addressed, and the resources and change needed to address it.

Leadership and Communication

Bennis, Warren and Patricia Biederman. *Organizing Genius: The Secrets of Creative Collaboration.* Reading, MA: Addison-Wesley, 1997.
   A leadership expert examines how the leaders of six Great Groups created a 'collaborative advantage'.

Greenleaf, Robert. *Servant Leadership: A Journey in to the Nature of Legitimate Power and Greatness.* New York: Paulist Press, 1977.
   Greenleaf's hypotheses—true leaders are chosen by their followers based on skills in awareness, foresight, listening, and ability to use power to benefit the organization—has influenced an entire generation of management experts and institutional leaders in determining the true servant roles of their organizations.

Bibliography

Hall, Edward T. *The Silent Language.* Garden City, NY: Doubleday, 1959.
> We can understand complex cultural data only when we understand various Primary Message Systems—so enculturated that we are not aware of the extent to which our responses are build upon it—including cultural aspects of interaction, association, subsistence, bisexuality, territoriality, temporality, learning, play, defense, and exploitation.

Block, Peter. *Stewardship: Choosing Service Over Self Interest.* San Francisco: Berrett-Koehler Publishers, 1993.
> Applying the principles of stewardship will radically change all areas of organizations from governance to management; organizations will succeed in their marketplaces by choosing stewardship over self-interest and redistributing purpose and wealth; individuals will choose responsibility over entitlement, holding themselves accountable to those over whom they exercise power.

Hesselbein, Frances, Marshall Goldsmith, Richard Beckhard, eds. *The Leader of the Future: New Visions, Strategies, and Practices for the Next Era.* San Francisco: Jossey-Bass, 1996.
> A collection of essays based on four principles: a leader is someone who has followers, who produces results, who sets examples, and who takes full responsibility.

Acknowledgments

Test Readers

Our secret weapon: test readers to whom we could turn, knowing we would get merciless and insightful criticism, as well as useful and creative suggestions for improvements. We wanted to write a book that would be useful to our friends, and anyone working on challenging projects. You made sure we did it:

Christopher Allen, Mindy Bokser, James CastroLang, Stephanie Corchnoy, Allan Drexler, Cay Drexler, Marie-Louise Kagan, Judy Merkle, Chip Morningstar, David J. Ross, Heidi Ross, E. Dean Tribble, Linda Vetter.

DesignShop Specialists

You took us inside your world of Key Facilitators and Knowledge Workers, of the Creative Process Cycle, and time traveling into the future. You were our exemplars of creative and cooperative teamwork. You shared with us the insights that you've gathered over several hundred years of combined experience in bringing people to their maximums and solving their problems.

It is said that you have to experience a DesignShop event to truly understand it: you've got to get on the boat and take the ride, not just hear about it. This is correct. But if we've succeeded in giving people even a hint of what the experience is about, it's because you helped us explain the unexplainable:

Kelvy Bird, Bill Blackburn, R.K. Bruce, Jr., Doug Cantrell, Bryan Coffman, Rob Evans, Jon Foley, Christopher Fuller, Pat Gibson, Frances Gillard, Todd Johnston, Gunner Kaersvang, Patsy Kahoe, Michael Kaufman, Scott Kjelgaard, Lisa Piazza, Chip Saltsman, Gail Taylor, Matt Taylor, Robert Taylor, Amelia Thornton.

Experienced Sponsors and Participants

First, they had the insight and courage to take their companies through DesignShop events and transformation. Then, they had the courage and heart to share their stories with us. When we demanded to know if this process really worked and where it failed, they unflinchingly gave us the inside view of the journey including the good and the bad, the troubles and the triumphs:

Bill Espinosa, Larry Ford, Lynn Galida, Ralph Graham, Keith Kushman, Greg "Deacon" Lewis, Elsa Porter, John Poparad II, Col. Bill Rutley, Lee Sage, Garry Singleton, Gary Strack, Jack Yurish, Jerry Wind.

Special Thanks

To Bryan Coffman who designed and wrote the exercises that follow each chapter and for the weblinks that he and Jay Smethurst added to enrich the text; to Chip Saltsman for comments, quotes, and feedback above and beyond the call of duty; to Jolynn Steffan for layout and editing labors; to Judy Hill for proofing punctiliously; to Pat Gibson for the massive transcription work intelligently and artistically done; to Patsy Kahoe for coordinating MG Taylor's immense assistance; to Sheryl Corchnoy for her assistance with our organization as authors; to Peter Durand and Christopher Fuller for their artwork that captures the emotion and essence of the DesignShop ride; and to Christopher for also contributing the cover design of the book.

To Matt Taylor and Gail Taylor for letting us rummage around through their life's work and harass them with endless questions about what, how, why, where, and "what do you mean by that?"

Index

Symbols

3D Model 11, 94, 149, 151
3D modeling equipment 93
3D modeling kits 140

A

Accelerated Solutions Environment 246
Act 179, 181, 76, 156 See also Scan, Focus.
AEDC 4, 50, 51, 52, 55, 101, 117, 139, 141, 148, 180, 205, 234, 250, 251
African Queen 37-38, 40, 76
Agency Group 48, 50, 56, 59, 81, 154
agenda 199, 217, 228
aha 180, 213
Air Force 226
ambiguity 7, 78
American Airlines 4
ants 129, 130 See also metaphors.
architecture 84, 86, 89, 95, 133
Army Corps of Engineer 141
Arnold, General Hap 102, 113
assumptions 201
AT&T 232
authors 201, 153, 156
Avis Rent-A-Car 5, 39, 40
axioms 95, 123, 177

B

Babcock, Bill 23
backcasting 205, 206, 36, 37, 38, 39, 62, 111, 147
badges 14
barrier 3, 13, 27, 40, 76, 90, 111, 115, 182, 214, 241
Basilio, General 251
Bell, Charlie 39
bibliography 201, 255
body language 68, 73
Boeing 107, 111, 115, 118, 119
Bogart, Humphrey 37
Bokser, Mindy 135
books 12, 14, 93, 153
Boulder County Development Office 5
brainstorming 7, 209
bury the hatchet 53, 54, 250

C

Camelot 239, 240
Cantrell, Doug 106, 114
Capitol Holding 48
Carl's Jr. 3, 16, 18, 19, 20, 23, 38, 44, 139, 140, 154, 180, 205, 250 See also CKE.
Carson Products 254
Carter, President Jimmy 74
cathedral 84
Challenge 10, 26, 60, 79, 99, 123, 157, 176, 221, 235, 256
Champy, Jim 253
chaos 224
CKE 15, 16, 20, 21, 250 See also Carl's Jr.
clothing 12
coffin 250
Coffman, Bryan 31, 74, 76, 140, 141, 169, 218, 224, 225, 226, 230
collaboration 45, 55
Common Experience 47-48
complexity 136, 208
conflict 21, 22, 32
core competency 248
Cortez 211
Covey, Stephen 109, 121
Creative Cycle 206-207, 214-215
Creative Process 22, 61, 78, 90, 99, 203, 219, 221, 255

Creativity 178
Csikszentmihalyi, Mihaly 178
Cushman, Keith 110, 114, 199

D

Death and Life of Great American Cities, The 86
Deming Management Method 61, 65, 109, 218
DesignSession 17, 32
DesignShop process 2, 6
Digital Equipment 247
Discovery Day 199
Discovery Session 200
Disneyland 18
Do or Die 204, 205
documentation 76
Drucker, Peter 105

E

education 73, 79

environment 1, 9, 11-12, 21-22, 26, 28, 30, 32, 48, 66, 84, 87-91, 96, 101, 132, 160, 164, 200, 213, 215, 241, 245
Environmental Pollution Agency 102
Ernst & Young 68, 140, 161, 178, 231, 243, 244, 245,
Escape from Los Colinas 168
Espinosa, Bill 15-16, 250
Evans, Rob 170, 201-202, 207, 210, 212
experience 73

F

F-15 6, 121, 141, 228, 252
F-16 103
FAA 4
facilitation team 173, 181, 200, 216, 217, 218, 230
facilitator 181, 212, 214, 217, 224
fear 231
feedback 219, 230
First Chicago and National Bank of Detroit 247
first-timer 8
flocking 162
Focus 179, 76, 139 See also Scan, Act.
Foley, Jon 4, 9, 50, 56, 81, 82, 111, 143, 154, 163, 218, 224, 225 See also Agency Group.
Ford 150, 153, 228
Forester, C. S. 37, 76
forming the problem 130
Fortier, George 251. See also Orlando Health System.
Fortune Magazine 39, 70
Fuller, Buckminster 98
Fuller, Christopher 32, 233
furniture 11, 93, 173

G

Galida, Lynn 33, 34
General Electric 107, 118
General Motors 150, 152, 153
Gibson, Pat 230
Gillard, Frances 32, 53, 109, 141, 224, 226, 230, 233, 250
Gossick Leadership Center 117, 121, 242, 246, 250
Graham, Ralph 110, 114, 242
Grannan, Bob 81, 82
grocery chain 4
group genius 1, 22
Gulliver 134

H

Hall, Edward T. 154
Hardee's 250
Harvard Business School 253
Hepburn, Katherine 37
Hertz 153
Hispanic Chamber of Commerce 74
Hitler, Adolph 84
Horatio Hornblower 37
hotel meeting room 11
hotel staff 165

hypertiles 91

I

InfoBroker team 57. See also Agency Group
Inside the Third Reich 85
Inventing the Problem 141-143, 147-148
iteration 147, 208, 209

J

Jacobs, Jane 86
Johnston, Todd 226
journal 237

K

Kaersvang, Gunner 227, 230
Kahoe, Patsy 162, 165, 166
Karmen, Theodore von 113
Kaufman, Michael 109, 140, 167, 169, 218, 254
Kelly, Kevin 208
key facilitator 162, 163, 170, 171, 199
kinesthetic 72, 73, 84-85, 88
kiosk 92, 152
KnOwhere 254
knowledge base 237
knowledge lead 164
Knowledge Wall 167, 63, 92
knowledge work 160, 176
knowledge worker 13, 64, 90, 109, 166, 216-217, 242, 250

L

Learning Organization, The 144
lighting 91
Lion King, The 243
logistics 165, 166, 199
Long John Silver 17
Lozanov, Georgi 28

M

Maccoby, Michael 74
Management Center 242
management consultants 171
management consulting 246. See also Ernst & Young.
Medicaid 65
meme 169
Merlin 239, 240
Merrill Lynch 254
metaphor 7, 72, 125, 127, 130, 137, 145, 210, 214, 216
Meyers/Briggs 107
MG Taylor Corporation 257
Michelangelo 78
Mitsubishi 49
modeling 72, 79, 135, 149, 170
Mongol Horde 212
Morningside Capital 254
music 12, 28, 162

N

NASA 112, 115, 119, 136

Index

National Car Rental 5, 150, 254
Navy 119
nonlinear process 207-208

O

ocean 210
Orlando Hospital 211
Orlando Regional Health Care System 65, 251
Out of Control 208

P

PanAm 4
paradigms 207
Pergamit, Gayle 140, 257
Peterson, Chris 257
Philadelphia 8, 177. See also Wharton.
physical activity 12
Poparad, John 52, 53, 54, 104, 107-108, 110, 117, 120, 129, 161, 168
Porter, Elsa 15, 61, 74, 129, 231
Post-it Note™ 92
potter's wheel 209
Pratt & Whitney 107, 112, 118
Process Facilitator 162, 163, 164, 171, 199
Project Manager 164
prospect 91

R

radiant room 25, 43
rainforest 128, 211. See also metaphors.
read-aheads 19, 146, 216
Reengineering the Corporation 253
refuge 92
Report-Out 64, 68, 130
Rilke 35
rivers 211. See also metaphors.
Rolls Royce 118
Rutley, Col. Bill 51, 52, 53, 54, 101, 103, 108, 111, 113, 115, 120, 228, 233, 242, 252, 253

S

Sage, Lee 244, 245, 249, 68
Saint Simon Engineering School 126
Saltsman, Chip
    164, 169, 172, 178, 180, 182, 201, 204, 207-208, 211, 215-216, 218, 227, 238, 249
Scan 66, 67, 69, 73, 74, 79, 110, 123, 134, 139, 143, 146, 174, 179, 200, 210, 227. See also Focus, Act.
Scan/Focus/Act 43, 60, 61, 110, 202, 203, 216, 221, 227
scenario 204, 223, 247
schedule 28, 30, 32-34
scribes 168, 169, 170-171
sensor 219
Share-a-Panel 44, 46, 63, 200
ships 132
Silicon Valley 255

simulations 142
sleeping on the problem 31
South Africa 4
Speer, Adolph 84
sponsor 30, 33, 181, 199, 200-201, 212, 219, 223
sponsor meeting 226
staff 33, 53
stakeholders 8, 14-15, 17, 21, 25, 56
Star Trek: The Next Generation 49
Store 2000 18, 24, 38
stovepiping 103, 120
Strack, Gary 251

T

tactile 88
Take-a-Page 10
Take-a-Panel 200, 44, 45, 62
Taylor, Gail 36, 39, 46-47, 50, 65-66, 71, 77, 97-98, 128, 143, 145, 177-178, 204, 216, 218, 245, 247
Taylor, Matt 37, 48, 55, 95, 110, 115, 130, 133-136, 159, 170, 172, 177, 180, 201, 206, 219, 225, 228-229-230, 245
Taylor, Robert 131
temperature 88
Thompson, Tom 19
time 23, 24, 28, 29, 30, 35
time compression 35, 36, 59
Time Travel 35
Time Warp Machine 83
tool kit 1, 7, 9, 31, 60
tools 1, 29, 32, 90, 160
Total Asset Management System 5. See also National Car Rental.
Total Quality Management 3, 104, 107, 121, 238
touch screen ordering 20
toys 11, 12, 111
tsukubai 84
Tullahoma 250, 102. See also AEDC.
TWA 4

U

Unbounding the Future 155
United Airlines 4

V

vantage points 31, 55, 62, 201, 210
verbal learning 72, 73
Vetter, Linda 70
visual learning 72-73, 88, 90

W

Wall Capture Team 164
Wall Street Journal 36, 109
Wasik, Vince 254
Weak Signal Research 154, 220
Wharton 8, 15, 25, 33, 40, 43-44, 61, 94, 101, 121, 125, 137, 145, 147, 153, 155, 162, 174, 177, 202, 206, 210-

211, 228, 237, 244, 250, 252
white wall 58
Wind, Jerry 43
work product 237
WorkWall™ 200, 217
World Wide Web 11, 14, 63, 91, 128, 257
Wright, Frank Lloyd 91, 95

Y

Yurish, Jack 254

Z

Zeviar, Dorothy 128